KING OF THE GODFATHERS

KING OF THE GODFATHERS

ANTHONY M. DESTEFANO

PINNACLE BOOKS
Kensington Publishing Corp.
http://www.kensingtonbooks.com

Some names have been changed to protect the privacy of individuals connected to this story.

PINNACLE BOOKS are published by

Kensington Publishing Corp.
850 Third Avenue
New York, NY 10022

All Kensington Titles, Imprints, and Distributed Lines are available at special quantity discounts for bulk purchases for sales promotions, premiums, fund-raising, and educational or institutional use. Special book excerpts or customized printings can be created to fit specific needs. For details, write or phone the office of the Kensington special sales manager: Kensington Publishing Corp., 850 Third Avenue, New York, NY 10022, attn: Special Sales Department, Phone: 1-800-221-2647.

Pinnacle and the P logo Reg. U.S. Pat. & TM Off.

ISBN-13: 978-0-7860-1893-2
ISBN-10: 0-7860-1893-3

First Hardcover Printing: September 2006
First Mass Market Paperback Printing: June 2007

10 9 8 7 6 5 4 3 2

Printed in the United States of America

Contents

CHAPTER 1

"No Sleep Till Brooklyn"

He knew they were coming.

As he walked the snow-crusted streets near his home in Howard Beach, Queens, on the night of January 8, 2003, the middle-aged man could sense the many pairs of eyes that followed his every move.

Street smart since leaving school in the eighth grade, he had acquired a finely tuned sense of when trouble was stalking him. Walking around on what was an unseasonably warm night along Cross Bay Boulevard with his youngest daughter, Joanne, the rotund grandfather had noticed cars he knew were those of the Federal Bureau of Investigation. The sedans and the vans with tinted windows, the "bad cars" as he would say, had been around a lot recently. This night they shadowed him constantly.

He went to the Target department store and the cars were there. He went to the Cross Bay Diner and the cars were there. His daughter walked into Blockbuster Video and even she saw the cars.

Looking like Jackie Gleason with a big frame that carried 300 pounds and sporting a full head of graying hair, the old man whose grandchildren called him by the pet name Poppy had a habit of returning to his own place every evening. In his younger days, he might have spent the nights with his overeating friends. Lately, his high blood pressure and diabetes, as well as the toll of obesity, kept him closer to home. So when the agents parked at the end of the block and watched him enter the dark brick home on Eighty-fourth Street for the final time that day, they were certain he was in pocket for the night.

The agents would stick around until morning. It was standard operational procedure for the FBI just before a big arrest to make sure a target stayed in place no matter how long the surveillance team had to be on the street. Poppy was the kind of man they would take as much time as needed to make sure he was in the bag.

Poppy, the affable grand dad who delighted in belly flopping and swimming with neighborhood kids in his backyard pool on Eighty-fourth Street, was better known to law enforcement as Joseph Massino, born January 10, 1943, and branded with FBI number 883127N9. He was the secretive and elusive boss of the Bonanno crime family, the last American Mafia don of substance to be free on the streets. The Dapper Don was dead. The Chin and the Snake were in prison. But Massino had flourished.

A crafty and perceptive man who could be as gentlemanly as he could be vicious, Massino was a throwback to an era when Mafia leaders acted like patricians rather than ill-bred street thugs that had come to symbolize the public face of organized crime. Yet, Massino was not above having blood on his hands—lots of blood if truth be told—and in a few hours that dark side would change his life forever.

In terms of FBI tradecraft, putting someone to bed in the way the agents monitored Massino that night was an example of a crucial surveillance ritual that preceded an arrest. Seeing the subject enter a home and not leave allowed the next day's arrest team to know with certainty that the person who was to be apprehended was at a particular place when the warrant was to be served. By midnight, Massino was at his faux Georgian-style home. The agents outside the house sat in their car at the location, fortifying themselves with cups of coffee and donuts from the Dunkin' Donuts a few blocks away.

Surveillance duty is usually given to newly minted agents fresh out of the FBI Academy in Quantico, Virginia. It is a way for the new agents to learn the geography of a place like New York City while at the same time making observations of people and places that might prove crucial in some investigation months or even years down the road. Any observation, even those made at a distance so great that nothing could be overheard, might prove important if it later corroborated something a witness might say in court or to a grand jury.

Special Agents Kimberly McCaffrey and Jeffrey Sallet had done their share of surveillance drudgery when they joined the FBI some years earlier. But early on January 9, 2003, the two agents had a different task. Dressed in dark blue raid jackets that were embossed with the large yellow letters that spelled out "FBI," McCaffrey and Sallet exited an official government sedan and walked up the front walk on Eighty-fourth Street. Accompanying them were three other law enforcement officials—an Internal Revenue Service agent, a state police officer, and another FBI agent.

The IRS agent made his way stealthily around the back of the house, taking care to avoid the covered swimming pool. McCaffrey and Sallet led the others up the walkway. The morning was chilly and at 6:00 A.M. the neighborhood was quiet.

McCaffrey rang the door bell. It might have been early but it was Massino, his hair neatly combed and fully dressed in a black pullover and large-sized sweat pants, who opened the front door. It was at that very instant that the two FBI agents, who had been studying and watching Massino from a distance for over four years, finally came face to face with their quarry. Though his pasta belly and mirthful grin gave him a genial appearance, Massino had a gaze that could be penetrating, steely, and cold. It was a look that could pull you in and captivate with its strength. It could also scare you. Slightly arched eyebrows made him always look as though he were expressing surprise. Yet, on this particular morning, Joseph Massino was not surprised.

"How are ya," he said.

He surveyed the agents and police arrayed on his doorstep and looked out at the black government sedan in front of his house. Since he had seen the other government vans in the neighborhood over previous days and had been arrested before, Massino knew that something was coming down. The numerous cars that had shadowed him the night before also added to his feeling of apprehension. After McCaffrey flashed her FBI credentials, Massino replied quickly, almost glibly.

"I was expecting you yesterday."

McCaffrey, a diminutive woman whose dark hair, black eyes, and fair skin bespoke her Irish roots, had to chuckle at his bravado. Here was a man who was hijacking trucks in the 1970s, before she was even born, a killer who is said to have boasted about being a one-man killing machine. But she also knew he could be a gentleman, a charmer, and certainly there was no hint of him causing any trouble. He will go peacefully, McCaffrey thought.

So began the day that Joseph Massino, the boss of one of New York City's five legendary Mafia families and "The Last Don," left his home in Howard Beach to live courtesy of the U.S. government in jail for the rest of his foreseeable life. Massino's wife of forty-two years, Josephine, a petite and stylish, titian-haired Sicilian, dressed in her pajamas and housecoat, could do little but watch stoically and tight-lipped as her spouse walked down the front way toward the government car.

Josephine Massino had witnessed this trip into incarceration before when Massino had been arrested in the 1980s. It led to a wearying routine of jailhouse visits and uncertainty. In recent days, as her husband's sense of apprehension grew, she felt her own anxiety mount. The timing couldn't have been worse. She was expecting an important call that very day from her oncologist. She would have to face that without him.

× × ×

It was more than just the presence of the government surveillance cars, long a common fixture in a neighborhood that was home to other gangsters, that had tipped Massino to impending trouble. Federal investigators had been snooping around Massino and his businesses for years and word had gotten back to him fairly quickly when subpoenas started landing around town.

Then there were the arrests. One by one FBI agents started picking off some of Massino's old cronies. Frank Coppa was in prison on securities fraud charges when he found himself indicted again in October 2002 for extortion. That particular indictment allowed the FBI to cast its net wider and arrest a number of other Bonanno crime family members like Richard Cantarella, one of Massino's captains and trusted aides.

Massino wasn't touched in that roundup. But it was clear that the government investigation was making a concerted push against a crime family that had survived much of the earlier onslaughts of federal prosecutions that began in the mid-1980s. Massino knew from the tally of arrests in recent months that it was only a matter of time before someone from a circle of mobsters he had confided in over a four-decade career in La Cosa Nostra would weaken and deliver him to the government.

Compared to his one-time neighbor John Gotti, the flashy but disastrous boss of the Gambino crime family, and Vincent "the Chin" Gigante, the Genovese crime family boss (who dressed in a bathrobe and mumbled as he walked through Greenwich Village in Manhattan in a crazy act), Massino was a relatively unknown face of the Mafia. True, he had been indicted in big cases in the past—once for plotting some gangland murders in the early 1980s and again in 1985 for labor racketeering. He also had a few mentions in the news media, usually accompanying his arrests or occasionally in speculative newspaper stories about the inner workings of La Cosa Nostra.

But if he was a mystery to the public, Massino, through his skill in mob politics as well as the ability to earn money, made for a steady rise through the ranks of the mob. Unlike Gotti, who taunted law enforcement with illegal fireworks displays in Ozone Park every Fourth of July and liked being a celebrity, Joseph Massino remained low key and avoided the flashy Manhattan night life. He liked to pad around the house in terry cloth shorts and cotton t-shirts. He filed his tax returns on time and declared income as high as $500,000 some years. When the police or FBI talked with him, Massino acted like a gentleman. He seemed almost boring.

But he was crafty. Massino knew that law enforcement surveillance techniques had advanced so much that talking to anyone except in the most circumspect way was suicidal. Gotti, having felt secure in an apartment above his Mulberry Street social club in Little Italy, talked openly about the Gambino family crimes and didn't dream that the FBI would have bugging devices in the room.

Yet hours of Gotti's conversations intercepted on FBI bugs all but wrote the federal indictment that led to his conviction and life sentence for racketeering in 1992. Later investigations of the Genovese, Colombo, and Lucchese crime families also relied on mountains of wiretap evidence that made the job of prosecutors as easy as shooting fish in a barrel. The old Mafia may have become the stuff of legend and hit television shows like *The Sopranos*, but it had also become easy pickings for law enforcement.

Massino could not completely avoid wiretaps. One of

Gotti's close associates, Angelo Ruggiero, an overweight and compulsively talkative mobster, had been so indiscreet that FBI agents not only wiretapped his telephone but also planted a bug in the kitchen of his Cedarhurst, Long Island, home. Massino was caught on some of the tapes though not enough to get him in serious trouble. But it was a wake-up call for him about the pervasiveness of surveillance. After that, Massino kept his mouth shut and decreed that his name should never be used in conversations, particularly in places where there may be wiretaps or listening devices.

There were a few slips in that rule. Cantarella was once overheard speaking to an informant. He said that it was Massino, who he referred to as "Joe," who helped him become a made member of the crime family. The informant was wearing a recording device at the time. But for the most part, Massino's name was discreetly kept out of incriminating conversations: a tug on the earlobe was how someone signaled he was talking about Massino without invoking his name. As a result, federal agents like McCaffrey and Sallet had no tapes that captured Massino's voice saying anything incriminating.

Sallet, a sandy-haired New Englander and diehard Red Sox fan whose crew cut made him look like a high school athletic coach, picked out a favorite CD and put it in the player. He might be an accountant, but Sallet was no nerd. He liked the Beastie Boys, a group of New York white rappers, and in the minutes before he had arrested Massino, he was listening to the last cut on the disc. The title of that song, "No Sleep Till Brooklyn," had been quite appropriate under the circumstances. That was certainly going to be Joe Massino's day.

It was to the sound of Generation X music of three white Jewish boys from upper-middle-class parents that the maroon Buick Regal with tinted windows carrying mafioso Massino headed out from the quiet residential block where he lived and made its way to the Belt Parkway for the trip west toward lower Manhattan and FBI headquarters. Sallet and McCaffrey were relatively new agents with six years and four years respectively on the job, but arresting Massino was clearly a career-defining move. It would be all over the news before lunchtime: Joseph Massino, the last of old mob bosses, had finally been taken down. No one was listening to the radio though as the government car traveled westward. Sallet's music selection droned on instead as he drove.

While sandwiched between McCaffrey and one of the police officers, Massino engaged in some small talk. Conversation about food was what Sallet found best for chitchat with someone being arrested. He asked Massino where he thought the best pizza in town could be found.

"CasaBlanca," Massino answered. It was his restaurant by Fresh Pond Road in Queens and he knew the sauce was the best in town. Massino was a pretty good sauce man himself. Family dinners at his house would find him holding competitions with his wife over who was the better cook. His daughters were the judges. Massino's ravioli was often the winner.

It had been inevitable with all the snooping McCaffrey and Sallet had been doing around town that Massino had heard of them.

"You must be Kimberly and you must be Jeffrey," Massino said to the pair. They politely confirmed this.

Massino also told them he knew they had convinced his wife's business partner, Barry Weinberg, a chain-smoking Queens businessman who held interests in parking lots all over New York, to wear a recording device. Now Massino, chastened by the Ruggiero tapes, knew that there was no chance that he had been picked up on any recording device Weinberg had been wearing. He never really talked with the man, particularly after some in the Bonanno clan had become suspicious of him. But Massino figured that the only reason he found himself sandwiched between two FBI agents and headed to Manhattan to be booked on an indictment was because somebody close to him had squealed.

"Frankie Coppa got to work quick," Massino said to the agents as the sedan made its way through traffic.

To the uninformed that terse remark meant nothing. But by blurting it out, Massino was letting Sallet and McCaffrey know that he knew his old friend, Frank Coppa, a Bonanno captain, had become a cooperating witness. Once Massino's closest of friends, Coppa had been moved from the prison facility at Fort Dix, New Jersey, where he had been serving time for securities fraud, to a federal witness protection prison. It was there that Coppa had been telling investigators what he knew of Massino and the crime family.

Massino now had enough information to know that his predicament was serious. McCaffrey told him that among the many racketeering charges being unsealed that morning in the Brooklyn federal district court were those involving the murders of three rival Bonanno captains in 1981.

"That was a long time ago and I had nothing to do with it," Massino said.

In fact, Massino had been acquitted of conspiracy to commit those murders in an earlier racketeering trial. The killing of the three captains—Dominick Trinchera, Alphonse Indelicato, and Philip Giaccone—was part of one of New York's most legendary Mafia power struggles. The remains of the three captains were found in a weedy lot on the Brooklyn-Queens border not far from Massino's home. Some other crime family members were convicted of the murders in 1983. But in the trial of Massino and his brother-in-law, Salvatore Vitale, the government's case was weaker and they beat the rap.

In the mob, all friendships could be dangerous. If Coppa or anyone else had been telling investigators what they knew of the deaths of the three captains, they could come back to haunt Massino. McCaffrey thought it curious that right after being told that he was charged with having actually participated in those killings that Massino asked if his brother-in-law had been arrested as well.

Yes, he had been, Massino was told.

Though he didn't respond or show any emotion when told of Vitale's arrest, the news must have caused Massino's already high blood pressure to spike. The brother of Josephine Massino, Vitale had been Massino's childhood friend and over the years had become a close confidant. Massino shared a lot with him, from learning how to swim in the Astoria pool to introducing Vitale to the illegal scores with truck hijacking. Eventually, as Massino rose in the ranks of the mob, Vitale rode his coattails, rising to the rank of underboss. "Good Looking Sal" or "Sally," as Vitale was known, relished the aura of being a mob boss. His vanity was a subject of gossip. His favorite cologne seemed picked as if to symbolize his status: it was the "Boss" fragrance of designer Hugo Boss.

Normally, the underboss position is a powerful one in the Mafia, but over the years Vitale had chafed at the paltry power Massino had given him, going as far as to forbid Vitale from speaking to the captains in the crime family. The trust that once ran deep between the two men had evaporated. Some of the Bonanno captains thought Vitale was too dirty and knew too much to be trusted. Better off with Vitale dead, some said. Privately, they wondered if Massino's judgment about Vitale was clouded by the fact that he was his wife's brother.

Vitale had been involved in a number of murders—"pieces of work," as wiseguys would call them. Knowing what he knew about the crime family business, Vitale could be dangerous if he weakened. And Massino knew that. Just three weeks earlier, a few Bonanno mobsters voiced distrust of Vitale.

"Sal is gonna rat on every fucking body," said Anthony Urso, one of Massino's key captains, who was overheard on a surveillance bug.

Rats were the bane of the Mafia. La Cosa Nostra was riddled with them and it made Massino even more paranoid. If he suspected any man was a rat, Massino gave him a ticket—

he called it a "receipt"—to the grave. Joseph Massino was from the old school of tough guys who never turned on their friends. You never squeal: it was a creed that Massino even taught his daughters to live by. It was the way of life and you swore to it with your blood the day they made you a wiseguy by burning the card with a saint's picture in the palm of your hand.

Massino would tell people he was proud of his crime family, the only one that had never had an informant or rat in all its years of existence. *Omerta* had never been violated within the family until old man Joseph Bonanno revealed some of La Cosa Nostra's secrets in his 1980 autobiography *A Man of Honor*. Massino had become so angry over Bonanno's tale that he wanted to change the name of the crime family to Massino. Time in jail, not tell-all books, went with the job of being a mob boss. John Gotti, Vincent Gigante, Carlo Gambino, Anthony "Tony Ducks" Corallo, Anthony "Fat Tony" Salerno, Carmine "the Snake" Persico—they all took their medicine and didn't rat out anybody. Massino would be a stand-up guy. That was part of a boss's job. Everybody knew that.

It turned out McCaffrey was wrong in her characterization of the charges against Massino during the car ride back to Manhattan. It might have been a ploy to see if Massino talked, but the indictment in the process of being unsealed that morning by Brooklyn federal prosecutors did not mention the killings of the three captains. In reality, Massino had been indicted for the 1982 slaying of another old friend: Dominick "Sonny Black" Napolitano. The killings of Trinchera, Giaccone, and Indelicato, as well as several others, wouldn't be laid at Massino's feet until much later.

The FBI car in which Massino rode went through the Brooklyn-Battery Tunnel, north on West Street, left onto Worth Street, and then headed into the basement of the forty-five-story federal office building known as Twenty-six Federal Plaza. A 1960s-style soaring rectangle of glass, stone, and chrome on Foley Square, the building housed most of the federal law enforcement agencies in the city. Anyone arrested in a major FBI operation—and Massino's bust was big—was usually taken to "Twenty-six Fed" and put through the ritual processing: fingerprinting, photographing, and the recording of personal information. One thing the agents decided against was a "perp walk," that is, parading Massino before prying newspaper photographers. They had decided to treat him with a little dignity.

For the Bonanno squad known by the designation C10, the processing of defendants all took place on the twenty-second floor and although it was serious business, Massino couldn't help joking with the agents as he was fingerprinted, saying he probably wouldn't get bail if he hired one attorney he knew from the old neighborhood. The agents knew at that point that bail was the remotest long shot for Massino, but they let his remark pass. Spotting one of the squad supervisors, Nora Conely, Massino had a flash of recognition. He remarked that he had seen her talking once to his old friend Louis Restivo, one of the owners of CasaBlanca Restaurant, about a fugitive.

She was second in command of the squad, McCaffrey explained to Massino.

"Like an underboss," Massino answered McCaffrey, putting it in lingo he understood.

Massino was going to spend the rest of the day shuttling between the FBI offices and across the Brooklyn Bridge to the U.S. District Court, where he would eventually be arraigned on the charges before a federal magistrate. It would take hours for that to happen. In the meantime, as the rest of the city awakened, another ritual was getting underway. Federal officials began to alert news agencies that they had a big announcement and at One Pierrepont Plaza, an office tower in downtown Brooklyn, copies of a four-page press release were stacked on a table in the law library of the office of the

U.S. Attorney for the Eastern District of New York, a fancy way to describe Brooklyn and everything to the east.

The document had a long title: Boss and Underboss Charged with Racketeering, Murder, and Other Crimes in Culmination of Four-Year Investigation and Prosecution of the Bonanno Organized Crime Family—Murders Include Retaliation for Infiltration of Family by "Donnie Brasco."

Press releases from prosecutors don't just relate the news; they also mention who the big shots are in law enforcement who want credit, or at least hope to get some mention in the news accounts that will follow. This press release was no exception. It listed Roslynn R. Mauskopf, U.S. Attorney for the Eastern District of New York; Kevin P. Donovan, Assistant Director in Charge, Federal Bureau of Investigation, the man who was McCaffrey and Sallet's boss; Paul L. Machalek, special agent in charge of the criminal investigations unit of the Internal Revenue Service; and James W. McMahon, the superintendent of the New York State Police.

The next four names listed in the press release told the world who was in trouble. First named was Massino, "who is the only boss of the five LCN families in New York not currently incarcerated." In law enforcement jargon the initials LCN stood for La Cosa Nostra, the Italian expression commonly used to describe the American Mafia. Though the public, press, and even police refer to organized crime composed of men of Italian heritage as the Mafia, purists are quick to point out that the term *Mafia* really refers to the organized crime based in Italy. The term *la cosa nostra*, which loosely translates as "our thing" or "this thing of ours," is actually what the FBI prefers.

Rounding out the list of those arrested that morning was, as Massino already knew, Salvatore Vitale, "who serves as the family's underboss." Also nabbed was Frank Lino, a mean-spirited, fireplug-sized Brooklyn man seven years' Massino's senior who had somehow survived mob infighting to become a *capo* or captain. Finally, there was Daniel Mongelli, a pubescent-looking thirty-seven-year-old who made up for what he may have lacked in intelligence with loyalty to a life of crime. His reward was the title of acting captain in Massino's regime.

As she gripped the podium before the assembled reporters and photographers, federal prosecutor Mauskopf said that the arrest of Massino and Vitale meant that the leadership of the Bonanno family was either in prison or facing the prospect of a lifetime behind bars. This was Mauskopf's first major organized crime indictment and her statement included such usual obligatory prose. She reminded everyone that the government was committed to eradicating the influence of organized crime in the city and that the case demonstrated this resolve.

But she also noted that this was a superseding indictment, meaning it built on an earlier set of charges that had led to the arrest of other Bonanno crime family figures like captains Anthony Graziano, Richard Cantarella, and Massino's old friend, Frank Lino. In all, Mauskopf noted, twenty-six members and associates of the Bonanno clan had been charged in the previous twelve months. Clearly, the crime family was facing big trouble. Time, she said, had not been good to the mob.

"In the early years, the middle years of the twentieth century, the structure of traditional organized crime was formulated, in large measure right here in Brooklyn," Mauskopf told the reporters assembled in her office. "At the beginning of the twenty-first century, as a result of federal law enforcement's efforts, their determined, their sustained, and their outstanding efforts, the heads of the five families and a significant portion of their members had been brought before the bar of justice."

Such self-congratulatory comments by law enforcement were common at such news events. But Mauskopf's attempt to give the case a touch of history caught the attention of many journalists who had been following the machinations of organized crime. The reference to "Donnie Brasco" and the murders that surrounded him tied Massino's arrest to one of the most legendary sagas of latter-day Mafia history. Brasco was in fact Joseph Pistone, who as an FBI agent beginning in the late 1970s infiltrated a branch of the Bonanno family. (Pistone's role was celebrated in the 1997 film *Donnie Brasco* starring Al Pacino.) Working undercover, Pistone posed as Brasco, jewel thief. With the patience of a crafty spy, he ingratiated himself with Bonanno soldier Benjamin "Lefty Guns" Ruggierio and his captain, Dominick "Sonny Black" Napolitano.

For three years Pistone gathered evidence against his mob friends, fooling them so completely that he was even proposed for membership to the crime family, a state of affairs that had angered Massino if only because no one really knew this Brasco fellow. In hindsight, Massino's wariness about Pistone demonstrates his survival instincts. When Pistone's undercover role was dramatically and publicly revealed in 1981, the results were predictable. Like the dark days of some Stalinist purge, the Bonanno family went through bloody days of reckoning. Those who had allowed Pistone to infiltrate the family had to pay the price. Napolitano was high on the list and federal officials believed he was murdered for the unpardonable sin of vouching for Pistone. The indictment charged that Massino, along with Frank Lino, engineered Napolitano's slaughter.

Pistone's infiltration of the Bonanno family had made it not only the laughing stock of the Mafia but also a pariah. Believing they couldn't trust the Bonanno hierarchy, the other mob families in New York kept the wounded family at bay and cut it out of some rackets. Among the fruits denied the Bonanno family was a cut of the lucrative "concrete club" that had evolved in the early 1980s. The club members were the four Mafia families who took a percentage through kickbacks of every cubic yard of concrete that was poured in

New York City. This amounted to millions of dollars in illegal profits and contributed to what critics said was the inordinately high cost of doing construction in New York.

It was in May 1984, in a private home on Cameron Avenue in Staten Island, that the boss of the Gambino family crime family, Paul Castellano, lorded over a meeting of representatives of three other Mafia families—the Genovese, Colombo, and Lucchese families—to hash out business disputes over their construction rackets, including the concrete shakedown. Investigators were also watching and recorded the men going to the meeting. In 1986, federal prosecutors in Manhattan secured convictions for the concrete racket against the leadership of the Mafia Commission: Anthony "Fat Tony" Salerno (Genovese crime family), Anthony "Tony Ducks" Corallo (Lucchese crime family), Carmine "the Snake" Persico (Colombo crime family), and their assorted lieutenants for taking part in various rackets.

But the Bonanno family, having been denied a cut of the concrete scheme, escaped conviction in the Commission case. True, Philip Rastelli, the Bonanno boss at the time, had been indicted. But Rastelli's case had been severed from the Commission trial and was never convicted. (He was found guilty in an unrelated Brooklyn federal racketeering trial.) Ironically, by being kept out of the loop by the other crime families in the concrete case, the Bonanno clan dodged a big bullet and continued to operate with much of its leadership intact. While other crime families were knocked off balance, the Bonannos were able to consolidate and recover from the disaster of L'Affaire Brasco.

But that honeymoon was over. The news release that accompanied Massino's indictment listed more murders. Vitale, investigators said, had set up the murder of Robert Perrino, a delivery supervisor at the *New York Post*, in 1992. After Manhattan District Attorney Robert Morgenthau began an investigation into the Bonanno family's infiltration of the newspaper's delivery department that investigators believed had become a mob fiefdom, Vitale panicked. The indictment charged that Vitale and others, fearing Perrino might cooperate with law enforcement, arranged for the newspaper supervisor's death in 1992.

Daniel Mongelli was charged with killing Louis Tuzzio in 1990. Tuzzio was a crime family associate whose death had already been charged in an earlier indictment against Robert Lino, Frank Lino's cousin. Tuzzio was murdered as a favor to John Gotti, payback for a bizarre shooting stemming from the death of Everett Hatcher, a Drug Enforcement Administration agent, at the hands of aspiring Bonanno family member Gus Farace in 1989. Tuzzio didn't die because Hatcher had been killed but rather, investigators said, because one of Gotti's associates had been wounded during the killing of Farace. Gotti had to be appeased. The mob can police its own as payback for screw ups—Hatcher's murder brought a lot of law enforcement heat on the mob—but it better be done cleanly.

There were some other charges against Massino involving gambling in cafés in Queens. Joker Poker machines and baccarat games were profitable staples of the crime family along with loan-sharking, which Massino was also charged with. But loan-sharking and gambling charges against a mob boss were an old story. What really had Massino tied up was murder. While more killings would be laid at Massino's feet in the months to come, prosecutors only needed one—the Napolitano hit—to make the case that Massino should not be given bail.

"It has taken over two decades to get the goods on Joe Massino for the murder of 'Sonny Black' Napolitano, but justice delayed is not always justice denied," said Kevin Donovan, the top FBI boss for New York City, to reporters.

Donovan referred in passing to a pair of agents who had doggedly tracked Massino for years. But he didn't mention their names. Sallet and McCaffrey didn't seek adulation and preferred to keep a low profile.

× × ×

Massino's youngest daughter, Joanne, had walked her own daughter to the nearby parochial school on the morning of January 9 as she always did. The child had often accompanied both her mother and grandfather on shopping trips to Cross Bay Boulevard in Howard Beach, Queens, near Kennedy International Airport. Joanne had felt the peering eyes of the FBI and, like her father, had spotted the numerous cars that seemed to be following them.

It was a little after 8:00 A.M. when Joanne came back to her home on Eighty-fourth Street in Howard Beach. Both she and her eldest sister, Adeline, had decided to stay close by their parents after each girl got married, so it was almost a daily ritual that the Massino girls saw their parents. (A middle sister had moved out of state.) Now that Joanne was divorced, she remained in the home she once shared with her ex-husband, who had moved to Long Island. As soon as she returned from escorting her daughter to school, Joanne spotted her mother in front of her own home a few doors away. The older woman didn't say a word, she just gestured.

"Come here, quick, I have something to tell you about your father and it isn't good," Josephine Massino seemed to say with an urgent wave of her hand toward her daughter, who knew in an instant that there was trouble.

Adeline, who lived about four blocks north of her parents, was at the Dunkin' Donuts store on Cross Bay Boulevard, the very same place the FBI agents would visit to pick up snacks for the long surveillances of her father. It was the morning ritual of this particular Howard Beach Little League mom to get her cup of coffee there and then visit her folks.

Though Joanne had the dark Neapolitan eyes of her father, Adeline took after her mother, right down to the auburn tint of the hair (which if truth be told, they both had done at the same beauty salon on the boulevard). Walking with her embossed coffee cup through the front door of her parents' house, Adeline was oblivious to the tumult that had begun to envelope her family. She would find out about it soon enough.

CHAPTER 2

Amici

When Roslynn R. Mauskopf, the federal prosecutor, told the news reporters that La Cosa Nostra got its start in the borough of Brooklyn, she really was telling the truth. But she may not have realized all the historical details. There were a few twists and turns before Brooklyn became the Mafia's American holy land.

The roots of Italian organized crime in New York City were tied closely to the great waves of immigration in the early part of the twentieth century. To understand what Joseph Massino inherited nearly 100 years later, one has to look at those early days, when the mob was evolving and its values were being adapted to life in America. The story of what became the Bonanno crime family was like some long, medieval tapestry, a continuing saga interwoven with the life stories of many of the Mafia's key personalities and bloody events.

By the turn of the twentieth century and continuing into the years immediately after World War I, Italians were among the largest group of immigrants coming to the United States. It was a largely economic immigration to be sure, pulling Italians from the economically depressed southern areas of

Italy, the *mezzogiorno* region composed of Naples, Calabria, and Sicily. While Italians settled in many cities, New York was a main attraction. It became a cliché image, the mass of immigrants dressed in Old World–style garb, gazing in awe at the Statute of Liberty as the crowded passenger liners sailed into New York harbor and made their way to Ellis Island, the first point of entry into the United States. Earlier immigrants who settled in the five boroughs of New York served as the seed for the later arrival of *amici,* relatives and friends from the same villages and towns in southern Italy.

Because a substantial number of Italian immigrants settled in Brooklyn, the borough attracted its share of new arrivals—a trend that continued late into the twentieth century. When World War I ended, one Italian man became the top Mafia figure and lorded over an enterprise of young criminals who he ruled with an iron fist. Joe Masseria was known in the underworld as Joe the Boss. A fat, short man, Masseria was known for his prodigious appetite for food and drink. Dinner with Joe the Boss saw his underlings try in vain to keep up with his devouring of plates of pasta and meats, washed down with Chianti.

Old mug shots show Masseria with a fat, round face and small piglike eyes. He was one of the "Moustache Petes," though he was clean shaven, the derisive name given to the old-timers who rose to the upper levels of Italian organized crime and were known for keeping with their Old World mentality. A peasant in manners—Masseria was said to have spewed food as he talked with animation over dinner—he had a retinue of young, ambitious mob toughs who ensured that his orders would be followed. Their names should be very familiar. Among them was Al Capone, Salvatore Lucania, better known as Charles "Lucky" Luciano, Vito Genovese, and Frank Costello (Francesco Castiglia), men who in their own right became major Mafia leaders and legends of their time. Masseria recruited men like Luciano, Genovese, and the others to beef up the ranks of a Mafia organization that was actually run by Ignazia "Lupo" Saietta. Known as a sadistic Sicilian, Lupo emigrated from Sicily to avoid a murder prosecution, and as a Mafia member he took over the Unione Siciliane, a sort of fraternal organization and mutual-aid society of Italian immigrants.

In 1910, Lupo was sentenced to thirty years in prison and Masseria was essentially the boss of the American Mafia in his absence. He consolidated his power and saw to it that fellow Sicilian immigrants had key positions of power under him as a way of ensuring fealty and obedience. It was after building an organization that owed its loyalty to him that Masseria is reported to have made a bold political maneuver that removed Lupo from the picture—without a shot being fired. According to Tony Sciacca in the book *Luciano: The Man Who Modernized the American Mafia,* Masseria convinced Lupo that even if he were to be paroled on the counterfeiting charge that he risked being arrested again for a parole violation.

"Joe the Boss would run the American Mafia, with Lupo as an unofficial advisor, immune from reimprisonment by remaining in the shadows," Sciacca states. "The legend in Little Italy has it that Lupo agreed to accept retirement."

Through the intercession of Harry Daugherty, the U.S. attorney general, Lupo was paroled in 1921 by President Warren G. Harding. Free from a prison cell, Lupo came to Little Italy, kissed Masseria on the cheeks, and then left for a year's sabbatical to Sicily. He was never a factor again in the American Mafia.

With the help of Luciano, Genovese, and others, Masseria became the undisputed boss of the Mafia in the United States. Under his leadership, the organization developed its own corner of the drug trade, bringing opium into New York City, bootlegging, and protection rackets in the Italian community. But it was not enough.

The Italian immigrants were not all alike in that they brought with them to America old clannish ways and prejudices. A Sicilian might hold secret resentment of the Neapolitan and vice versa. Among the Sicilians, of which Masseria was one, suspicions developed as well. Some of those aligned with Masseria traced their origins to the area around the town of Castellammare del Golfo in western Sicily. This was not the area where Masseria traced his roots, and the various Castellammarese who took up residence in Brooklyn viewed another charismatic Sicilian named Salvatore Maranzano as their leader. Tall, lean, and sporting a thin moustache, Maranzano was the physical opposite of Masseria. He seemed like a banker, in sharp contrast to the short, burly, and voracious Masseria. Maranzano, who was something of an intellectual among the immigrants, kept in his apartment volumes about the Roman Empire under Julius Caesar, including his battle tactics.

Many of the Castellammarese who settled in Brooklyn did so in the area around Roebling and Havermeyer streets, near Metropolitan Avenue. It is a part of Brooklyn known as Willliamburg and it was in this area, close to the waterfront, that Maranzano held court with fellow Sicilians. Among them were many who would come to hold their own place in the genealogy of the Mafia: Thomas Lucchese, Joseph Profaci, Stefano Magliocco, and Stefano Magaddino, a mafioso from Buffalo. There was also a young, handsome Castellammarese who at the age of nineteen had arrived in New York in 1924 after taking a circuitous smuggling route that led from Sicily, Tunisia, Marseille, Paris, Cuba, and then by a small motorboat to Tampa, Florida. He had fled Sicily at a time when the government was trying to crack down on the Mafia. His name was Joseph Bonanno.

Living with relatives in Brooklyn, Bonanno passed up opportunities to toil in the decent obscurity of lawful occupations and instead saw his destiny in the world of crime. It was of course a calculated choice of Bonanno's to seek his fortune in ways the vast majority of his fellow immigrants shunned. In his classic biography of Bonanno, *Honor Thy*

Father, author Gay Talese says Bonanno sought respect and saw himself as a leader of men. He was prepared to do what he needed to pursue his goals.

"He did believe that the ruling classes of America as in Sicily had great respect for two things—power and money—and he was determined to get both one way or the other," Talese states. "So in his first year in Brooklyn, Bonanno affiliated himself with the neighborhood Mafiosi, who were obviously doing well; they were driving new cars and wearing finer clothes than their humble countrymen who got up each day at dawn to toil in factories or work in construction gangs."

Aligned with Maranzano, Bonanno made a name for himself in the rackets of the time. There was bootlegging, gambling, and smuggling of weapons. The Brooklyn Italian lottery was also controlled by Bonanno, and it was his organizational ability, as well as his polished, diplomatic manner that earned him respect. Wise enough not to squander his earnings, Bonanno invested in other legitimate businesses such as garment factories, cheese producers, and even a funeral parlor.

Success of Castellammarese men like Bonanno served to make Masseria suspicious of the growing strength of Maranzano and his followers. Historians of the Mafia are unanimous in saying that Masseria, concerned about the independence being shown by Maranzano and his men, planned to strike against them to eliminate their rivalry. Larger tribute payments were demanded by Masseria. These were rebuffed by Maranzano's allies and Masseria knew by 1930 that he had to annihilate the competition.

But just as he was preparing to go to war against the Castellammarese, Masseria's hunger for money and power led him to make a big tactical mistake. Masseria attempted to extort the ice-making business of one of his own crime captains, Gaetano Reina. When Reina resisted, Masseria had him killed in February 1930, just as the ice merchant was leaving a building on Sheridan Avenue in the Bronx. The killing of Reina prompted his gang members to ally with Maranzano and a period of Mafia assassinations and gunfights known as the Castellammarese War broke out in New York. It was a time of bloodshed that would ultimately go a long way to shaping the modern Mafia in the United States.

The killings went on for over a year as Masseria struck against the bootlegging businesses of the Maranzano crowd. With allies like Thomas Lucchese, Carlo Gambino, Vito Genovese, and, of course, Lucky Luciano, Masseria seemed in a stronger position. But Maranzano had important alliances as well, including the help of a young mob associate known as Joseph Valachi, who would eventually marry the daughter of the assassinated Reina. There was intense mob bloodshed in the war, with some estimates saying over fifty men died on both sides. Whatever the body count, the war proved bad for business and the costs were troubling Luciano and Genovese. They reached out to Maranzano in an effort to stop the fighting.

In return for setting up Masseria for the kill, Maranzano agreed with Luciano and Genovese that the war would stop and that they would be safe. Masseria had escaped death a number of times, so he would not be an easy target. It was Luciano who rose to the task of setting the old man up for the kill. What happened next was reminiscent of a scene right out of *The Godfather*. Convincing Masseria that it was safe to have dinner outside of his Manhattan apartment, Luciano accompanied his boss on the afternoon of April 15, 1931, to Coney Island. The restaurant was a well-known Italian eatery run by Geraldo Scarpato. Masseria's prodigious appetite was on display as he consumed plates of pasta and drank Chianti. After lunch Luciano convinced Masseria to play some cards and then excused himself to go the bathroom.

With Luciano out of the room, several armed men suddenly arrived outside Scarpato's at around 3:30 P.M. in a car driven by Ciro Terranova, the mafioso known as the "Artichoke King" because of the way he extorted the myriad pushcart peddlers in East Harlem. With Terranova remaining behind the wheel, a handful of gangsters—no one is certain just who took part—entered the restaurant and blasted away at Masseria, who died as soon as he hit the floor. When police arrived, Luciano told them he had been in the bathroom, a fact corroborated by the restaurant staff. Apart from a commotion when the shooting started, Luciano said he saw and heard nothing.

With Masseria out of the picture, Maranzano moved quickly to consolidate his power and bring the other mobsters under his control. It was at a meeting in a Bronx social hall that Maranzano threw a big dinner attended by hundreds of Mafia members and associates. It was an event that for all practical purposes marked the formal organization of Italian organized crime in the United States as it would be known for decades. Though powerful mobsters like Capone in Chicago and Luciano were said to be against the idea of a big boss lording over the crime families, Maranzano pushed the idea of himself being anointed the Caesar of organized crime. According to the recollection of mob turncoat Joseph Valachi, Maranazano spelled out an organization of criminals that was modeled on the legions of ancient Rome.

"Mr. Maranzano started off the meeting by explaining how Joe the Boss was always shaking down members, right and left," Valachi said in his memoirs, the *Valachi Papers*, which were written by Peter Maas. "He told how he had sentenced all the Castellammarese to death without cause."

"He was speaking in Italian," Valachi recalled, "and he said, 'Now it is going to be different.' In the new setup he was going to be the *Capo di tutti Capi*, meaning the 'Boss of All Bosses.' He said that from here on we were going to be divided up into new Families. Each Family would have a boss and an underboss."

Beneath the top echelon of bosses were to be lieutenants

or *capodecini* under which were the regular members or soldiers. Instilling a military-style structure to the crime families, Maranzano set up a chain of command that required soldiers to talk about problems with their lieutenant who might then go higher up the chain to the underboss or boss.

Surrounded by a large crucifix and religious pictures, Maranzano talked continuously to the multitude of gangsters about the code of conduct that mafiosi must live by. The Mafia came before everything, and its members who violated the secrecy of the organization and talked to outsiders about its business would be killed, Maranzano said.

As a result of the Bronx meeting, bosses for five Mafia families emerged with Maranzano's blessing. They were Luciano, Thomas Gagliano, Joseph Profaci, Vincent Mangano, and Frank Scalise. By his own account, Joseph Bonanno was part of Maranzano's family and was an aide-de-camp to the crime boss. But while Luciano and the others should have felt comfortable with the power they now had and the relative peace in their world, they saw Maranzano as a power-hungry despot who threatened their rackets. Maranzano proceeded to shake down other mobsters under the guise of requiring them to buy tickets for banquets in his honor, affairs that netted him more than $100,000, a princely sum in 1931. Luciano in particular thought that the rule of a supreme boss lording over the crime families was an anachronism. Maranzano had turned out to be as much of a destructive force as Masseria had been. If Valachi was accurate in his recollection, Maranzano saw Luciano, Capone, and Genovese as threats and wanted them killed.

Maranzano's plan was to summon Luciano and Genovese to his office at 230 Park Avenue for a meeting and then have an Irish gangster by the name of Vincent Coll kill the both of them. But in a classic double cross, one of Maranzano's associates tipped off the intended victims. Luciano then moved quickly and turned to his Jewish cronies from the East Side of Manhattan to set up a counterattack to take place the day of the meeting. Meyer Lansky, who would become the fabled financial wizard of the mob, hired four other Jewish gangsters who dressed as policemen, and on September 10, 1931, they confronted Maranzano in his Park Avenue office. The crime boss had been expecting Luciano and Genovese, but when two of the fake cops said they wanted to talk business, Maranzano went with them into an inner office. Using knives and guns, the assailants killed Maranzano.

Mob folklore has it that the day Maranzano died there was an orgy of blood in which as many as sixty of Maranzano's men in New York and other cities died. Even Bonanno subscribed to the story in his autobiography. The murders became known as the Night of the Sicilian Vespers and while that label has a certain grandiose ring harkening back to Sicilian history, the factual basis for the bloody legend appears way more modest. One historian checked police records in thirteen major cities for the days around the killing of Maranzano and found no indication of a large Mafia bloodbath—only three other mob homicides. Those three victims were Maranzano associates who author Peter Mass, in his book *The Valachi Papers*, identifies through police records as James LePore, Samuel Monaco, and Louis Russo. LePore was shot dead at an Arthur Avenue barber shop in the Bronx the same day as Maranzano, while the bodies of Monaco and Russo were pulled out of Newark Bay in New Jersey on September 13, 1931, three days after the Maranzano assassination.

With Maranzano out of the picture, Luciano was the top mobster in New York City, but unlike his now deceased rival he was smart enough to realize that the old ways of having one big boss were outmoded and unworkable. There was too much money to be made in the rackets and everybody could have a cut, if only they worked together. Bonanno, who had been part of Maranzano's inner circle, was the strongest man in his particular crime family and was elected the new boss by acclamation.

"I had the choice of rejecting Luciano's olive branch or of accepting it in good faith. If told to fight, the men in my Family would have fought," Bonanno later said. "But what good would it have done to fight Luciano? He had claimed self-defense in the killing of Maranzano. Now he mainly wanted to be left alone to run his enterprises. He was not trying to impose himself on us as had Masseria. Lucky demanded nothing from us."

At first, Luciano wanted to carve up territory in the garment district with Bonanno, a move that the latter rejected. According to Bonanno's son, Salvatore or "Bill," who later wrote his own book *Bound by Honor*, his father and Luciano worked out a system of consensus and settlement of disputes that involved a so-called *Commizioni del Pace*, or Committee of Peace. This later became known as the Commission, the governing body of the mob.

The idea was for the five Mafia families to have a representative on the Commission and eventually over time this encompassed the heads of the families. Bill Bonanno, who anointed his father with the grandiose title "Angel of Peace" because of the way he brokered the idea of a commission, said the setup kept things relatively quiet between the crime families for decades.

"The heart of it was live and let live," Bill Bonanno explained. "Let each Family run its own business in its own way, don't interfere, and if any disputes arise, mediate them through the Commission. When a matter came up in one Family that might have a spillover effect for all, *mediation*, not *warfare*, was the ruling word."

There wasn't total peace, even with the Commission set up, as mobsters got caught in disputes within the families and occasionally paid for it with their lives. However, beginning in 1931, there was relative peace and prosperity among the Mafia families in the United States, a period that lasted nearly three decades. It was during this period that Joseph

Bonanno ran his family the way he saw fit, remaining one of the premier crime bosses of his time.

It was also a time when Bonanno got married. In a wedding at which many of the Mafia leaders were invited and attended, Joseph Bonanno married Fay Labruzzo on November 15, 1931. The reception was at the Knights of Columbus Hall in Prospect Park, Brooklyn. Just before the ceremony there was a bit of consternation as the ring Bonanno was to give to his bride went missing. It later turned up in the pants cuff of Natale Evola, one of Bonanno's wedding ushers. From that day forward, Evola, a garment trucker who lived in Brooklyn, was known by the moniker of "Joe Diamond."

Though Bonanno got married during the Depression, things were good for his businesses, both legal and illegal. Talese reports that a cash cushion, acquired during the earlier years, allowed Bonanno to buy up real estate at bargain prices. He had homes in Arizona and New York and by all accounts was a respected member of whatever community he called home. While Vito Genovese had to flee the country in 1934 to escape murder charges and Lucky Luciano was convicted in 1936 for running a prostitution business, Bonanno seemed to adroitly avoid trouble. The only rub with the law came in the late 1930s when a Brooklyn clothing factory he was a partner in was hit with a federal wage and hour violation. Bonanno was fined $50.

Despite the troubles confronting some top mafiosi in America, the period before and after World War II in New York was one of prosperity and power for the mob. It was the start of the mob's Golden Age, when gangsters in New York held sway with politicians, judges, and prosecutors in a way that would become unthinkable—and impossible—in the twenty-first century. Bonanno, the consummate Castellammarese who combined a business acumen with a political shrewdness, did well in this halcyon time, even though he kept out of the limelight.

In its own way, World War II was a fortuitous event for

the Mafia and allowed a number of American bosses a cushion of several years from legal trouble. Though it was a well-kept secret at the time, it is now well documented that U.S. officials turned to some of New York's mob bosses for help in the war effort. The first approach came after the passenger liner *Normandie* burned and foundered at its mooring on the West Side of Manhattan. Anxious to combat sabotage on the waterfront—something suspected of having caused the *Normandie* to burn—military and government officials turned to Joseph "Socks" Lanza, a Genovese man on the waterfront along the East River, including the Fulton Fish Market. Though under indictment for extortion, Lanza was seen as the right man for the job. While it is impossible to say if his efforts thwarted any sabotage or scared away any Axis spies, nothing akin to the *Normandie* incident happened again during the war.

Officials also turned to Luciano, who during the early part of the war was serving his sentence for prostitution-related offenses in the tough Dannemora prison in upstate New York. Luciano agreed to help and used his influence with his associates to help security on the West Side docks. But the really important help Luciano gave the Allied war effort came when from prison he established contact with his amici in Sicily. He instructed them to serve as spies and guides for the invading U.S., British, and Canadian forces who landed on the island in the summer of 1943.

After the Allies were able to take Sicily in five weeks, they leapfrogged to the Italian mainland with the invasion of the Salerno-Naples area. Again, the Allies had the help of another New York Mafia boss, Vito Genovese. Living in Naples since he fled New York following his indictment for murder of an old business partner, Genovese had become something of a stellar citizen. He even reportedly arranged for the murder on a Manhattan street in 1943 of one of dictator Benito Mussolini's most vocal opponents, Carlos Tresca. For the Allies, Genovese worked as a translator and, as

Talese later reports, was able to provide information about the Italian black market profiteers.

Genovese's wartime efforts didn't insulate him from problems. The FBI had him extradicted back to New York to stand trial for the Fernando Boccia murder. But conveniently, the key witness against Genovese was poisoned to death in the Brooklyn jail cell where he was being held as a material witness. Deprived of the witness's crucial testimony, prosecutors dropped the case against Genovese. He was free to live and work at his pleasure in New York.

The war assistance by some of the mob bosses didn't give them carte blanche to do business as usual. Luciano had Washington's gratitude and won his freedom from prison when New York Governor Thomas Dewey, the very man who while working as Manhattan's district attorney secured Luciano's conviction, signed an order commuting his sentence on February 2, 1946. But as part of the deal, Luciano had to agree to voluntarily depart the United States (he was not a naturalized citizen), which he did shortly after Dewey signed the commutation order. Before setting sail on the *Laura Keene*, an old Liberty ship, Luciano, in another example of how the mob guys could get one over, was able to leave the immigration station at Ellis Island and attend a farewell party in his honor at the Village Inn in Greenwich Village. Mafiosi, judges, and politicians attended and reportedly gave Luciano thick envelopes presumably stuffed with cash. After sailing back to Italy on February 9, Luciano had to work through his emissaries, chief among them being Genovese, who was out from under the yoke of his legal troubles.

The war years had emboldened the mob, having seen how its effective power on the street and the docks had worked to its advantage. Crime families, including that of Joseph Bonanno, also developed rackets by trading in rationed goods, including precious gasoline stamps. But other core (and illegal) Mafia businesses in New York such as the docks, labor unions, and the garment industry were also prospering. Despite prosecutions by Dewey, the Mafia families also enjoyed a tremendous amount of connection to New York politicians and judges.

By the end of the war, Luciano had control of his family through Genovese and was a major force. Rounding out the leadership of the New York families were four other bosses from the time Maranzano was deposed: Joseph Profaci, Vincent Mangano, Thomas Gagliano, and, of course, Joseph Bonanno. However, Genovese had an ambitious Frank Costello to contend with and that created problems. It was Costello who had cultivated friendships and allegiances at a time when Genovese had been ducking prosecution in Italy. Profaci, Mangano, and Gagliano all had aspiring and power-hungry underbosses and associates to deal with. But Bonanno had no such complication of leadership and command. He was the sole power in his crime family, unchallenged by any upstarts or intrigue.

CHAPTER 3

The Toughest Kid on the Block

Traveling east along Metropolitan Avenue from Williamsburg where Joseph Bonanno got his start as a criminal, you will soon cross into the area of New York City known as Maspeth. The origin of the neighborhood's name is obscured within some mix of the old Dutch and Indian languages. It was once a swampy area, the Indian name meaning "the place of bad waters." In the nineteenth century, it contained large trout ponds that were drained over a century ago. Today, the largest body of water in Maspeth is the Newtown Creek, an estuary officials have been gamely trying to clean up for years.

When western parts of what is today known as Queens became accessible by the railroad and ferries in the nineteenth century, industry grew and Maspeth saw a large influx of working families. Factories sprung up where workers spun hemp into rope and processed fertilizer and flooring. The neighborhood became another magnet for immigrants. The cheap housing and residential character of the place drew Italian, Irish, and Polish immigrants. Well into the twenty-first century Maspeth was one of the main residential areas for firefighters, sanitation workers, laborers, and truck drivers who traced their ancestry back to Italy.

It was immediately after World War II that an Italian immigrant family with the surname of Vitale took up residence close to Maspeth. Giuseppe and Lilli Vitale had emigrated from the village of San Giuseppe, some forty miles south of Palermo in the western part of Sicily. Life in the old country had not been easy, particularly when faced with the infant mortality rates that Sicilian families experienced. Like most Sicilian households, the Vitale family had hoped for a son. They already had a name. The boy would be called Giuseppe or "Joseph" in English.

Male offspring were favored by parents since they could guarantee the family name would be passed on. But the Vitale family was not going to be blessed with a son, certainly not while living in the hardscrabble hills of the Sicilian countryside. Two baby boys died, either in childbirth or shortly after. Twice the Vitale parents had to bury the tiny bodies as their three daughters watched.

In Maspeth, the Vitale family lived in the kind of working obscurity that immigrants found as their niche. They weren't rich but they had by all accounts a quiet, nurturing home life where the three daughters—Anna, Betty, and the youngest Josephine—thrived. Giuseppe, also known as Joseph, and Lilli Vitale took one more chance at having a son. Seemingly cursed with bad luck with sons named Giuseppe, the parents decided that if another male child came into their lives he would be named something different. On September 22, 1947, Lilli Vitale gave birth to a son, and he was baptized as Salvatore. He survived. The family had great hopes for him.

Both employed, Giuseppe and Lilli spent a great deal of time out of their house and entrusted the care of Salvatore to their daughters. Josephine was four years older than her baby brother but even at such a young age, with her parents spending so much time out of the house making a living, she became a surrogate mother.

The Vitale girls fussed over Salvatore in ways that were certain to spoil him. He got what he wanted when he wanted it, usually from Josephine. Yet, family members would later remember that despite all the doting from his siblings, Salvatore Vitale did not respond in kind to his sisters. Sure, he may have been spoiled, but he seemed to lack affection, his relatives would later recall. He didn't do anything terribly wrong as a child. But while the Vitale women centered their lives around the home, Salvatore seemed distant and cold. He should have been another girl, his father would say of his only son, according to one family member.

Maspeth is bisected by the Long Island Expressway, the concrete ribbon of a roadway that became over the years the crowded conduit for much of the traffic going to and from New York City. The part of Maspeth north of the expressway—where the Vitale family would buy a house on Sixty-eighth Street near Grand Avenue—retained its residential character. The same was largely true of the southern part of the community, although residential development was hemmed in by large cemeteries.

It was a few blocks from the main shopping boulevard of Grand Avenue in Maspeth that another working-class family took up residence. Like the Vitales who lived about five blocks away, Anthony and Adeline Massino were Italian Americans. But while the Massinos traced their heritage to the city of Naples and its environs, they were second-generation Americans born and raised in the United States. They had three children, Joseph, John, and Anthony. Their father worked in a neighborhood grocery store.

Joseph Massino was a boy comfortable on the streets. Big boned, trim, and muscular, he was athletic but not very good in school. Friends would later recall he became very adept in math. In a working-class neighborhood where as a kid you had to hold your own to make your mark, he earned a reputation of being one of the toughest on the block. He could kick ass with the best of them.

Joseph Massino only got to the seventh grade in what is now Intermediate School 73 on Fifty-fourth Avenue. Bored with school, Massino took a variety of jobs, including as a summer lifeguard at beach clubs in Atlantic Beach on Long Island and in Florida. In something of a Maspeth legend, which Massino himself would insist was true, he supposedly once swam from Breezy Point in the Rockaways to Manhattan Beach, a distance of over one mile. Stories also circulated that he would jump off the Cross Bay Bridge, which connected the Rockaways to the mainland, and swim for hours.

With a reputation for being a tough guy and with a full head of wavy black hair, Massino's rugged looks caught the eye of neighborhood girl Josephine Vitale, who was seven months younger. She had been voted the best looking in her eighth grade class. The year was 1956.

Around the time Joseph Massino and Josephine Vitale were getting acquainted in working-class Maspeth, the American Mafia was on the verge of some big changes. Bonanno was shuttling back and forth between Tucson, Arizona, and New York. He made one side trip to Havana, Cuba, which in those days was a playground for the rich and infamous. As he recounted the Havana trip in his autobiography, Bonanno hooked up with the financial mob wizard Meyer Lansky, who owned a piece of the Hotel Nacional, and spent his days wandering the streets of old Havana, where he stayed in some flophouse hotel in 1924.

The way Joseph Bonanno recounted the Havana trip it was nothing more than a nostalgic trip away from home of some "Ulysses," as he likened himself, who had his fill of adventure in life. His son, Bill, in his 1999 autobiography, put a different spin on the Havana trip on which he accompanied his father. Bill Bonanno said that his father met up with not only Lansky but also New York Mafia bosses Albert Anastasia, Frank Costello, and Joseph Profaci. "We were there for pleasure, not business, but business came up," the younger Bonanno said. Cuba's dictator Fulgencio Batista met with the mobsters and tried to get them to somehow influence the Eisenhower administration to take a more active role against the insurgency led by Fidel Castro. According to Bill Bonanno, Castro figured the mafiosi had an interest in the island's drug trade, aside from the millions made in the casinos.

The conventional wisdom about the American Mafia's stance on drugs has been that the bosses were against narcotics trafficking. But if it was a hands-off policy, it was riddled with holes like Swiss cheese. Bill Bonanno asserted that in 1947 in a clandestine Mafia Commission meeting on a yacht off Florida—and not in Havana as widely believed—the bosses argued about drugs. According to Bonanno, the "liberal" faction of the Commission, composed of Vito Genovese and Thomas Lucchese, wanted to get involved in heroin. The conservatives, led by Joseph Bonanno, thought it was a bad idea and prevailed on the Commission to pass a resolution prohibiting narcotics trafficking. The elder Bonanno, his son stated, believed drugs would destroy the families.

Despite such prohibitions, a number of New York Mafia leaders began to push harder and allowed some of their men to get involved in narcotics. The same divisiveness over drugs also split the Sicilian Mafia. When Joseph Bonanno made a trip to Sicily in early fall of 1957—again part pleasure and part business—he learned that New York Mafia families were involved in the trafficking of heroin and its opium base, according to his son. Impossible, the elder Bonanno responded when told of the New York connection. "They are up to their asses in it," an old friend explained. "They couldn't care less about our glorious tradition."

The main violator of the Mafia drug ban was certainly Vito Genovese, who finally got Frank Costello out of the leadership role in their family by ordering an assassination attempt of his rival. The plot to kill Costello culminated in a shooting in May 1957 as the dapper Costello was returning to his apartment in Central Park West. The gunman has long been reputed to have been Vincent Gigante, whose bullet grazed Costello in the head but didn't kill him. Getting the message, Costello retired as boss of Lucky Luciano's old family. From then onward, Genovese pushed the narcotics connections, ultimately pushing so hard that he was arrested on narcotics charges by federal officials in 1958 and after his conviction was sent to prison where he died in 1969.

It was very soon after the Costello assassination attempt that one of the other conservative bosses, Albert Anastasia, was targeted for death. The plotters were rival Vito Genovese, who conspired with Carlo Gambino, then a rising captain in Anastasia's family. Gambino had already arranged the murder of Anastasia's underboss Frank Scalise, the first step to seizing control of the family. The assassination of Anastasia as he sat in a barber's chair at the Park Sheraton Hotel on October 25, 1957, became one of the legendary mob murders in New York.

Anastasia's murder was splashed on the front page of all of New York's major daily newspapers—there were more than ten of them at the time—and Joseph Massino couldn't have missed seeing the big story. But Joseph Bonanno did, at least initially. He was in Sicily when Anastasia was killed and only learned of it when he returned to New York. For a startled Bonanno, the killing of one of his conservative allies on the Commission was a bad sign. "The Pax Bonanno, that I was so proud of having forged was on the verge of disintegration," he said years later.

Immediately after Anastasia's death, the American Mafia leaders called a massive summit conference in the town of Apalachin in upstate New York, which had been the site of a Commission meeting in 1956. The setting was the home of Joseph Barbara, a mafioso with ties to local politicians and police. Bonanno was opposed to the 1957 meeting, thinking it was ill advised and the location not the safest place for mob bosses to gather. Evidently, Barbara reported having trouble with greedy local law enforcement officials.

Nevertheless, the meeting was held on November 14,

1957, and on the agenda were three items: the ratification of Gambino's takeover of the Anastasia family; ways to deal with the new, tough federal narcotics control law that took effect in 1956; and aggressive unionization of garment factories tied to the mob in eastern Pennsylvania.

The meeting turned into a disaster for the mafiosi who attended. Local police noticed the traffic going into Barbara's property and set up a roadblock, checked the cars, and noted the names on the driver licenses. Bosses like Vito Genovese, Carlo Gambino, Joseph Profaci, and Joseph Magliocco were noted by police. Bonanno, who had tarried in nearby Endicott with his cousin, Stefano Maggadino, said he heard about the roadblocks on the news reports and avoided the meeting altogether. In total, about sixty members of various Mafia families were listed by police as being at Barbara's home and while no one was immediately arrested, investigation of the meeting spawned further investigations that led to arrests for years to come.

While Mafia politics can sometimes move with the speed of a bullet, in the case of Anastasia's murder, the full ramifications would not be felt for years. Things moved in convoluted fashion and ultimately the changes in two leadership positions in the space of a few months meant that the so-called liberal wing of the Commission, composed of Thomas Lucchese, Vito Genovese, and Carlo Gambino, who took over from Anastasia, was equal in number to the more conservative men of tradition represented by Joseph Bonanno, Joseph Profaci, and Stefano Maggadino, from Buffalo.

For Bonanno, the new alignment in the Commission was a sign that the old traditions of the Mafia were changing in ways that he found distasteful. While the Castellammarese, who shaped the American Mafia since the 1930s, were bound by Sicilian traditions of loyalty and honor, others seemed seduced by the constant chase for money. The descent into narcotics was the clearest indication that the production of capital through risky enterprises was viewed by some as worth the danger. The publicity and law enforcement interest in the Mafia after Apalachin also painted what Bonanno saw as an honorable way of life as nothing more than a conspiracy bent on destroying America.

Bonanno also believed that the Mafia was hurting its own image with the public assassinations like that of Anastasia. The year 1961 was a case in point. Upstarts in Profaci's family, a group of young Turks led by the Gallo brothers—Joey, Albert, and Larry—revolted against the boss. The Gallos were really nothing more than mob toughs who went around strong-arming businesses to take their jukeboxes. Investigators even determined that the Gallos had set up their own union of jukebox repairmen as part of the racket. But as former New York Police Department (NYPD) detective Ralph Salerno recounted, the publicity the brothers received from a 1957 U.S. Senate hearing chaired by Senator John McClellan gave them an inflated sense of self-importance.

Salerno was part of a NYPD investigation that used wiretaps and bugs to discover that the Gallos were unhappy with the way they were being treated by their boss Profaci. According to Salerno's account in his own book *The Crime Confederation*, the Gallos became angered when Profaci asked them to kill a gambler named Frank "Frankie Shots" Abbatemarco in November 1959. Abbatemarco was killed, but his gambling interests went to Profaci and his friends while the Gallo crew got nothing.

The Gallo gang engineered a bold kidnapping of five key leaders of the Profaci family and had also targeted Joe Profaci himself, although he escaped. Salerno said the kidnappings were never reported to police, although informants kept Brooklyn detectives up to date. The hostages were held for two weeks as Commission emissaries tried to broker a settlement. Joey Gallo, the hothead, didn't want to negotiate but was ordered to take a trip to California by his older brother Larry, a move that led to a release of the hostages.

In early 1962, the Commission met to deal with the Profaci-

Gallo dispute and it was Bonanno who convinced the members to allow Profaci to remain as head of the family. There had been a push by Gambino and Lucchese to get Profaci to retire. But Bonanno said the families had to trust each other to take care of their internal problems. A truce lasted for about six months, but Salerno said he and his fellow investigators discovered that Profaci was quietly working to strike back at the Gallos. After Larry Gallo escaped a strangulation attempt at the Sahara Lounge on Utica Avenue in Brooklyn, a full-fledged war broke out, unlike anything seen since the days of Masseria and Maranzano in the 1930s. The Gallo brothers went to the mattresses, barricading themselves in two apartments on President Street in Brooklyn, armed to the teeth with rifles and shotguns. In his telling of the Gallo War, Salerno counted no fewer than fourteen attempted assassinations and killings involving Profaci and Gallo loyalists. The war continued even after Profaci died in June 1962.

With the death of Profaci, his underboss and brother-in-law Joseph Magliocco tried to get the Commission to ratify him as the new boss. He had the support of Bonanno, who no doubt saw a continuation of the alliance Bonanno had with the late Profaci. The Commission, however, denied Magliocco approval. Bonanno chalked that up to the fact that the Gallos had support on the Commission from the Gambino-Lucchese faction. Still, Magliocco persisted and intrigue continued.

Both Joseph and son Bill Bonanno, in their separate accounts of Magliocco's struggle for power, believe this was a significant episode in the Bonanno family's growing disillusionment with the New York mob scene. Joseph Bonanno said that his son Bill, at a time when he was seeking guidance about his marital problems, stayed briefly with Magliocco, his wife's uncle. The Magliocco estate was a walled compound on Long Island that at this time in 1963 was heavily fortified and guarded, much the way Vito Corleone's home was depicted in the *Godfather*.

In a classic mob maneuver, Joseph Bonanno related that Magliocco appeared to have planted his own spy, a mobster close to Gambino and Lucchese. According to the elder Bonanno, both Magliocco and Bill Bonanno met this spy at a Long Island railroad station one particular day.

"Magliocco and the man briefly exchanged a few words," Bonanno recalled. "Magliocco used this man to keep tabs on his enemies and to let him know what Gambino and Lucchese were saying about him."

Sixteen years after his father's account of that brief encounter, Bill Bonanno related a somewhat different, more sinister version of that day at the Brentwood railroad station. The man who got off the train and spoke with Magliocco was Sally Musacio, a relative by marriage to the aging Magliocco. According to Bill Bonanno, Magliocco asked, "Is everything set?" When Musacio answered yes, Magliocco said, "Okay, start."

According to Bill Bonanno's account, that brief exchange was a command by Magliocco that a mob war was to start, with Lucchese, Gambino, and Maggadino being the targets. But a young captain in Magliocco's crew named Joseph Colombo tipped off Lucchese and Gambino about what Magliocco—and the Bonannos—planned. To undo the political damage, Bill Bonanno met Lucchese at his home in Long Beach, Long Island, and explained that it was sheer coincidence that he was present in Magliocco's company. The wily Lucchese didn't buy the explanation.

Shortly after the assassination of President John F. Kennedy in November 1963, Joseph Magliocco died without ever being officially recognized by the Commission as boss of the old Profaci family. As his reward for ratting out Magliocco and the Bonannos, Joseph Colombo was blessed by the Commission with leadership of the family. But while the likelihood of serious mob warfare had been averted, the Bonanno family continued to be the object of scorn by the other New York bosses. According to Joseph Bonanno, his cousin from Buffalo, Stefano Maggadino, was leading the opposition.

Portrayed as an insecure man in the face of the elder Bonanno's business ventures in Canada, Maggadino saw his cousin as a threatening interloper into his territory of Toronto. Joseph Bonanno, who had been expelled from Canada in a legal dustup with authorities there, insisted he had no such designs, but his relationship with his cousin continued to sour. Things did not improve when Bonanno installed his son Bill as consiglieri, a move that angered older family captains such as Gaspar DiGregorio.

For years, Joseph Bonanno had been growing increasingly disillusioned with the mob life. He felt that the old Sicilian traditions of his kind of men of honor were on the wane. He was spending more time outside of New York, mostly in Arizona. A man of intelligence, Bonanno had a curiosity about many things and felt comfortable talking about any number of subjects. But he was also arrogant and condescending, seeing old friends and relatives such as Maggadino as intellectual inferiors. Bonanno also came to view the Commission, which was firmly in the hands of the Lucchese-Gambino alliance, as illegitimate and meddling in his own family affairs. So in 1964 when Maggadino had three Commission emissaries summon Bonanno to a meeting to hear grievances against him, the elder Bonanno refused to show up.

The flouting by Bonanno of the Commission's demand for a meeting was a cardinal sin. The severity of the repercussions were noted by Sam "the Plumber" DeCavalcante, the Mafia boss of New Jersey. Though he didn't know it, DeCavalcante's office in Kenilworth, New Jersey, had been bugged by the FBI for a four-year period between 1961 to 1965. DeCavalcante was picked up on the recordings telling associates just how poisoned Bonanno's relationship with the Commission had become. It seemed to DeCavalcante that Bonanno had been the source of the problem. Among

Bonanno's sins, DeCavalcante said were his attempts to muscle in on other families and his elevating his son Bill to the role of consiglieri. But it was Bonanno's ignoring of the Commission request for his presence at a meeting that did him in, DeCavalcante claimed.

"The Commission doesn't recognize Joseph Bonanno as the Boss anymore," DeCavalcante told his friend Joe Zicarelli, a Bonanno crime family member who lived in New Jersey. "They [the Commission] can't understand why this guy is ducking them."

DeCavalcante told an incredulous Zicarelli that neither Bonanno, nor his son Bill, would be recognized as leaders of the crime family. That rang ominous for Zicarelli, who suggested both men might be in danger. However, DeCavalcante said Bonanno wasn't in any danger unless he made any tricky moves.

Joseph Bonanno's challenge to the Commission and Maggadino set the stage for one of the most bizarre episodes in American Mafia history. On October 20, 1964, the day before Bonanno was to appear before a federal grand jury in Manhattan probing him on a possible conspiracy charge, he was accosted by two men on Park Avenue near Thirty-sixth Street in Manhattan.

"Come on Joe, my boss wants you," one of the burly men said as they hustled Bonanno into a waiting car.

The grab took place around midnight outside the luxury apartment building of Bonanno's attorney, William Maloney. Maloney tried to chase after the intruders, but one of them fired a single shot from a handgun at Maloney's feet, sending him scurrying for protection inside the lobby of his building. Bonanno was bundled into a car that sped off toward Lexington Avenue.

The New York newspapers went into a spasm of sensational stories about Bonanno's abduction and for months stories appeared, fed by police sources, that Bonanno had been spotted in Europe, was hiding in Arizona, or was secretly in the protective custody of the federal government. There was plenty of speculation that Bonanno had staged his own kidnapping to avoid having to testify before the grand jury. Some news headlines had Bonanno written off as dead. DeCavalcante held to the theory that Bonanno staged his own disappearance and a month after the incident FBI recordings show him saying as much to his own underboss.

"He pulled that off himself," DeCavalcante said. "It was his own men. We figure it was his kid and Vito."

For sixteen months Joseph Bonanno was missing, at least in the eyes of police and federal investigators who couldn't find him. What happened? The only account of what happened to Bonanno was the one he provided in his autobiography. He recounted that his abductors were men he knew, both relatives of Maggadino. Crossing the George Washington Bridge, the car went over the Hudson River and traveled for several hours over the rain-slicked roads. The next morning at a farmhouse in the woods "somewhere in upstate New York," he was told by his captors to make himself comfortable and wait.

"In the afternoon, I heard a car pull up to the farmhouse. This was it. My nemesis had arrived. I was summoned to the main room of the house," Bonanno recounted. "Stefan Maggadino tromped in—an old spry and portly man with ruddy cheeks and an amiable smile."

According to Bonanno, his cousin was alternately sardonic, angry, solicitous, concerned, and beseeching in what were weeks and weeks of conversations about their relationship and the fact that Maggadino suspected that his New York City relative had designs on his territory upstate. But more important for Bonanno, the talks revealed that Maggadino had a deep-seated envy of his cousin and feelings of insecurity and inferiority.

Bonanno later speculated about whether Maggadino had acted with the consent of Gambino and Lucchese, or the entire Commission. He never stated whether he had any answer about what support his cousin had for the kidnapping. After a few weeks, Bonanno said he was driven by the same two men who abducted him to El Paso, Texas, where he asked to be let out of the car.

How true is Bonanno's account? No one knows, but it is likely that Bonanno staged his own kidnapping. If the snatch was real, they would have killed him. Years after Bonanno's autobiography was published with the account of his disappearance, Bill Bonanno recounted receiving a cryptic telephone call from an unidentified man about two months after the Park Avenue kidnapping. The call was made to a public telephone Bill Bonanno said he and his father had arranged years earlier to use if either of them ran into trouble. In essence, the caller told Bonanno's son that the Mafia boss was okay and to "just sit tight." His father, the younger Bonanno was told, would see him in a few days.

As far as can be determined, Joseph Bonanno remained out of sight of law enforcement and his son for approximately another seventeen months. Then, on May 17, 1966, after being dropped off by a friend at Foley Square in lower Manhattan and in the company of his new attorney, Albert Kreiger, Joseph Bonanno walked into the U.S. District Court for the Southern District of New York. Taking a side entrance to avoid being spotted, Bonanno walked into a third-floor courtroom and surrendered himself to the judge on duty. Since federal prosecutors had been notified by Kreiger, federal marshals placed Bonanno under arrest.

In the months that followed his dramatic surrender, Bonanno would have to deal with a trial on charges he willfully failed to appear before a federal grand jury. But it was quite clear that Bonanno was finished as a key New York Mafia boss. He had no backing on the Commission and his arrogant attempt to have his son step in as leader and the snubs of the other bosses destroyed his ability to lead. He made no secret in relaying a message to the Commission that everything stemmed from problems he had with Maggadino. With a gun held to his head by the Commission, Bonanno then haltingly moved into a forced retirement. He was lucky to get away with his life.

This strange period of strife between Bonanno and Maggadino led to the final distancing of Bonanno from playing any active role in what he called "our tradition." Bonanno's continued absence also brought on leadership instability within the crime family that saw various men attempt to assume the role of boss. Backed by Maggadino, one of Bonanno's captains, Gaspar DiGregorio, made a brief pretense as boss and was able to profit from the defections of some crime family members and associates who didn't want to be frozen out of rackets by being loyal to the Bonannos.

As a tool of Maggadino, DiGregorio tried to set up Bill Bonanno for assassination in January 1966 in what became known as the Troutman Street shootout in Brooklyn. The younger Bonanno escaped unscathed. An aspiring mob gunman named Frank Mari was later credited with firing some of the dozens of shots that never found a target. Ultimately, DiGregorio lost face because of the botched hit and suffered a heart attack; his role as factional leader was taken over by Paul Sciacca, a garment manufacturer who had been a Bonanno consiglieri years earlier. Sciacca, while not considered a powerful leader, was nevertheless acceptable to Maggadino and his allies on the Commission, namely Gambino, Lucchese, and Colombo, who by then was firmly set as leader of the old Profaci family.

Though considered by the Commission to be boss of the Bonanno family, Sciacca was really just the leader of a number of factions fighting for power in the clan. Out of a crime family believed in 1966 to number 400 members, Bonanno loyalists were estimated to have comprised about half that. DeCavalcante was recorded on one FBI tape saying that as soon as the Commission voted Bonanno out as boss in 1964 at least sixty members had already defected. Though he was tapped by his father to be among a group of three or four trusted aides to watch after crime family affairs, Bill Bonanno was distracted by his own legal problems and concerns about the safety of his wife and children. The Troutman Street shootout had also shown that Bill was in personal danger. Because Bill had to be absent quite often from New York during this period, it fell to Natale Evola, who had been an usher at his father's wedding, to steer those loyal to Bonanno.

Times were dangerous, yes. The destruction of what Joseph Bonanno once called the Pax Bonanno had resulted in numerous shootings and murders. Aside from the abortive Troutman Street incident, there were a number of other mob killings and shootings during the "Banana War," as the crime family clashes were known. Among those wounded was Frank Mari, one of the men believed to have been involved in the attempt on Bill Bonanno's life.

Joseph Bonanno had prided himself on the decades of relative peace he had imposed on New York's Mafia scene. In his view, it was the convincing force of his personality and the political ties he had to other Castellammarese leaders that made the Mafia thrive. The peace allowed each crime family to conduct its rackets and make money. But as Bonanno would say, it was because the individual members of the Mafia were restrained by shared values of respect, trust, loyalty, and honor that the families maintained discipline. However, toward the end of his tortured reign, Joseph Bonanno saw that change.

"Everyone likes to have money, but in the absence of a higher moral code the making of money becomes an unwholesome goal," Bonanno said in his autobiography. As Bonanno saw it, the "individualistic orientation" encouraged disrespect for authority and family values. In many ways then, the old crime boss sounded like any conservative man who felt in the face of a changing world that he had become an anachronism.

The debacle with the Commission showed that Bonanno

had lost his touch as a mob politician. The internecine warfare that erupted in Bonanno's last years as boss—the Banana War—littered the streets of New York with bodies until well into 1968. By this time, though, the elder Bonanno had lost his taste for the battle. The fragmentation of his once-powerful family was also too much for its founder.

"There is no *Bonanno* Family anymore," he bemoaned in his book. He was right—to a point.

CHAPTER 4

Maspeth Joe

Those old enough to remember can recall what they were doing and where they were when they heard that President John F. Kennedy was assassinated on November 22, 1963. Bill Bonanno certainly did. He said he was in a Manhattan steak house with a number of mafiosi. Among them was Philip "Rusty" Rastelli, one of a stable of Bonanno loyalists from Williamsburg, Brooklyn.

Destined for a life of crime, Rastell: had the credentials at an early age. A juvenile delinquent by the age of eight, Rastelli had his first big arrest in 1936 at the age of seventeen for homicide. It was later reduced to assault and he was sent away for a term in a reformatory school. The time upstate didn't help him since it was only four years later that he drew a full-fledged adult prison term of five to ten years for assault and robbery. Through the 1940s and 1950s, Rastelli was arrested a few more times but saw those charges dismissed.

The eldest of three brothers who all would go on to be criminals, Rastelli, when he wasn't in jail, was busy developing an interesting business niche. Williamsburg and its environs like Greenpoint and Maspeth were filled with trucking terminals, warehouses, and factories. The workers needed to eat but never had the time—particularly with thirty-minute lunch breaks—to do anything adventuresome. So, a service industry of food wagons developed to fill the need. Loaded with drinks, sandwiches, pastries, and coffee, the silver-bodied lunch wagons were vital to industrial New York. It would become Rastelli's calling and his own racket.

In the 1920s and 1930s, mobster Ciro Terranova wasn't subtle in his extortion of the pushcart vendors in Manhattan's East Harlem and elsewhere. He would shake them down for payoffs and those who didn't comply found themselves the object of a good beating while their pushcarts were trashed. Rastelli had a more intricate form of extortion. Beginning in 1966 he founded the Workmen's Mobile Lunch Association. Among the benefits offered the food vendors who operated the lunch wagons was the guarantee of a daily route with no competition. Business could be so good that even some of the association officers took over routes.

Rastelli kept some routes in reserve and doled them out as favors for friends. Of course, there was a catch for such a guarantee of livelihood. The vendors had to pay $10 to $15 a week—not an insignificant sum in the 1960s—for membership (protection) to Rastelli's association. But it was the wholesale suppliers of the lunch wagons who were really cash cows. They had to pay off Rastelli's crowd as well, sometimes over $900 a month, for the privilege of supplying sandwiches and drinks to the lunch wagons. If those payments weren't made, the suppliers would see their lunch wagon customers dry up. It was classic racketeering activity, maybe not the most flashy stuff around but it suited Rastelli well.

When the great Banana War sputtered to a close in 1968 and Joseph Bonanno and his family decamped for Arizona, Joseph Massino was a strapping twenty-five-year-old man with a wife—he had married Josephine in 1960—and young daughter. For work he ran a lunch wagon, taking a cue from his mother's side of the family, which began outfitting the trucks to carry snacks to factories. Since he lived in Maspeth, Massino didn't have far to travel to service the factories that lined Grand and Metropolitan avenues. "Joe Maspeth" was how the lunch wagon crowd knew him. Friends remember that it was a struggle at first. Massino was strapped for cash and in the wintertime he took to standing around Grand and Metropolitan avenues selling Christmas trees to earn a few more dollars. He even had to borrow a few hundred dollars from relatives to pay the medical bills for the birth of his first child. But Rastelli liked him and that counted for something.

The lunch wagon business might have been a racket, seeing how Rastelli controlled things, but for his friends like Massino things worked out. The lunch business could be a living and for a thrifty husband and father like Massino the work was enough to get by. In 1966, records show that Joseph and Josephine Massino took out their first mortgage for $16,000 at 5.5 percent interest from the Greenpoint Savings Bank to purchase a house on Caldwell Avenue in Maspeth, just a few doors down from where his parents lived at number 71-21 Caldwell. Joseph and Josephine Massino, who had been living a few blocks away in a two-story frame house on Perry Avenue just off the Long Island Expressway, needed the extra space since they had a five-year-old daughter, Adeline, and were planning for more children. The payments for what appears to be Massino's first tangible stake in the American dream of home ownership amounted to $98.26 a month.

Anyone connected to Philip Rastelli and his brothers, Carmine and Marty, had an easy entrée to mob life. Philip Rastelli wasn't flashy, but his rackets were solid. Massino was close to Rastelli's brother Carmine, who ran a depot where the lunch wagons filled up with supplies, so he was guaranteed good deals and fresh pastries. Massino's spot for his coffee stand was on Remsen Place in Maspeth, right around the corner from the house on Perry Street and just a short walk from his new house on Caldwell Avenue. The lunch wagon Massino had was dubbed the "roach coach," which may or may not have reflected the level of hygiene practiced in the food trade. Gradually, through the Rastelli connection, Joseph Massino, the beefy food vendor who also earned the nickname "Joe Wagons," became intertwined with the Bonanno crime family. It would prove to be an auspicious time for Massino to build such ties.

The war for leadership of what had been the crime family of Joseph Bonanno had led to a confusing situation to say the least. By the spring of 1967, law enforcement officials in the United States and Canada believed from their surveillance reports and other investigations that Bonanno had maneuvered a comeback of sorts because of the weakness exhibited by the leadership of Gaspar DiGregorio, the man who was backed by Stefano Maggadino for the role of boss when Bonanno disappeared. But even a top NYPD inspector in charge of intelligence had to admit that in the end investigators were groping to understand what was going on in the crime family.

DiGregorio's abdication after he suffered a heart attack only months after he was chosen as boss led the way to power plays by Bill Bonanno, which had resulted in the Troutman Street shootout and the open warfare that followed. But by late 1968, police perceived a different situation in the Bonanno family, one in which Joseph Bonanno accepted Paul Sciacca as the new boss and had agreed to move permanently with his family to Arizona. MAFIA LEADERS SETTLE "BANANA WAR" was the headline of a November 24, 1968, *New York Times* story about the development.

Police-organized crime investigators, like Kremlinologists of the cold war period who studied the Soviet Union, looked to social circumstances and public appearances to divine what was taking place behind the scenes in the Mafia. In terms of the Bonanno family, it was a September 14, 1968, wedding on Long Island that led police to believe that the crime family war had been settled. As police told the *Times*, Bonanno loyalists and Sciacca supporters who had been on hostile terms were "disported together convivially" at the wedding reception of Sciacca's son, Anthony, to Florence Rando, a niece of Frank Mari.

The Sciacca-Rando wedding wasn't the nuptial of the century, but it drew a lot of attention from law enforcement because such celebrations are places where mobsters want to be seen and do business. The guest lists for such functions are studied because they provide clues to who is in and who is out in the mob hierarchy. In this case, there were 200 guests who attended a reception at the Woodbury Country Club and detectives filled nine pages of notes with their jottings of the various car license plates.

There is no evidence that Joseph Massino, who at that stage in his life was nothing more than an associate in the crime family, attended this particular wedding. But his mentor Rastelli was spotted by police at the reception and his presence signaled that those who had once been loyal to Joseph Bonanno and his son had buried the hatchet with the Sciacca faction. Rastelli was clearly safe and in his role as captain had not lost any stature. A peace of sorts had blossomed.

However, Sciacca suffered from a bad heart. So he wanted to stop his involvement with the crime family and was in the process of grooming Mari to become his successor. A triggerman and reputed dope dealer, Mari was elected family boss during a sitdown in a restaurant in Manhattan in May 1969. His reign was short. In September 1969, Mari, his bodyguard James Episcopia, and Sciacca loyalist Michael Adamo disappeared. There bodies were never found. Police suspected Mari had been killed as payback for having a role in the murder of Joseph Bonanno's bodyguard Sam Perrone a year earlier. Another theory was that some mobsters simply resented the way Mari was pushed forward, particularly since he hadn't distinguished himself.

The Bonanno family could have lurched into another period of disarray, but the Commission took the unusual step after Mari's disappearance of appointing a triumvirate to rule the family, at least temporarily. The three leaders who were to work as a team were Natale Evola, who had weathered a narcotics conviction to maintain his power in the garment trucking industry, an obscure crime captain named Joseph DiFilippi, and the none-too-flashy Philip Rastelli.

As a member of the crime family's governing committee, Rastelli's stature within the mob had grown and those like Massino who had hitched themselves to him began to see their lives tightly intertwined with his fortunes. It would take years for the importance of this connection between Massino and Rastelli to become apparent. Much of what would later happen to Massino could be traced to Rastelli's influence. Theirs was a mentoring relationship and the ties that developed would endure for a lifetime.

It was also in 1970 that a Brooklyn kid with straw blond hair and a Germanic name started hanging around Massino's Remsen Place coffee trucks. The youngster with the pale complexion stood out among the darker Italians in the neighborhood. He was barely a teenager when he met the twenty-something Massino, but their relationship would take its own fortuitous turn. Duane Leisenheimer, whose fair hair earned him the nickname "Goldie," was really up to no good and going nowhere when he met Massino. A student at Brooklyn's Automotive High School on Bedford Avenue in Williamsburg, Leisenheimer was on his way to becoming an auto mechanic but could only make it through his sophomore year before dropping out. Still, he liked cars and noticed that Massino's Oldsmobile had cracked windows, which was odd since an auto glass business where the youngster worked was around the corner from Massino's coffee stand.

Leisenheimer liked cars so much he started stealing them. He said he was sixteen years old when he stole his first vehicle and started doing some work in a local chop shop.

For those unfamiliar with the term *chop shop*, it is a place where stolen cars are stripped for parts that can then be resold at double or even triple the value of the complete vehicle. Leisenheimer made $150 for each stolen car. In no time, he was stealing them at the rate of fifteen vehicles a week—not bad money for a high school dropout. But it could be bad for the neighborhood to have a budding car thief hanging around, so Massino told Leisenheimer not to steal cars from the area or park them around the stand.

"I don't want your heat," Massino told him.

Massino also didn't want his own heat, his own troubles, to burn the youngster. Of course, Massino had plenty of heat to worry about. Though he had a nice business with the coffee and sandwich stands he acquired, he sold more than food out of the lunch truck. The neighborhood workers who came for a bite to eat were also able to play the numbers with Massino, who used the trucks as a small gambling location. For them it was the poor man's lottery. He undoubtedly was kicking up some of the proceeds to Rastelli.

Massino had another side job that was a natural for Maspeth. The area around Grand and Metropolitan avenues was riddled with factories, warehouses, and trucking depots. It was New York City's loading dock. Trucks were all over the place and they were laden with consumer goods that everybody wanted and would pay good money for. Apparently, with Rastelli's blessing Massino started hijacking trucks and needed help. He asked around about the young car thief in the neighborhood.

"He is a stand-up guy," said one of the local toughs about Leisenheimer. In plain English that meant the kid from Brooklyn wouldn't rat anybody out.

It was all Massino needed to hear. So even though he couldn't steal cars from the neighborhood, Duane Leisenheimer could be a hijacker, courtesy of Joe Massino and Philip Rastelli. In just one night the car kid from Brooklyn could make up to $2,000 helping Massino move truckloads of stolen television sets, men's suits, Huckapoo shirts, and Farberware. That was more money than Leisenheimer might make in a week of stealing cars. Maspeth was turning into a nice place for the Brooklyn high school dropout.

Leisenheimer wasn't the only young man who gravitated to Massino. Salvatore Vitale, the younger brother of Massino's wife, Josephine, had bonded at an early age to the budding lunch wagon entrepreneur who was five years his senior. In 1968, Vitale ended a short tour of duty in the army as a paratrooper. He tried going straight and spent two years serving as what he would later say was a job as a "narcotics correction officer," which was ironic considering the involvement over the years of some of the Bonanno family in narcotics. When he left that job, Vitale approached Massino for work. There was plenty to do with the hijacking business, as well as with part-time work as a burglar, and Vitale was a willing recruit for both types of work.

"If you are going to do scores, do them with me," Vitale remembered Massino telling him. It would lead him into another world of big-time break-ins, hijacks, and fur district rip-offs in Manhattan. The commodities stolen ranged from coffee to air conditioners to tennis rackets. Sometimes Vitale and Massino would become very daring and inventive. In one episode later recounted to investigators, Vitale remembered how he rented a storage vault under a fake name in Manhattan's fur district just south of Thirty-fourth Street. During summer nights in August, Vitale said, he would get the locks off other storage vaults, remove furs, and store them in his locker. Another time, he, Massino, and a Colombo crime family member made about $34,000 in the theft of watches from a store in Livingston, New Jersey. For that job, Vitale said, they cut some telephone lines.

Inevitably, Rastelli, by virtue of his leadership role, was a high-profile target for law enforcement, and he made it easy for the cops. In July 1970, Rastelli was indicted by a Suffolk County grand jury. The secret panel met in such secrecy and with such concern for witnesses that the windows of the district attorney's office were covered with paper and some of the hallways were closed to the public and patrolled by armed guards. Rastelli was among five men charged with usury. The indictment stated that Rastelli's loan sharks charged interest up to 300 percent a year (25 percent was the legal limit) and terrorized nearly two dozen customers. One customer was a local Suffolk County bail bondsman who got so far into debt that he was forced to bring in extra customers to Rastelli and his crew.

Rastelli was convicted in December 1972 on loan-sharking charges and was sentenced to prison. His incarceration deprived the crime family of one part of the leadership troika, but Rastelli was still able to participate and get information through the visits of his brothers, Carmine and Marty, as well as through associates like Massino. This kept Rastelli in the loop at a time when—unbeknown to many—Natale Evola was in serious trouble.

In 1972, federal officials began a series of ambitious undercover operations in Manhattan's garment district. Long a stronghold for the Mafia, the garment area surrounding Seventh Avenue was honeycombed with factories, cutting rooms, showrooms, and innumerable small businesses that supplied the clothing companies with everything from bolts of cloth to zippers. The mob had gained its influence over the industry through labor racketeering in which the unions used the services of mob toughs to go along with the union demands. On the other side, employers used Mafia associates to help set up shadow companies and operations that were nonunion to avoid paying workers contract wages and benefits.

Garment manufacturers also worked on extremely tight profit margins and had to be able to change their production operations to meet the shifting fashion styles and the sudden rush of orders from department stores. It was a tough business and when banks and factors (companies that lend money against a firm's accounts receivable) were reluctant to come up with cash, Seventh Avenue executives turned to Mafia loan sharks for quick infusions of financial help. Never mind that interest rates could go over 300 percent a year. Manufacturers hoped that the orders they would be able to fill after getting mob financial help would bring in enough quick payment from retailers to have the mob debts paid off quickly. Sometimes it worked. Other times a financially stressed manufacturer had to take on the mob as a silent partner.

The trucking companies were vital to the industry because cut goods, the separate pieces that made each item of apparel, had to be shipped to contracting firms where the clothing was actually assembled. Once that was done, the finished goods had to be sent back to the manufacturer for shipment to warehouses and retailers. It was all done by trucks and it was the truckers who provided the lifeline for so much of the industry. As such, truckers like Evola had inordinate power over the garment industry because they could create transport bottlenecks through which everything passed.

Garment truckers policed themselves with a "marriage" system. As far back as any one could remember, the truckers had a cartel-like arrangement in which no one stole accounts. Sometimes separate buildings, and all the dress manufacturing firms within, were considered the territory of one trucker. The manufacturers were essentially "married" to a certain trucker. There was no "divorce" from the relationship unless the manufacturer went out of business for six months. If the trucking company closed, the manufacturer's account was taken over by another hauler.

Evola was not the only Mafia boss involved in the garment trucking industry, but as a caretaker of the Bonanno family he was certainly the most prominent. To target the coercive marriage system among truckers and other crimes in the garment district, federal prosecutors in 1973 established two undercover companies in Manhattan: a mom-and-pop trucking firm and a coat manufacturing company. The coat company, known as the Whellan Coat Company, employed as its chief executive a veteran garment district executive who was able to lead investigators to Evola and his cronies.

The plan was to see if Evola would try to coerce the new company into using certain trucking companies. There were some tantalizing leads, particularly when one of Evola's cronies, an elderly Austrian immigrant named Max Meyer, indicated to an undercover agent that there was indeed a trucking cartel. But as soon as the undercover operatives visited Evola at his trucking depot on West Thirty-eight Street in Manhattan they noticed he was walking with the assistance of a cane and walker. As the weeks went by, he appeared in the office less and less. The old Bonanno boss was ailing with cancer and the investigative game plan, which also called for the undercover agents to get a meeting on garment district business with Rastelli, had to be revised. Evola died on August 28, 1973, and investigators were never able to implicate him in any coercion.

Evola's death left Rastelli as one of the powers in the Bonanno family. DiFilippi, the other part of the ruling triumvirate, did not have the stature or support to challenge Rastelli. Had he been able to stay out of trouble, Rastelli might have been able to cement his leadership with the passing of Evola and build his own dynasty, avoiding some of the strife that would follow. But while he was able to play the deadly Machiavellian game of mob politics, Rastelli had not been very astute about the cops. For much of his adult life Rastelli had been in prison and in 1974 the prospect of his seeing freedom continued to recede. The problem was the lunch truck business.

By 1974, Rastelli's coercive racket with the lunch trucks caught the attention of federal investigators in Brooklyn. Although the Workman's Mobile Lunch Association aspired to get its forty-eight charter members benefits like group insurance and discounts on truck repairs, nothing like that happened. Instead, with Rastelli operating in the background, the association was engaged in a classic shakedown. Suppliers of the lunch wagons were pressured for kickbacks amounting to a percentage of the dollar value of the items sold to the mobile canteens. Truck owners who were in the unfortunate circumstance of not being part of Rastelli's association were persuaded by "implicit threats of violence," as one federal court stated, to stop coming around to certain lucrative locations.

Rastelli was indicted in March 1975 on charges that he directed a protection racket in the lunch wagon industry. The bad luck rubbed off on Massino. All the hijacking around Maspeth had also caught the attention of federal investigators who gathered evidence that the lunch wagon vendor was trafficking in goods stolen from interstate commerce. The bad luck that hit Rastelli and Massino in 1975 came at time when the Bonanno crime family was entering another period of flux and instability. While it was true that Rastelli was considered by the Commission to be a major power in the crime family, that didn't mean he had no rivals.

Carmine Galante, like Rastelli, might as well have been born on probation for the way his life had been going. A native-born American who grew up in East Harlem, Galante got into a life of crime at an early age. He was eleven when he got his first rap for robbery and at the age of twenty he had become enmeshed with the Castellammarese crowd of Bonanno in the Williamsburg area of Brooklyn. A fight with a policeman during a truck hijacking led to Galante earning a twelve-year sentence to state prison. He served about nine years and was released in 1939.

Galante, who became known by the moniker "Lilo" for the cigars he smoked, stayed with the Bonanno clan and rose fairly high up in the hierarchy. Police considered him a key suspect in the 1943 assassination of Italian antifascist writer Carlos Tresca. By the end of World War II Galante was an underboss. Though at the time he was not a household name among famous gangsters, Galante's mob stature and importance in the crime family was shown by his attendance at a 1957 meeting of top mafiosi in Palermo, Sicily. The meeting was also attended by Joseph Bonanno, another family underboss named Frank Garafola, an exiled Lucky Luciano, as well as Sicilian leaders Gaetano Badalementi and Tomasso Bucetta. The latter two would come to some prominence later in heroin dealing.

The exact nature of the meeting has never been determined by officials, although Bonanno said in his autobiography that it had to do with trying to get the Sicilians to think corporate and to set up an American-style commission to govern their activities. That never happened. But it appears that during this Sicily conclave Galante developed deeper ties to his amici in the ancestral land. It wasn't long before a number of Sicilian mobsters, young men known as "Zips," a term believed to be referring to the speed at which they talked in their Sicilian dialect, immigrated to the United States and gravitated to the area around Knickerbocker Avenue in Brooklyn. They would prove to be a source of power and support for Galante later—as well as a cause in his eventual downfall.

But before Galante had time to begin exploiting his relationship with the Sicilians, he was caught up in a major heroin bust in 1959. It was a major investigation that nabbed not only Galante but also John Ormento of the Lucchese family and Vito Genovese. Their undoing was due to the bitterness of Nelson Cantellops, a Puerto Rican drug dealer in Manhattan who had been arrested for selling drugs and became an informant to get out from under a possible five-year prison term. Cantellops's information proved accurate and showed how brazen top echelon mobsters had become in handling narcotics and how ignored the supposed Mafia edict against drug dealing had become.

Galante, like Ormento and Genovese, was convicted. Just at the point when he could have been developing a substantial power base and easily surpassed Rastelli, Galante was sent away to spend a twenty-year sentence in a federal penitentiary. When he was paroled in 1974, Galante immediately began trying to consolidate his power. In one signature event that is now firmly part of New York Mafia lore, Galante supposedly had the door to Frank Costello's tomb blown open with a bomb as a way of signaling his own return from prison.

But Galante didn't have to try anything more drastic with Rastelli or with Massino for that matter. After a two-week trial in the Brooklyn federal court, Rastelli was convicted in April 1976 of extortion and restraint of trade. Already serving time for the Suffolk gambling case, Rastelli learned that as soon as he was to be released from state prison he would be the guest of the federal government for another five to ten years in custody for being the Maspeth lunch wagon robber baron. His release date was to be in 1983. But in Mafia power struggles things are never clear-cut and even prison will not stop the politics of mob bosses. So Galante and Rastelli became locked in their own deadly game for the leadership of the family. It was a battle that would take nearly three years to play out and in which Massino would play a significant role.

CHAPTER 5

A Piece of Work

The problem with Mafia bosses is that they get an inflated sense of self-importance. Paul Castellano, the greedy boss of the Gambino crime family, was a case in point. He thought of himself as if he were the president of the United States, which is what he once told his Colombian house maid when he wasn't trying to impress her with his virility, something that came late in his life with the help of a penile implant.

Castellano also couldn't take a joke and that could prove deadly. One of his daughter's boyfriends found out about that the hard way. Joseph Massino, it seems, had a hand in that.

Castellano's legitimate businesses were in the meat and poultry industry. As a young man, Castellano had a full head of dark wavy hair and in his old police mug shots he actually looked handsome, despite his thick, pronounced nose. As Castellano aged, he lost a lot of his hair and what was left around the sides turned gray. His nose took on more of a prominence, and in 1975 he looked a bit like another poultry expert, Frank Perdue. With an aggressive television advertising campaign and a distinct, high-pitched whiney voice, Perdue became one of Madison Avenue's darlings. His Perdue chicken ads drew instant recognition. Vito Borelli, a boyfriend of Castellano's daughter, Connie, took a look at Perdue's face in an ad and thought he noticed a similarity.

"He looks like Frank Perdue," Borelli said of Castellano, who at the time was waiting for a sickly Carlo Gambino to die so he could take over the crime family.

That comment was not a good thing to say, especially when the remark got back to Castellano. A person of normal sensitivities would have laughed off the comment or even viewed it as a compliment. But Castellano took offense and according to police turned not only to his boys in the Gambino family but also to Joseph Massino to teach Borelli a lesson.

Over the years, Massino had become close to a number of up and coming stars in the Gambino family. That he also got to know Castellano is a clear indication that Massino was himself a rising power in his own right. It was those Gambino ties that appear to have led Massino at the age of thirty-two to carry out his first "piece of work": a murder. The victim was the loose-lipped Vito Borelli.

Unlike some of the fabled mob assassinations where a victim is spectacularly gunned down on the street or in public, many Mafia homicides are handled like secret production lines with clear divisions of labor. Somebody will arrange transportation. Another will procure a murder weapon. Yet a third person might arrange to clean up the crime scene while more people may help dispose of the body. Of course, there are always those who will entice or inveigle the victim to show up at the place where he will lose his life.

In mid-1975, investigators learned, Massino turned to his trusted brother-in-law Salvatore Vitale and the fair-haired Duane Leisenheimer for help. Vitale was told by Massino to pick up a stolen car from Leisenheimer and bring it to—of all places—a cookie storage facility in Manhattan. The keys of the van, which Vitale had parked outside the storage location, were left under the seat.

The night of the killing, an exasperated Massino called Vitale to complain that the van wouldn't start. So Vitale drove his own car back into Manhattan and pulled up to the storage location. He saw that Massino was there in some very good company. Outside the building were John Gotti, then a young soldier in the Gambino family, his friend Angelo Ruggiero, another Gambino associate, and Frank DeCicco. Vitale also recognized Dominick "Sonny Black" Napolitano, a powerful Bonanno crime family captain. A killer who also liked to raise racing pigeons, Napolitano was one of Rastelli's allies and as such could count on Massino for help.

According to a law enforcement intelligence report, once outside the Manhattan location, Vitale was told to back up his vehicle and what appeared to be a body wrapped in a tan drop cloth was placed in the trunk. Then, Ruggiero and De-Cicco got into Vitale's car and told him to drive to a garage. When asked later about the incident by the FBI, Vitale couldn't recall exactly where the garage was. He thought it might have been in Ozone Park. But what he did remember was that when the body was taken out of the trunk he saw it was Vito Borelli, with his head and body showing signs of repeated gunshot wounds. The corpse was clad only in its underwear.

Vitale later recalled that he didn't see what happened to the body. Whatever transpired with poor Vito Borelli's remains was likely nothing sacred since Vitale would also remember seeing another Gambino associate, Roy Demeo, at the garage. Demeo's forte was that of butcher and he seemed to relish the dismemberment of bodies. Demeo did it all over the city and sometimes got so frenzied in the disembowelments that ears of his victims would fly off, only to be retrieved later by dogs who happened upon the crime scene. It was his special line of work. Borelli's body was never found.

Vitale dropped off Ruggiero and DeCicco at Gotti's infamous Bergin Hunt & Fish Club in Ozone Park. That was a misnomer since the girth of club patrons like Ruggiero and

DeCicco showed they did very little outdoor sport or exercise of any kind beyond pulling a trigger or working the espresso machine. Their only hunting was that of the likes of human victims like Borelli. As he remembered it, Vitale was told a few days after the murder that the victim was indeed Borelli. His offense had been the Frank Perdue joke that Castellano saw as an insult.

The Borelli murder and the body disposal indicated to Massino that his brother-in-law could be trusted to carry out an assignment for the mob with no questions asked. Vitale was basically a catering truck driver for Massino, but his childhood friend was connected to a world that was wild, dangerous, and exciting. He knew Massino was living a double life: as a married father with a stable business and as a Mafia associate on the rise. It was hard for Vitale to walk away from that, not only because Massino was married to his sister, Josephine, but also because his friend was the closest male companion he ever had growing up in a household filled with older women.

The Borelli killing also showed that Massino had made his bones—he killed for the mob when asked. The timing couldn't have been better because around the time Borelli was killed the ranks of the Mafia were opening up for new members. The bosses opened up their books around 1976 to 1977 and Massino was put up for membership in the Bonanno family and made it in easily. He wasn't just big Joe Maspeth anymore, the guy you would see in the lunch wagon to play the numbers or score some hijacked goods. Now, as police learned, Massino was a full-blown wise guy, and if Rastelli or anybody else introduced him around, they would say he was "a friend of ours," which was a coded expression to mean he was a true-blue gangster.

From his Maspeth base, Massino developed a number of rackets. The more he did on the street, the more people Massino met. He developed ties not only to the Gambino family but also to the Colombo group through Carmine

Franzese, a soldier known as "Tootie." One of Massino's sidelines was in the trafficking of untaxed cigarettes, always a hot commodity. Federal and state taxes could drive up the price of a carton of cigarettes by as much as 30 percent, and this was before the smoking industry was hit with the affects of the 1990s' antismoking litigation.

Massino's partner in the untaxed cigarette business was an associate of the Colombo crime family known as Joseph "Doo Doo" Pastore. The product was smuggled in from South Carolina without any tax stamps and when he wasn't working that racket Pastore would hang around Massino's deli on Fifty-eighth Avenue, which opened in the 1970s, sampling the coffee and cakes. Massino owned the small building—real estate was not overpriced in that area of Queens—and sometimes he would use the upstairs apartment for business with Pastore, who was generally flush with cash. The street was a crease in the city, a small byway barely 100 yards long that was easily overlooked by motorists passing by on the larger avenues. Any strange cars on the block would be easily noticed, although that didn't stop the FBI from eventually setting up a surveillance post a mere twenty or thirty yards away from the shop's front door.

The FBI was in the area a lot because Maspeth was a haven for hijackers and the bureau's truck squad got to know the main traffickers in stolen property. Pastore was known to the agents as an "action guy," a man who would take a truck any way he could and bring it back to the alleyways of this industrial part of Queens, where the reputed middlemen like Massino could move the goods to buyers or find a warehouse. By the early 1970s, Pastore was known to the FBI hijack experts to a greater extent than Massino. In June 1972, Pastore was arrested with two other men on charges he possessed a load of stolen trucking cargo. But the case against Pastore was slim and in February 1973 the government asked that the indictment against him be dismissed.

Massino, apparently reluctant to ask directly for a financial favor from his cigarette partner, had Vitale borrow several thousand dollars from him instead. The money Vitale borrowed in the spring of 1976 from Pastore, about $9,000, was never paid back. It was never paid because Pastore was simply no longer around to collect. While the precise reason is unclear, investigators learned that Massino had become disenchanted with his old cigarette smuggling and hijacking friend and decided to end their partnership in a less than amicable parting. It is possible, seeing that the FBI had focused on Pastore, that Massino feared that his business relationship might make him vulnerable to becoming an informant. Whatever the reasons, Massino turned to Vitale, who had already proved himself in the Borelli murder.

Like many wiseguys, Pastore was a habitué of strip clubs—"Go-Go" bars as they were known at that time. At one club on Forty-forth Street in Manhattan he met a young woman named Gloria Jean Young. An aspiring singer, Young had gravitated to the city in the hopes of advancing her career but instead began working as a Go-Go dancer. The night she met Pastore things began to happen fast. As she later told investigators, she spent the night with him at the Plaza Suite Hotel and from then on Pastore was a constant factor in her life. She explained that the mob-connected smuggler put Young up in an apartment, furnished it, and paid her rent.

But in mid-May 1976, Young remembered, things changed drastically. She drove with Pastore to a brownstone house somewhere in Queens and waited in the car while he went inside. After about ten or fifteen minutes, Pastore exited the building and returned to the car. He looked frightened.

"He didn't feel very well and he felt bad and said something was coming down," Young later recalled in court testimony. The young dancer said the incident also left her rattled and afraid for her own safety, so she decided to leave Pastore and the life they had together. The next day a girlfriend drove Young to the airport and she left town, never to see Pastore again.

Whatever had unsettled Pastore was a bad omen. Vitale later told investigators that he had barely a day's notice that Carmine Franzese was going to "take care" of Pastore in the apartment above Massino's deli on Fifty-eighth Road. Vitale was told to complete his regular rounds selling coffee and donuts from one of Massino's mobile lunch wagons and then return to the deli.

Dutiful as ever, Vitale drove back to the deli the next day after the workday and met Massino. It was done, Massino told his brother-in-law, who then climbed the flight of stairs to the empty apartment. There was blood all over the floor of the little kitchen and the cabinets. Even the refrigerator had some spatter inside. However, there was no body in sight since it had already been moved to a dumpster a few blocks away on Rust Street. Picking up some towels that had been left in the apartment, Vitale later told the FBI he used them to soak up the blood and wipe down the cabinets. When finished, he took the blood-soaked towels, put them in a bag, walked around the corner to another dumpster, and tossed them all away. Good job, Vitale remembered Massino telling him.

It was on June 1, 1976, outside 58-77 Fifty-seventh Avenue in Maspeth, literally around the corner from Massino's social club and deli, that Pastore's body was found. Massino told police he had last seen his old friend on May 19. Since he said he was a family friend, Massino went with Pastore's half-brother, Richard Dorme, to identify the decomposed body. Dormer threw up in the morgue after the body was shown.

Massino would always deny he had any role in the killings of Pastore and Borelli, although Vitale would insist his brother-in-law told him he fired two shots into Pastore's face. So in less than a year, Vitale had graduated from Massino's trusted gofer, by his own admission to investigators, to an accomplice in two homicides. Since the Pastore killing seemed to have been a strictly personal situation, it is doubtful Massino improved his standing with the crime family in having it arranged. But the Borelli killing was another matter since it ingratiated Massino with Castellano, the rising power and soon-to-be boss of the Gambino family, and it showed to both the Bonanno and Gambino clans that Joe Maspeth was a man who could do a piece of work. With Rastelli in prison and the Bonanno family in a state of tension over its leadership, it was not a bad time for Massino to develop alliances and to earn his stripes as a crime family member. But there is a point where gangsters, no matter how careful, get into trouble and Massino was no exception.

CHAPTER 6

"I Don't Do Nothing"

On the morning of March 11, 1975, Salvatore Taboh went to his job as a truck driver in Mahattan at around 7:00 A.M. so he could grab some breakfast before he started his work shift at the Hemingway Trucking terminal. By the time he clocked in at 8:00 A.M., Taboh had been fed and was then able to answer a call from the dispatcher to get his assignment for the day. There was no real surprise at that time because Taboh got his usual rig, tractor-trailer number 897.

The Hemingway terminal was on Leroy and West streets in lower Manhattan, an area where a lot of trucking firms marshaled their rigs. Taboh warmed up his tractor—the part of the rig with the engine—and hooked it up to the trailer part that contained myriad number of packages of merchandise. Pulling out at about 8:30 A.M. from the terminal area, Taboh drove uptown to his first stop at Twenty-seventh Street between Fifth Avenue and Broadway. He parked his rig and went upstairs to make the delivery. Since he was early and the business that was supposed to accept the package wasn't open, Taboh went to the next office where a woman who was working agreed to accept the item. Taboh went back downstairs to retrieve the package. He couldn't find it because the entire tractor-trailer was gone, the whole thing, package included. Just like that.

While rushing over to a nearby phone booth, Taboh spotted a police car and told the officers what had happened. The cops called in the stolen rig and Taboh then called his dispatcher to report what had happened. The time was about five minutes to 9:00 A.M. He couldn't have left the truck for more than five or ten minutes.

Across the East River in Queens, FBI agent Patrick Colgan was in his official bureau car when he got a radio transmission about the stolen Hemingway truck at about 9:20 A.M. Colgan was in Queens a lot because he was part of the FBI truck hijack squad and he knew that the borough had become a haven for hijackers. Though higher-ups in the FBI didn't think cargo theft was a big racket for the mob, street agents like Colgan thought otherwise. Queens in particular was a hijacker's paradise with John F. Kennedy International Airport and numerous trucking terminals, notably in Maspeth. Associates and members of the Gambino and Colombo crime families saw hijacking as a relatively low-risk crime with the potential for quick cash. One of the most prominent of reputed truck thieves, Colgan knew, was a big guy from Maspeth who had some businesses by Rust Street. Playing an educated hunch, Colgan, a five-year veteran of the agency, quickly drove to the area where Rust Street intersected with Grand Avenue. He knew the number and name on the truck he was looking for.

What luck. At around 9:45 A.M. Colgan spotted the very Hemingway rig he was looking for parked on Rust Street, just north of the Maspeth Avenue intersection. Driving by the truck, Colgan noted its license plate number, A80808, which corresponded to the radio report. There was no one in the driver's seat and the rig was pointing north. Colgan parked his car about 150 feet away from the stolen vehicle. His car was pointing south. Colgan waited.

About twenty minutes after parking, Colgan saw a man

walk out from a street by the nearby Clinton Diner and walk over to the waiting Hemingway tractor-trailer. The guy was Raymond Wean, a denizen of the Maspeth world of hijackers who just so happened to be on probation for a conviction on a federal hijacking charge. The time was about 10:15 A.M., less than an hour after the apparently befuddled Taboh noticed the truck missing in Manhattan.

The rig was driven a short distance north on Rust when it suddenly made a U-turn and headed south, passing Colgan, who got a good look at Wean's face. The FBI car fell in behind the truck rig and followed it a short distance until it came to a stop light. It was then that a blue Cadillac pulled up to the driver side of the tractor cab and Colgan noticed two men occupying the car talk with Wean. After the Hemingway rig turned right on to Grand Avenue, Wean parked it, got out, and started to walk away. He was a big, imposing man who stood well over six feet tall and weighed about 300 pounds. Wean was a working man with hands the size of ham hocks. Colgan pulled up to him, got out of the FBI car, and arrested Wean for possessing the stolen truck.

"I was not in any truck, I was just simply walking down the street," Wean responded.

"Well, I not only saw you get out of it, I saw you get into it," Colgan answered.

"Give me a break, I'll do anything. I am on parole in the Eastern District," Wean pleaded.

Wean's wrists were so big that Colgan couldn't put handcuffs on the suspect. So he ordered Wean to sit in the FBI car and not try to escape. As Colgan was placing Wean in the bureau vehicle, he noticed the blue Cadillac drive by. The agent's eyes locked a glance with those of the driver, who seemed to instantly recognize that Colgan was with the FBI. A startled Joseph Massino then drove away in the Cadillac.

As he later told a federal judge, Colgan also recognized Massino as the man who was known to the FBI as a truck hijacker and fence of stolen property. Actually, among the FBI agents Massino was not known as a strong-armed guy who would stick a gun in a driver's face. Rather, he was known to investigators as a middleman, a broker of stolen commodities. Street agents working the hijack world said Massino was known to specialize in ground coffee, liquor, and clothing. So when Colgan suddenly saw Massino appear around the Hemingway truck, it raised suspicion that he was involved with the theft of the vehicle.

Massino should have kept on driving away. Instead, he came back and was himself arrested. The Hemingway incident then became the first time in Massino's life that the federal government had nabbed him. Granted, the Hemingway heist wasn't the biggest crime around. The trailer was filled with blankets and clothing. But it led to Massino's first federal indictment. What also made the case noteworthy was that it was the only time Massino would ever take the witness stand in his own defense, perhaps the only Mafia leader of note to ever do so in his career. By testifying, Massino won a dismissal of the first serious set of charges ever lodged against him.

Massino and Wean, who lived in Whitestone, were indicted by a Brooklyn federal grand jury in 1975 on charges that they conspired to receive 225 cartons of merchandise stolen from an interstate shipment contained in the Hemingway truck. They were also both charged with possessing the stolen shipment. In addition, Massino, because of his drive by and return to the scene when Wean was being arrested, was charged with trying to hinder Wean's apprehension. Records show both men made bail, with Massino posting a $10,000 bond secured by one of his business properties.

Massino's lawyer was Eugene G. Mastropieri, a city councilman who also practiced law (as city rules allowed). Court records show that Wean's and Massino's cases were severed, meaning one would be tried without the other. Wean went to trial first.

It was close to Thanksgiving in 1976 that the Brooklyn

federal judge Edward Neaher impaneled a jury in Wean's case. By that time the case had been simplified even more because prosecutors had decided to drop the conspiracy charge and just try Wean on the one count of being in possession of stolen property. The government used Colgan and some other FBI agents, as well as the truck driver, Salvatore Taboh, as their key witnesses. There was some suspicion among the agents that the driver might have given up the truck too easily and thus was complicit in the crime. But that was never proven. In reality, the credibility of the agents was crucial for the case; the defense attorney, Robert Weisswasser, attacked Colgan in his opening statement as an "out right fabricator, a liar, a perjurer." The defense would also make an issue of the fact that the agents didn't immediately dust the keys found in the truck cab for fingerprints.

Weisswasser's tactics of attacking law enforcement didn't work. The jury quickly found Wean guilty of the charge of possession of the two hundred and twenty five cartons of stolen property found in the truck.

For Massino, the situation became more interesting. Judge Neaher held a hearing to determine a rather fundamental legal issue: was Massino read his Miranda rights when he was arrested on March 11, 1975? If the agents didn't properly Mirandize him, then his statements during the arrest would be invalid and that could destroy the case against him. Since the groundbreaking U.S. Supreme Court ruling in the *Miranda* case in 1963, law enforcement officers were under an obligation to tell defendants a series of warnings, among them that they had the right to remain silent, that anything they said could be used against them, and that they had a right to have a lawyer appointed to represent them if they couldn't afford to pay for one. The giving of the warnings had become elementary for all agents and cops but sometimes there were screw-ups or the circumstances were ambiguous, all of which led to so-called suppression hearings being held by the court.

Suppression hearings often boil down to a defendant's version of events being pitted against those of the arresting officers. On February 10, 1977, Massino himself took the witness stand before Judge Neaher in the Brooklyn federal court. Since Mastropieri had brought the motion to get his client's statements tossed out as evidence, it was Massino who testified on direct examination.

Massino's testimony was fairly brief. He remembered being arrested by Agent Colgan on March 11, 1975, and then asking why he was being taken into custody.

"What did he say to you and what did you say to him at the time he placed you under arrest?" Mastropieri asked.

"I told him, 'What am I under arrest for,' and he said, 'You will find out.' He handcuffed me and put me in a car and they took me away," Massino said.

In the car, Massino said he sat with two other agents but said they didn't advise him of his rights. At FBI headquarters in Manhattan near Sixty-ninth Street Massino said some agents gave him some paper but he pushed it back to them, unread.

"Did he ask you to sign that paper?" Mastropieri asked.

"No, he did not," replied Massino.

"You heard the testimony over the course of the last two days," Mastropieri finally said. "At any time were you given your rights by any one of the agents that testified here in court?"

"No, I was never given my rights," answered Massino.

Assistant U.S. Attorney Jonathan Marks then asked Massino if he knew before the arrest date that he had a right to remain silent if asked questions by the FBI.

"Only from watching television," said Massino.

"Well, did you understand that you had a right to remain silent?" Marks pressed.

"I was never told of it," Massino replied.

While a person may know, even from television shows, about the Miranda rights, the law remains clear that the arresting officers or agents have to explicitly advise a defendant, no matter how widely known those warnings have become in popular culture. By insisting that he had never been warned as required by Miranda, Massino was saying the FBI had screwed up on something fairly significant.

Marks continued to press Massino, showing him a document that court records indicate may have been either a standard form that listed the Miranda warnings or perhaps a waiver of the right to be Mirandized. But Massino stuck to his story and said that while he remembered an agent shoving a piece of paper at him at the FBI offices he didn't read it.

"How long did you have that piece of paper in front of you," asked Marks.

"Just put it in front of me. He says, 'Look at it.' I said, 'I don't look at anything. I don't do nothing,'" Massino said.

FBI agent Richard Redman, who rode in the bureau car with Massino back to Manhattan, gave a different story. Massino was not only advised of his rights in the car but also he said he understood them, Redman testified. During the drive to the FBI offices, Massino said he knew Wean for over twenty years and explained that the reason he drove away when Colgan spotted him in the Cadillac was that "I had to take a shit and I told him [Colgan] I would go and come back," said Redman.

At the FBI offices, according to Redman, Massino turned chatty and told the agents they really had Wean good when they caught him with the truck. When asked why he drove his Cadillac alongside the truck as Wean was driving, Massino responded that he had to tell his friend that the FBI was following him and "I had to shout at the dumb fuck because he didn't hear me," Redman remembered Massino saying.

In essence, Massino testified that he was never given his Miranda rights by the FBI. The government contended that Massino volunteered the remarks he made to Redman and the other agents and so the Miranda rule didn't apply. In the end, Judge Neaher said that since the agents had continued to question Massino after he said he didn't want to talk and wouldn't sign the form the court would suppress any statements Massino made the day he was arrested. Since the government's case rested largely on Massino's statements, there was little evidence remaining, so prosecutors moved to dismiss the indictment against Massino. The case was tossed out, and Massino was in the clear.

When Neaher ruled in Massino's favor, the big man from Maspeth was known as a hijacking leader to the FBI. But it appears that Massino's status as a made member of the Mafia (his induction is believed to have occurred in 1976 or 1977) was still under the radar at that point. This was true even though, as Vitale later recalled, Massino had been involved in the Vito Borelli and Joseph Pastore killings.

However, Wean was now a two-time loser in federal court and Neaher sentenced him on March 10, 1977, to three years in prison. Wean had some serious thinking to do. Life on the street and hanging around with Massino in Maspeth had not been good for him, especially since he had three young kids, a wife, and an ex-wife. There had to be a better way to get by in life.

CHAPTER 7

Power Play

On an afternoon in 1977, a group of about a half-dozen adult men stood outside a restaurant on Mulberry Street in Manhattan's Little Italy. To a casual observer, the group was doing nothing in particular. Sometimes one of the men from the crowd would sneak a look inside. But for the most part they hung out, which was not unusual for the neighborhood.

Mulberry Street had been the spine of this Italian neighborhood for decades. Italian immigrants as far back as the mid-ninteenth century had populated the area and the immigration continued well into the 1900s, attracting its fair share of Mafia members and associates. Ethnic neighborhoods like Little Italy provided a base of support, through people and cooperating merchants, for the Mafia. The clannish nature of the streets, where dialects of Italians from Naples, Sicily, Calabria, Genoa, and Tuscany textured the conversations, gave some assurance that outsiders like police would stand out and be spotted.

The men outside the Casa Bella Restaurant on Mulberry Street were keeping a lookout not only for cops but also for any signs of danger that might threaten the people inside. Among the inside crowd on this particular day were

Carmine Galante, the recently freed Bonanno crime family captain, and Mike Sabella, another captain who just so happened to own the place. Guard duty in Little Italy to protect a high-echelon mobster like Galante could be nerve wracking. Even though he was armed, Bonanno soldier Benjamin "Lefty Guns" Ruggiero, one of the men in the group outside Casa Bella, seemed to constantly fidget. Thin faced, lean, and always exhibiting a sense of nervous expectation, Ruggiero knew political undercurrents were at work in the family, and since Galante was hated by many mobsters, at any moment he could turn into a target of opportunity for his rivals. Since he was part of Galante's security detail, Ruggiero could find himself in a gun battle in which he was expected to protect the man at all costs.

One of the other men standing in the crowd outside Casa Bella with Ruggiero was a trim, muscular man who looked the part of an aspiring street hood, although he wasn't armed. Curious about what was going inside, he peeked through the window. He spotted Galante's bald head and trademark cigar as he talked with Sabella and a few others. Ever since Galante had attended the Palermo meeting in 1957 with Joseph Bonanno, he had been popular with the Sicilian men who he convinced to immigrate. These heroin-dealing Zips, as the Sicilians were called, were some of the only people Galante felt comfortable around. Everybody else could wait outside.

The curious thing about the man who peered inside Casa Bella was that even though he had all the trademark looks of a wanna-be mafioso—the gold chains, rings, and stylish sports clothes—he was actually the furthest thing from it. Known to Ruggiero as "Donnie Brasco," he was actually Joseph Pistone, an undercover agent for the FBI. He was damn good at what he did.

It was in 1976, having already done a few stints with the FBI in short undercover assignments, that Pistone and his supervisors wanted to exploit the possibility of a deeper penetration of the underworld. The decision was made for Pistone to go undercover in New York City as Donnie Brasco, a jewel thief who could make a score. After establishing some connections with the Colombo crime family, Pistone made the acquaintance in March 1977 of Ruggiero and Bonanno soldier Anthony Mirra at Mirra's place, the Bus Stop Luncheonette on Madison Street, a few blocks east of Little Italy. A cold killer, Mirra had become a feared man in the crime family because of the ease with which he committed murders.

Pistone started off handling some stolen property for the mob, and in the process he gleaned intelligence information about the Bonanno family hierarchy for his FBI handlers. Where possible, Pistone pretended to move stolen property for his unsuspecting mob cohorts but actually turned it over to his FBI handlers. In turn, the agents gave Pistone some government cash that had been earmarked for the investigation so that he could turn it over to his wiseguy connections. This not only allowed Pistone to show that he sold the stolen property but also to build more credibility with his mob connections.

With luck, patience, and lots of bravado, Pistone became a close friend of Ruggiero and began to gather plenty of evidence for the FBI. But, unknown to Pistone, his fellow agents were carrying out a separate intelligence gathering operation in lower Manhattan that also targeted the Bonanno family.

Local social clubs, storefronts with windows emblazoned with signs saying "members only," were sprinkled around Little Italy and seemed to exist only as convenient meeting places for the mob. The Bonanno family had one club incongruously named Toyland Social Club at 94 Hester Street, which was run by Nicholas Marangello, the underboss of the crime family. Marangello had poor eyesight and needed thick glasses, which earned him the monikers "Eyeglasses" and "Nicky Glasses." He had started out at the age of fifteen with a juvenile delinquency record, and by the age of nineteen he was sent to Sing Sing Prison for a ten-year term for robbery. By the time he was forty-three years old, and with a few more convictions under his belt, Marangello was in charge of some extensive gambling operations run by the Bonanno family.

The FBI set up continuous surveillance of the Toyland club, and what they discovered was that the club was like the set of some mob movie. The club was used not only by the Bonanno crime family but also by the other families, particularly the Colombo and Gambino clans. Hidden FBI cameras took hundreds of photographs to document the mobsters who showed up. Intelligence gathering operations such as the Toyland probe are started to find leads that might later prove useful in future investigations. For instance, a wiretapped conversation might reveal to police that two mobsters agreed to meet at Toyland on a particular day to plan a crime. If surveillance confirmed that meeting, the resulting photographs might later prove useful as corroboration. But until then, the surveillance reports, known in FBI jargon as form "Ninety-twos," and photographs from the Toyland investigation resided in government files in the hope that someday they would prove useful.

Pistone didn't know it at the time, but some of his visits to Toyland and to other crime family hangouts in Manhattan, were captured by the FBI cameras. Pistone would later learn that security was so tight about his undercover role that surveillance agents and police had him picked as a mob associate known only as Donnie Brasco. Having established good rapport with Ruggiero and other made members of the Bonanno family, Pistone in 1977 was soon treated like one of the guys.

"I knew most of the regular wiseguys down on Mulberry Street, not only Bonannos but guys from other crews," wrote Pistone in his autobiography. "I was given the familiar hugs and kisses on the cheek that wiseguys exchange. I could come and go in any of the joints I wanted."

So by the time Pistone had stood with Ruggiero and others outside Casa Bella to watch over Galante in the summer of 1977, he had also rubbed shoulders with a lot of other Bonanno members. Among them was the thirty-four-year-old Joseph Massino, who Pistone viewed as a rising star in the crime family. With a growing pasta belly and broad shoulders developed through his teenaged years as a lifeguard, Massino cut an imposing and intimidating figure. Surveillance photos of that period showed Massino with a head of thick, wavy black hair as he stood outside the Holiday Bar on Madison Street, just across from Tony Mirra's luncheonette. Massino was also spotted at Toyland with his brother-in-law, Salvatore Vitale, Carmine Franzese, and, of course, Marangello.

By now, Massino was no longer just Joe from Maspeth. In fact, having proved to the mob that he was an earner, Massino moved uptown—so to speak—buying a home on Eighty-fourth Street in Howard Beach. By then, he and his wife had their youngest of three daughters, Joanne, and it seemed right that his family move to a newer, more modern home than he had on Caldwell Avenue. As a made member, Massino's place in the family was assured, assuming he didn't screw up or insult the boss.

In the summer of 1977, with Philip Rastelli in prison, law enforcement officials began to consider Galante the effective boss of the family. Rastelli, it seemed to police, had more or less given up on trying to fight for the top spot, even though he retained the loyalty of Massino, Marangello, and a substantial number of other captains and soldiers. Galante was a more ruthless character who was known to quote Plato, Augustine, and Descartes; he also had been diagnosed as being psychotic by prison psychiatrists.

Galante's main mission revolved around his attempt to build the crime families' narcotics operations. After having spent nearly fifteen years in prison for trafficking in heroin, it might have been that Galante would be gun shy about peddling narcotics again. But drugs, particularly heroin, had become lucrative markets for the Mafia and intelligence reports placed Galante in the middle of things. He traveled to Florida to cement deals with drug dealers and reportedly reached an agreement with Harlem's drug kingpin, Nicky Barnes, to have heroin distributed in the predominately black community. With Carlo Gambino's death in 1976, there really was no old-time Mafia leader to stand in Galante's way when it came to narcotics.

If there had been any doubts that Galante was considered to be one of the preeminent leaders of the Mafia in the city, they were dispelled by a front-page article in the *New York Times* on February 20, 1977, which trumpeted his rise to power with the headline: AN OBSCURE GANGSTER IS EMERGING AS THE MAFIA CHIEFTAIN IN NEW YORK. While Rastelli had his loyalists like Massino, Galante had a small army of Sicilian cohorts who populated Knickerbocker Avenue in East New York, a part of Brooklyn that had become a magnet for the young men who migrated from Sicily. It was the Sicilians, who were lead by Salvatore "Toto" Catalano, a puffy-faced, dark-haired immigrant baker, who formed the backbone of Galante's heroin operation.

But as might be expected, Galante let power, or his perception of it, go to his head. The heroin operation was lucrative, yes, but Galante wanted more. Police believed he started to covet the operations of the other crime families, particularly in the emerging territory of Atlantic City, which had been under the purview of Philadelphia's mob boss Angelo Bruno. The Sicilians on Knickerbocker Avenue had been Galante's workhorses with heroin, but his greed was fueling their disloyalty. Something had to give.

Police surveillance can be very good at spotting Mafia characters holding meetings and monitoring prison visits, but the substance of those meetings may be unknowable, if at all, for years. Such was the case in the months before July 1979, when officials noticed a steady stream of visitors to

Rastelli at the federal penitentiary in Lewisburg, Pennsylvania. News reporters were leaked the names of some of Rastelli's visitors, and they included some prominent Bonanno crime family members: Nicky Marangello, Steven "Stevie Beef" Cannone, Philip Giaccone, Frank Lupo, and Armand Pollastrino. There was also mention made in those reports of a Bonanno soldier who had attracted little media attention until that point. He was identified as "Joseph Messino" and was said to be among a number of emissaries for Rastelli while he served his sentence.

Rastelli needed his contacts with the outside, otherwise he had little chance of asserting any sort of power and control over the Bonanno family. Mafia bosses could be incarcerated but rarely were they unable to exercise some leadership. Looking back, it might have seemed from the headlines that Galante had the upper hand in the family, but Rastelli was not to be discounted. In fact, the imprisoned mafioso had sources of strength and resources that even Galante didn't know about.

Knickerbocker Avenue in East New York had plenty of Italian restaurants and coffee shops. Since Galante had much of his business with the Sicilian wing of the Bonanno family, he could sometimes be found dining or taking his espresso in one of the many small establishments where the Zips congregated. Joe and Mary's Italian American Restaurant at 205 Knickerbocker had the added benefit of a small garden at the back where diners could take their repast amid tomato plants being raised for the salads.

On the afternoon of July 12, 1979, Carmine Galante entered the restaurant for what police said was a bon voyage party for owner Joseph Turano, who was leaving shortly for a vacation trip to Italy. Galante arrived shortly before 2:45 P.M. with his Sicilian immigrant bodyguards Baldassare Amato and Cesare Bonventre, a nephew of the old Bonanno crime family underboss John Bonventre. To get to the patio dining area, Galante's entourage went through two inner dining rooms, where some other diners where having a fish dinner. The artwork on one of the walls was a cheap reproduction of Leonardo da Vinci's renowned work *The Last Supper*.

Galante sat with the two Sicilians at a table in the patio area covered with a tablecloth embossed with a floral design. He wore slacks and a light polo shirt and sat in a wooden chair with a curved back. Turano joined Galante at the table, as did Leonardo Coppolla, Galante's forty-four-year-old friend and bodyguard. Some wine, fruit, and rolls were brought to the table. Galante lit one of his ubiquitous cigars.

A blue Mercury pulled up in front of the restaurant and three men got out. Witnesses remembered them vividly because they all wore masks. They also noticed that one of them had a sawed off, double-barreled shotgun, another carried a regular shotgun, while the third seemed to be carrying a handgun, at least one and possibly two. The time was fixed by the witnesses at 2:45 P.M.

The three masked men went straight through the restaurant to the patio area. One of them, someone later recalled, shouted out, "Get him, Sal." Boy, did they ever.

A shotgun blast from one of the assailants hit Galante in the chest while another shot hit him in the face, blowing out his left eye from its socket. Coppolla was also shot and died instantly. Turano was hit as well, as was his seventeen-year-old son, Johnny. The killers exited with the same cold efficiency with which they entered. Two crash cars had sealed off Knickerbocker Avenue and the hit team made a high-speed departure from the scene with no trouble.

Galante died immediately where he fell. The blast had knocked him out of his chair. His cigar remained tightly clenched in his jaw, while his right arm was bent at his side and the left hand was drawn up across his chest as if he were soundly asleep. The elder Turano was mortally wounded and would never make it out of the hospital emergency room. His son survived. Meanwhile, Amato and Bonventre got away unharmed, a fact that didn't go unnoticed by the police.

At 4:08 P.M., teletypes in newsrooms around the city spat out an urgent bulletin: "Reputed Mafia Chieftain Carmine Galante and an associate were shot dead in an Italian restaurant in Brooklyn, police said." That was all it took for reporters and editors to launch into a frenzy of coverage. GALANTE EXITS IN (MOB) STYLE: GODFATHER BLOWN AWAY AL FRESCO IN B'KLYN, said the *Daily News*. News photographers snapped sensational shots of Galante's corpse splayed on the patio, complete with his bloody eyeless socket. Cops finally took a plastic table cloth and draped it over his upper body to give him a last bit of dignity and an escape from the prying cameras.

The photo of the blasted Galante that showed him dying with a cigar clenched in his teeth was sensational. But the police investigation that followed seemed to raise some suspicion that perhaps a cop had placed the cigar in his mouth to make it look good, especially for the news photographers who resourcefully went to neighboring rooftops and took the crime scene pictures. However, Kenneth McCabe, one of the detectives who investigated the case, later said that the medical examiner determined that Galante had indeed died with the his last smoke clenched in his jaw.

There was a lot of law enforcement speculation about Galante's killing. Undercover FBI agent Joseph Pistone wasn't in New York City when Galante was killed but was instead in Florida taking part in a related undercover probe in which he and other agents were running a nightclub as a way of attracting the mob's attention. Pistone only learned of Galante's death after he received a telephone call from his mobster friend Lefty Ruggiero. As Pistone later testified, Ruggiero was coy in giving away information.

"In the first conversation Ruggiero had asked me if I had read the New York papers, and I told him no, I didn't. I had not at that point," Pistone said during his testimony in the famous 1985 Pizza Connection trial. "And he instructed me to

go buy a New York paper, he said, 'You'll be in for a surprise.'"

Pistone picked up the papers and saw the news about
Galante and said he eventually made his way back to New
York later in July 1979, where he visited Ruggiero at his
club on Madison Street. It was at that point, Pistone said,
that Ruggiero said that with Galante out of the way there
were going to be big changes in the Bonanno family.

"He said now that Galante had gotten whacked out that
Rusty Rastelli was going to be the boss of the Family," Pistone recalled. That shouldn't have come as a big surprise
since Rastelli had been the only other power in the family
capable of challenging Galante.

According to Pistone, Nicky Marangello and Michael
Sabella, two Galante allies, were also on the hit list to be
murdered but some people intervened, and instead they were
demoted—Sabella to the rank of soldier and Marangello removed as underboss—Ruggiero said.

There were some other changes reported by Ruggiero:
among them was the fact that Joe Massino had been elevated
to the rank of captain. This was a major promotion, coming
a mere two or three years after Massino had been initiated as
a mob member, and was a clear indication that his stock was
greatly on the rise in the Rastellli regime.

But while Pistone was told what the promotions and de-
motions would be, he apparently wasn't told by Ruggiero the
how and why of Galante's killing. At least in the early
months and years after the Knickerbocker Street slaughter,
the FBI and police believed that the Galante hit was sanctioned by the Mafia Commission because such extreme action of killing a boss needed high-level authorization.
Evidence quickly emerged to support the theory that the
Commission was involved. Within a half-hour or so after the
killing, NYPD surveillance teams saw a number of Bonanno
captains such as Steven Cannone, Bruno Indelicato, and
Dominick "Sonny Black" Napolitano go to the Ravenite So-

cial Club on Mulberry Street, where they greeted and kissed Gambino crime family's aging underboss Aniello Dellacroce.

Police and FBI agents who studied the tape of the Ravenite gathering were alerted to what they believed was the butt of a gun sticking out from Indelicato's waistband. That meeting was a sign to some of the agents that the other crime families (i.e., the Commission) were involved in signing off on Galante's assassination. It is also important to remember that the Bonanno family was essentially being monitored by the Commission for years since the ouster of Joseph Bonanno. Finally, some years later an associate of the Colombo crime family testified that family boss Carmine Persico told him he had voted against Galante's murder but that the heads of the Gambino, Lucchese, and Genovese crime families had okayed the plan.

But from where did the plot to kill Galante emanate? The idea it seems came from Rastelli. With Massino and Napolitano as allies and using them as emissaries to other loyalists, Rastelli put together a pure Machiavellian power play. Galante may have been a ruthless killer in his own right but he had alienated many and his drug dealing had won him the contempt of some of the heads of the other families. In the end, Galante wasn't the boss but was living out what one FBI agent privately confided was a Napoleonic complex—Bushwick style. His Zip allies like Amato and Bonventre, knowing where the true power lay, set him up at the restaurant. Rastelli showed that he was the true boss and loyal captains like Massino, who one mobster later testified was actually outside the restaurant when Galante was shot dead, assured him the leadership.

The wake for Carmine Galante was at a small downtown funeral parlor on Second Avenue in Manhattan. His funeral was also modest. Like some other mobsters, Galante was buried at St. John's Cemetery in Queens, a burial ground run by the Diocese of Brooklyn. Over the years, famous crime bosses like Joseph Profaci, Vito Genovese, Carlo Gambino, Aniello Dellacroce, John Gotti, and even Philip Rastelli were interred there. They repose either within the immense cloister building or very near it in private mausoleums and well-tended graves that are tourist attractions. Sprigs of palm sometimes adorn them.

Galante is buried nowhere near the cloister building. Instead, his small grave is on the southern fringe of the cemetery, just yards from the busy Metropolitan Avenue. A modest granite stone with the carved image of Christ and the Sacred Heart marks the spot. "Love Goes on Forever," reads the inscription, along with the simple words "Beloved Carmine." It is very easy to overlook.

CHAPTER 8

The Three Captains

The most noticeable thing about the three-story building at the intersections of Graham and Withers streets in Williamsburg, Brooklyn, was the pigeon coop on the roof. When he needed time away from the street or the business in his social club on the first floor, Dominick "Sonny Black" Napolitano would retreat to the rooftop to be alone with his birds. Surrounded by his clutch of racers, Napolitano could take stock of the world and plan his moves as he looked out over the street scene outside his club, the Motion Lounge.

By 1980, there was a lot Napolitano had to think about. Both he and Joseph Massino had come out on top in the latest internecine struggle within the Bonanno crime family. They both had the ear of boss Philip Rastelli and were considered among the major captains of the family. They had been the imprisoned crime boss's conduit to the outside and records show that Massino had made a number of visits to the Lewisburg Penitentiary when Rastelli was housed there. Under the crime family reshuffling that went on after Carmine Galante was killed, Napolitano took over most of the crew of soldiers that had been run by the demoted Michael Sabella.

Among those who were put under Napolitano was Benjamin "Lefty Guns" Ruggiero.

Since he got out of state prison, Napolitano jumped back into the swing and ran his Brooklyn crew—Massino had one of the Queens crews—through deals involving stolen gems and artwork pilfered from JFK International Airport. Ruggiero had hooked up with a guy Napolitano had begun to admire as a newcomer who had proved to be a good earner for the family. It was a new face introduced to him by Ruggiero. This new guy was known as Donnie Brasco.

Aside from an unthinkable breach of FBI security or dumb slip up, there was no way Ruggiero could have known that Brasco was really undercover FBI agent Joseph Pistone. So when Ruggiero introduced Pistone to Napolitano, the FBI was in the process of tightening the noose on the Bonanno captain. The agency was doing that in ways Pistone didn't even know about. Other agents in the FBI had planted listening devices in a number of Bonanno social clubs and among those targeted was the Motion Lounge, the nondescript meeting place at 120 Graham Avenue where Napolitano held court. Not that Massino's haunts escaped such surveillance since a bugging device was also placed in his J&S Cake Social Club business in Maspeth on Fifty-eighth Road.

As fate would have it, Napolitano gave Ruggiero the option of being under Joe Massino, but Ruggiero decided to stay with Napolitano. It was a fateful choice because had Ruggiero chosen to go with the beefy guy in Maspeth, Massino's fortunes might have turned out much differently. But at least in the early days of 1980, Napolitano had done well with Pistone. The undercover agent had been able to steer Napolitano into an arrangement with Florida's crime boss Santos Trafficante. It was a deal that gave Napolitano a great deal of clout and put the Bonanno family into a nightclub in Florida known as the King's Court Bottle Club. It was actually an undercover business being run by Pistone's fellow agents in the Miami and Tampa offices of the FBI. Not only was the FBI watching Napolitano's deals in New York but also had him covered in Florida.

With Rastelli in prison, the Commission appointed an acting street boss, Salvatore "Sally Fruits" Ferrugia, to run things on a day-to-day basis. Of course, Napolitano was flying high, making connections with Trafficante. But Salvatore Vitale and others believed it was Massino who was the real power on the street in the crime family, the guy with the resources to make things happen. It soon became clear on the street that Napolitano and Massino were going through their own dance for power in the crime family.

"Sonny and Joey are feuding," Ruggiero told Pistone at one point, "because Sonny's got more power. So Joey's got an unlisted telephone number now. He ain't talking to anybody because of this feud with Sonny."

Just who had more power in the family depended on who you talked to. Massino could have just as easily taken an unlisted telephone number thinking it would deter surveillance. No matter what kind of power plays Massino and Napolitano were carrying on with each other, there was a more serious political undercurrent in the family, one that even the demise of Galante had not resolved. While Rastelli was considered to be the boss of the family, some of his captains began to view him as ineffective. His continued incarceration had denied the family a full-time boss and instead left it to the ministration of a caretaker, Ferrugia, who was no match for the dominant personalities of Massino and Napolitano. Eventually, Nicholas Marangello, the family underboss, and Steven Cannone, the consiglieri, took over as a committee running things while Rastelli was away.

Three captains in particular became disenchanted with this leadership, and they began to make noise. It was the kind of stuff Massino got wind of. One day in his social club near Rust Street Massino confided to Vitale the troubling news that the three capos—Philip Giaccone, Alphonse "Sonny Red"

Indelicato, and Dominick "Big Trin" Trinchera—were actually plotting to take over the entire Bonanno operation.

"Rastelli is a bum," was what the three captains had been saying about the incarcerated boss to justify their actions.

Vitale, who was only a crime family associate at that point in the early 1980s, had met Giaccone, who was known by the moniker "Phil Lucky." In the early days, Giaccone had actually been Massino's captain before the man from Maspeth won his promotion after Galante's death. Trinchera was another obese mobster who was close to 300 pounds. Indelicato's son, Anthony Bruno Indelicato, had been one of the three men suspected of doing the actual shooting of Galante in 1979.

Massino, Vitale told investigators years later, didn't tell him much about the plotting but did say that the Commission had intervened when the rumors became rife and decreed that there should be no bloodshed. The other Mafia families decided that everybody should wait for Rastelli to get out of jail and then work out the problem.

"Work it out among yourselves, no gun play," was how Vitale characterized the Commission's dictate.

That seemed to hold things in check for a while. Apart from Massino and Napolitano, the incarcerated Rastelli could count on the support of Cannone and Ferrugia. On the other side, the three captains were backed by the top Sicilian Cesare Bonventre and his Zip associates from Knickerbocker Avenue. With the Sicilians in their corner, the three captains were not to be trifled with, particularly since they had the support of Vincent "the Chin" Gigante, the Genovese family boss and his powerful Westside contingent. Had the Sicilians had their way, they could have pushed Salvatore Catalano, the heroin dealer, as a candidate for boss. In fact, for about a week Catalano was pushed forward as the boss. Catalano had been a made member of the Sicilian Mafia; therefore, under the arcane code of the American Mafia he could not become a boss in the United States: "You were either all Italy or all United States" as one mafioso put it. It also didn't help Catalano that his command of English was not that good.

Well wired with his own informants in the other crime families, Massino picked up rumors that the peace would not hold. Police later learned that a Colombo crime family member—Carmine Franzese, who had a close personal relationship with Massino—passed along the tip that Giaccone, Trinchera, and Indelicato were stocking up on automatic weapons to carry out a putsch against Rastelli and his supporters. Because the other side was loading up, the Rastelli faction had to do something. The Sicilians in particular had a reputation for being bloodthirsty and disloyal, factors that made them potent adversaries. A preemptive strike was needed.

As Vitale later told investigators, Massino turned to his old friend on the Commission, Gambino boss Paul Castellano, as well as Carmine Persico, head of the Colombo crime family. Their advice to Massino was simple and straightforward: Do what you have to do to protect yourselves. When Vitale heard that from Massino, he fully understood what the message from the Commission had been: Kill the three capos. That things had come to this point had troubled Massino, who believed, according to Vitale, that weakness on the part of Marangello and Cannone had allowed the three captains to think they could flout the crime family's administration.

× × ×

The thing about Mafia social clubs in New York City was that it was usually a safe bet that they would always have something going on. The clubs were thrones for the powerful and those who sought an audience with the kings of La Cosa Nostra. The clubs were also venues for planning, meeting, or just simply talking over a cup of espresso. Police and federal agents got into a habit of watching the comings and goings at the clubs much like Kremlinologists studied the lineup of Moscow's May Day parades for signs of where the power lay in the Soviet Union to discern who was up and who was down in the mob.

In Maspeth in 1981, any FBI agent worth his or her salt knew that Joseph Massino held court at the J&S Cake Social Club on Fifty-eighth Road. If any agent had no particular assignment but wanted to check out the boys in Massino's orbit on a particular day, a swing by J&S Cake wasn't a bad way to spend the time. You never knew what you would find.

It was at about 5:05 P.M. on May 5, 1981, that Special Agent Vincent Savadel decided to make a run by the Massino club in his government-issued sedan. He had already swung by another Massino hangout at 58-14 Fifty-eighth Avenue and jotted down one license plate when he went around the block to Fifty-eighth Road. Just as Savadel drove by, he spotted Massino coming out of the two-story building in the company of what he later reported were "several white men."

The body language of Massino and his associates seemed to convey that they were going someplace, Savadel thought. The agent drove a short distance to the corner on Rust Street and, figuring the Massino crowd was going to drive away, waited in his car.

It wasn't a long wait. A brown Cadillac came out from Fifty-eighth Road and made a right turn, northbound, on Rust Street. As the car passed him, Savadel noticed that there were at least four people inside. It was a car that had been outside Massino's social club.

Moments later a dark red, almost maroon-colored, Buick also came out from Fifty-eighth Road and made the same turn, following the Cadillac. As the car passed Savadel's parked FBI vehicle, the driver looked at the government agent. Savadel's and the driver's eyes locked on each other. The driver momentarily gazed at Savadel with a perceptive lingering glance that signaled recognition. Savadel also knew who he was looking at: Joseph Massino.

Making a U-turn, Savadel followed both cars north on Rust. Massino seemed to be looking in his rearview and sideview mirrors, checking out the FBI car. The two cars accelerated and then Massino's vehicle pulled on to the wrong side of the two-way street until he was next to the Cadillac. Savadel noticed Massino gesturing with his hands and talking. Then Massino gunned his accelerator and took the lead, with the Cadillac following.

Traveling fast on the back streets, Massino's car disappeared from sight, leaving Savadel to follow the brown Cadillac as it entered the Long Island Expressway going eastbound. The Cadillac quickly exited on to Maurice Avenue, leaving Savadel to continue eastbound on the expressway. As he did so, he glanced at the Cadillac. The men inside the vehicle looked at him as well.

Savadel couldn't follow the Cadillac because of traffic. He had also lost Massino's vehicle in the high-speed drive from Rust Street. The agent had no idea where the men were all going that evening when they launched into their sprint with the cars. Still, the agent remembered what happened. There was no telling when the car chase might become important.

After peeling off from the car chase, Savadel called the Bonanno investigators at the FBI operational center that was located not too far away in Rego Park. He related what he had just seen, likening Massino and company's driving antics to a "fire drill." What did it mean? Nobody in the office knew for sure. Instinctively, Special Agent Charles Rooney, who was working one aspect of the Bonanno crime family involved in major international heroin deals, scribbled down what Savadel had reported on a small Post-It note and stuck it on a chart in the office. You never know when all those gyrations with cars might mean something, he thought.

It was also on May 5, 1981, that Donna Trinchera spoke with her husband just as he left the couple's Brooklyn house. There was a meeting he said and he was going to it. The thin, blond woman didn't question her spouse too much. It was a meeting, that's all, he said. She expected him to be home at some point.

In fact, it was the third such meeting Trinchera and his two friends had gone to in recent weeks. One had been at the Ferncliffe Manor and the second at the Embassy Terrace at Avenue U and East Second Street in Brooklyn. Nothing had been resolved at either sitdown. The third meeting of the Bonanno crime family administration was set for the early evening hour at a social club in Brooklyn on Thirteenth Avenue. Since it was a conclave of the upper echelon of the crime family, neither Trinchera nor the two men he arrived with, Philip Giaccone and Alphonse Indelicato, were armed. The rules were that an administration meeting meant that no one packed a weapon, the better to avoid hotheaded reactions that might get out of hand.

But the three captains had always suspected that a meeting could be a death trap, so they took precautions. The night before the Embassy Terrace meeting the three captains, plus Alphonse Indelicato's son Bruno, stockpiled some guns at a bar owned by Frank Lino, an acting Bonanno captain, about two blocks away. In case the three captains were killed, Lino and Bruno Indelicato were told to retaliate and kill as many of the opposition as possible.

Unarmed, the three Bonanno captains walked to the building for the third meeting. They were followed by Lino. Nobody in that little group seemed to notice a fair-haired young man from Maspeth sitting in a car a block away with a walkie-talkie. If they had, it wouldn't have seemed so strange since Duane Leisenheimer was always around Joseph Massino, who had every right to be at an administration meeting. Trinchera rang the doorbell.

Inside, the sound of the bell let the men who were waiting know the visitors had arrived. Four of them were standing in a closet, and when they heard the bell they pulled ski masks over their heads. The closet door was open just enough so that those inside could see Trinchera walk in first to the big meeting room. He was followed by Giaccone. Then came Indelicato. He was the key. When the men saw Indelicato come into the room, they knew what they had to do. They had been told earlier that if Indelicato didn't show up it would be a regular meeting in the room. If he did show up, well, that would be that.

The three men, plus Lino, had come to the meeting to take a third stab to see if the bad blood and tension with their family could somehow be lessened. Everybody in their world knew that the Bonanno family had a power struggle so the meeting was called to iron things out. Joseph Massino had wanted it and the three captains who had arrived knew that he was a formidable power, a man with the clout to call everybody together. They, too, wanted to talk. Lino would be their witness.

The three late arrivals saw in the big room those who were followers of Massino and the other powerful captain Sonny Black Napolitano. Naturally, Massino was there. So was Joseph Zicarelli from New Jersey, known as "Bayonne Joe," and Nicola DiStefano, whose fights of yesteryear had earned him the sobriquet of "Nick the Battler." There was also a Sicilian gangster named Antonio Giordano, as were several other members of the crime family high echelon. Scanning the small crowd, the three captains would have noticed, perhaps oddly, that Napolitano wasn't there.

Gerlando "George" Sciascia spotted Indelicato in the crowd and ran the fingers of one hand through his hair. For the others in the closet that was the prearranged signal that meant they could start.

The four men in masks burst from the closet. One had a

Tommy gun, another a shotgun, and two carried pistols. Two of them ran to guard the exit door. Vito Rizzutto, turned to the three captains.

"Don't anybody move, this is a holdup," said Rizzutto.

Seeing the masks and the guns, Trinchera, Indelicato, Giaccone, and Lino reacted. They knew at that instant that their worst suspicions had been realized. They had been lured into a trap. Their survival instincts kicked in with a suddenness that surprised some in the room. Trinchera made guttural noise and charged the assailants.

Unarmed and unassuming, the three luckless men had nowhere to turn. Rizzutto and Sciascia opened up with a shotgun and pistol. Trinchera lost part of his abdomen in one blast. Indelicato tried to run out the exit but fell just short of the door when another shotgun blast hit him. Sciascia came over, pulled out a pistol, and shot him one more time in the left side of the head. Giaccone was lying dead in the big room.

Lino, the last man to enter the killing zone, turned around when the shooting started and in the confusion of those early seconds ran right past the two men who were supposed to seal off the exit. There was no stopping him. He moved so fast there was no use trying to follow him.

The shooting was over in seconds. There was blood and viscera all over the big room. Besides the gunners, the only one left standing in the middle of the chaotic scene was the big man himself, Joseph Massino.

× × ×

Early the next morning, May 6, 1981, FBI agent Charles Rooney returned to his office on Queens Boulevard in Rego Park. Many of the agency's organized crime squads worked out of the modern steel and glass building. It was a convenient location for them because so many of the targets of investigations lived and worked in Queens, Brooklyn, and Long Island. The location provided the agents with easy highway access to those areas. The office also housed several pen registers, devices that were able to note whenever a particular telephone was called or was being used to place a call. Pen registers were not wiretaps, so the FBI didn't need a warrant to tie them into a particular telephone number through the telephone companies.

Rooney was in his office by 8:00 A.M. All of a sudden, the pen registers started to click on, sounding like a bunch of electronic crickets. Then they started sounding like a bunch of adding machines as they quickly typed out on paper the telephone numbers that each of the monitored lines was calling. Since each machine had been linked to a particular telephone number in the Bonanno investigation, it was clear that the targets in the case were busy calling each other.

But what were they calling each other about? Rooney and his fellow agents could only watch in amazement as the machines recorded the various telephones making and receiving calls.

One of the machines registered calls on the telephone at Massino's J&S Cake Social Club. But without listening into the call the FBI could only guess what Massino and the other investigative targets were talking about. For all they knew, he might be taking a lot of orders for ham sandwiches. But Rooney and the others surmised it was something much bigger than that to make the pen registers so hot.

The pen registers were one of three strange clues Rooney and the other FBI agents noticed over the next three days. Another tantalizing lead for Rooney came from Pistone, who telephoned his fellow agents with the information that Benjamin Ruggiero, having dropped out of sight for a few days, had called him to say "everything is fine, we are winners." Then Rooney learned that an associate of the Bonanno family, Antonio Giordano, had been checked into Coney Island Hospital with a bullet wound. To Rooney, the fact that Giordano, a resident of Bushwick, in northern Brooklyn, would take himself to a hospital in the southern part of Brooklyn seemed odd. An FBI agent visited Giordano, who was suffering from paralysis after being shot in the back. The wounded man insisted to the agent he was shot in a traffic altercation. It was a story he stuck with.

Though seemingly disparate incidents—the frenzy of activity on the pen registers, Ruggiero's comment to Pistone, and the shooting of Giordano—they appeared more than just coincidental to Rooney and his FBI colleagues on Queens Boulevard. Something clearly had happened in the Bonanno crime family. But what?

Rooney found one more thing to puzzle over. An FBI surveillance team had photographed Massino outside the Capri Motor Inn in the Bronx the same day the pen registers went crazy. Massino was in the company of Vito Rizzuto, a Bonanno captain from Canada, and George Sciascia, another Bonanno member from Canada. Also present was Gianni Liggamari, a major Bonanno family drug dealer from Sicily. The Canadians were heavyweight Mafia members in a country where the Bonanno family long had representation. That Massino was meeting with them at a time of so much tantalizing intelligence only served to increase Rooney's curiosity.

CHAPTER 9

The Inside Man

Dominick Trinchera, Philip Giaccone, and Alphonse Indelicato didn't know they were going to die when they walked into the social club on May 5, 1981. But undercover agent Joseph Pistone certainly had enough indications that at least Giaccone was a target. Benjamin "Lefty Guns" Ruggiero had told Pistone that Giaccone was the object of a hit attempt as early as April but that it had been called off. The thinking was that all the three captains should be killed together.

In later court testimony, Pistone recalled that on April 23, 1981, Ruggiero explained that it was Dominick Napolitano and Joseph Massino who had put together the planned hit. Because of that, said Ruggiero, the Commission had assured both captains that Philip "Rusty" Rastelli would be the absolute boss. On top of that, Ruggiero told Pistone, the Sicilian Zips had come over to Massino, assuring that the Rastelli loyalists would have crucial support in the coming showdown.

Ruggiero dropped some more hints, Pistone later recalled, when he told the undercover agent that the three captains (who were still alive at that point) had lost the power play for the crime family. The deal had been ratified by the Mafia Commission, Ruggiero indicated.

"They lost, and they lost nationwide. New York, Miami, Chicago, they lost nationwide," Ruggiero told Pistone, cryptically.

"Rusty was the boss," Ruggiero added, referring to Rastelli.

In recounting later on the witness stand and in his book of the deadly days around May 5, 1981, Pistone said that when Ruggiero suddenly went missing, another FBI agent reported that informants were saying the three captains— Trinchera, Giaccone, and Indelicato—had been assassinated. It took about ten days but Pistone got called by Napolitano for a meeting at the Motion Lounge. What he learned there would answer the questions Charles Rooney and the other FBI agents had been puzzling over ever since their pen registers went hyperactive on May 6, 1981.

Pistone remembered a calm Napolitano sitting at the bar. There were the usual associates at the club: Jimmy "Legs" Episcopia and John "Boobie" Cerasani. Pistone also noticed a tall, stocky, thick-handed guy who had been around Massino a lot. His name, Pistone would later learn, was Raymond Wean.

After some greetings, Napolitano and Pistone sat alone at a card table in the club room next to a small pool table. Napolitano told Pistone that the three captains had indeed been murdered. There had been one complication though. Indelicato's son, Anthony Bruno, was still around and the information the mob had was that he was running around in Miami, coked up and bruising to avenge his father. If Pistone found him in Florida, Napolitano said, just have him killed.

"Be careful, because when he's coked up, he's crazy," Napolitano told Pistone.

Pistone later recalled that Wean left the club shortly after Pistone entered and made a telephone call to the FBI relating how a strange guy named "Donnie" had appeared and seemed very friendly and close to Napolitano. Wean made the call to his new best friend. He was Patrick Colgan, the FBI agent who had arrested him and Joseph Massino six years earlier over a hijacked load of clothing on Grand Avenue.

The problem for Wean though was that after his 1977 federal conviction he just couldn't stay out of trouble. Nassau County police picked him up on a felony charge and if convicted again Wean would have been a three-time loser and facing more jail time. As he cooled his heels in the county lockup, Wean's common-law wife reached out to Colgan.

"He likes you. He trusts you," Wean's wife told Colgan, as she pleaded with the agent to visit her lover in jail.

Out in Nassau County Wean knew that his only ticket out of a long prison term was to cooperate. He knew a lot about the Bonanno crime family and Massino, Wean said. He also didn't want to die in jail, a distinct possibility since Wean had already suffered from a heart attack.

"I'll cooperate and testify," Wean told Colgan. "I will go up against Joey."

Wean became an informant. He did so because Joe Massino had never really taken care of him. Wean had done some serious jail time for being a part of Massino's hijacking operations and in all of those years away from his family, one former FBI agent recalled, the lady love of the big-bodied truck robber never got anything from his Maspeth crony to ease the financial crunch. One of Massino's failings was that he didn't take care of the people he climbed the backs of in his steady rise as a gangster. It would be something that would come back to haunt him.

But before Wean could do anything, he had to make a $100,000 bail in the Nassau County case, a sum that he had no way of raising. To make Wean's release possible, Colgan and an assistant U.S. attorney from Brooklyn took the unusual step of testifying at a special secret court hearing before a state court judge about Wean's intended cooperation and the need for a lower bail. The court agreed to lower the bail to $40,000. Because the FBI wasn't going to post the bond, Colgan suggested to Wean that perhaps his parents could raise the cash. Wean contacted his elderly mother and father, and they agreed to help him. He made bail.

With a grateful Wean on his side, Colgan said he wanted him to try to hang around Massino and see if he could secretly tape him. But as it turned out, Wean spent more of his time around the Motion Lounge because Massino had told him to make himself useful to Napolitano, Pat Colgan later recalled. It was clear to many in the FBI at this point that Massino was the up and coming power in the family and he really didn't need to run around with a street guy like Wean. Neither Wean nor Pistone knew of their separate roles in what would soon become part of a nightmare for the mob. While the FBI had known almost immediately about the killings of the three captains, no corpses had surfaced. That changed on Sunday, May 20, 1981.

Ruby Street in eastern Brooklyn literally straddles the borough's border with Queens. It is an area of old detached houses and surrounding vacant spaces where tomato plants grow by the roadside. There is the feel of a forgotten neighborhood, a No-Man's Land in a city of over 8 million souls. It is also a place for secrets.

At the intersection of Ruby and Blake Avenue was a fairly large vacant lot that like most neglected spaces in the city became overgrown with weeds. Kids liked to play in it and did so on that particular Sunday in May. They were looking to amuse themselves when they noticed a peculiar object sticking up from the dry soil It was a human hand, and from the looks of things it had been hastily buried. It was as if whoever did the burial didn't care if the corpse was found.

When the police arrived, they discovered the rest of the partly decomposed body of a man who had been buried about two feet down. The corpse was wrapped in a tufted blanket used by moving companies to protect furniture, and a police officer who responded to the scene noted there was a rope around the body's waist. The corpse was clothed in an orange t-shirt, tan dress slacks, and brown cowboy boots. The body had two tattoos on the left arm: a heart pierced by a dagger and an inscription that read "Holland 1945 Dad." The dead man was wearing a stainless steel Cartier watch and had in his pocket a leather Gucci key case that contained keys to a Volvo.

Three gunshot wounds were found: two in the body and one in the head. The fatal shot appeared to be one in the back that had punctured the aorta. Though the body had suffered from some decomposition, one of the forensic experts injected some fluid into the shriveled fingers—a standard practice—so that fingerprints could be taken. The medical examiner took a few days but after a relative showed up to look at the body it was quickly confirmed that the corpse in the vacant lot was that of Alphonse "Sonny Red" Indelicato. One of the dead captains had been found.

CHAPTER 10

Up on the Roof

What a fuckup.

Dominick "Sonny Black" Napolitano had no other way of describing what had happened at the Ruby Street lot.

Neither Alphonse Indelicato's body nor those of any of the other dead captains was to have been found. But here it was, not even three weeks after they had been killed and the corpses were starting to surface. That was not supposed to be, Napolitano told his crew members, if Massino had done the job right.

The finding of Indelicato's body raised concern that the corpses of Dominick Trinchera and Philip Giaccone would also surface. If that happened, it would lead to more leads that could, even with the state of forensic science in 1981, provide evidence that could implicate the Bonanno faction, which had engineered and carried out the murders. Massino, police later learned, had farmed out the disposal of the bodies to the Gambino crime family, which did a sloppy job.

Disconcerted over the discovery of Indelicato, the Bonanno family became nervous. As the earlier episode with the pen registers in the FBI Rego Park office indicated, the agency needed to get some good wiretaps and to plum informants for clues. Joseph Pistone had been able to glean information showing how the Rastelli faction had clearly won the day, but there was still the need to gather more intelligence.

It also became clear to FBI officials that Pistone's long-running tenure as an undercover agent within the crime family was coming to an end. The politics of the family still remained dangerously unstable. Massino and Napolitano were vying for the job as the powerful captain in the family and it was evident there was friction between the two even though they had both won the backing of the Commission for Rastelli. Massino was also very wary and looking closely for signs of informants.

Napolitano had not just given Pistone a contract to kill Bruno Indelicato on a whim. The Bonanno captain had come to trust the undercover agent and became impressed with his ability to earn money through the King's Court Bottle Club in Florida, not knowing it was an FBI undercover company. By 1981, the books of the crime family, so to speak, were being opened again for new members and Napolitano told Pistone he was going to propose him for membership. The plan was for Pistone to be proposed to become a made member shortly after boss Philip Rastelli came out of prison later in the year after serving his sentence for the lunch wagon extortion case.

Napolitano didn't keep secret his plan to have his buddy Pistone become a made member. He talked about it openly. As Salvatore Vitale later told police, he and Massino learned of the plan to elevate Pistone during a visit to Napolitano's Motion Lounge. Vitale had driven Massino to the club on Withers Street in Williamsburg, where his brother-in-law got out of the car and approached Napolitano. It was clear from the body language of the two captains that they were having a heated conversation, Vitale noticed. Massino seemed very upset.

Walking away from Napolitano, an angry Massino returned to the car where Vitale was waiting.

Napolitano wanted to "straighten out" the brash new-comer Donnie Brasco, a fuming Massino told Vitale. What especially bothered Massino was that Brasco would be proposed for membership before Vitale. It also seemed odd to Massino, indeed imprudent, that Napolitano would even think about submitting this fellow Brasco's name for mob membership after only knowing him for a couple of years, Vitale recalled. It takes years of close association with someone for mob bosses to feel comfortable with a man before proposing membership. Brasco had rocketed into contention almost overnight and no one knew if he even did a "piece of work," meaning had a hand in an actual killing sanctioned by the crime family. Massino and Napolitano already had some friction between them and now there was the added problem of Brasco being favored over the ever loyal Vitale.

Though Pistone later said that he saw benefits to the FBI having one of its agents serving undercover as a made member of the Mafia, the law enforcement agency saw things differently. Killings from the Bonanno factionalism had spread to those outside the crime family when two other mobsters believed to have been friendly with Alphonse Indelicato were murdered. Things were getting dicey. The decision was made to pull Pistone from his undercover assignment at the end of July 1981. The man known as Donnie Brasco to the men in the world of the Bonanno crime family would cease to exist. Joseph Pistone would then resurface in his true identity on the witness stand.

Court records show that Pistone, as well as another FBI agent, Edgar T. Robb, who was known by the street name of "Tony Rossi," were officially pulled from their undercover roles on July 30, 1981. Robb had worked as the undercover agent at the King's Court Bottle Club in Florida, the place Napolitano and Benjamin Ruggiero had conducted business in and believed to be their racket. Pistone wanted to tell Napolitano himself about his true identity, but that was one final role he wouldn't play. FBI officials decided the Bonanno mobsters in New York had to be told of Pistone's true identity, by other special agents. Napolitano, Ruggiero, and any others involved with Pistone were to be told he was a government agent and not an informant because it was believed it would help safeguard Pistone from retribution.

"Our belief, again based upon experience, was that while members of La Cosa Nostra have readily killed any number of 'informants' or 'stool pigeons,' they would not threaten the lives of undercover FBI agents," said one of Pistone's supervisors.

Despite the high stakes in criminal investigations, FBI agents and police often developed working relationships with the mobsters they targeted. Not only did the agents of law enforcement come to know their targets but also the mobsters themselves saw the investigators as a form of brethren. Mobsters knew the cops had a job to do and for the most part respected them, particularly if they did the job well and treated the people they targeted with some respect. In return, the wiseguys in the crime families reciprocated the simple courtesies and respect they received.

On July 30, 1981, three veteran FBI agents took a trip to Williamsburg and parked not far from the Motion Lounge. Together, special agents Doug Fencl, Jim Kinne, and Jerry Loar, all dressed in summer blazers and suits, went to the building at the corner of Withers and Graham in Williamsburg, which housed the Motion Lounge. Fencl rang the bell to Napolitano's apartment on the second floor. Napolitano screamed out, asking who was calling.

"Doug Fencl, I need to talk to you," the agent said.

"Come up," said Napolitano.

Once inside the apartment, Fencl sat with Napolitano around the dining room table. The agents asked Napolitano if he knew Donny Brasco and Tony Rossi and he said he did. Fencl then told Napolitano that they were FBI agents.

Fencl pulled out a picture of Pistone, Robb, and other FBI agents. The photo showed a smiling Fencl and a total of four

other men including special Agent Loar posing against a
wood-paneled wall that had been brightly lit by the camera
flash. It wasn't a very arty shot. To the left of Loar stood Pistone in a stripped polo shirt and his hands clasped in front
of him. Pistone seemed almost expressionless in the picture
but looking closely you could see the slight suggestion of a
smile on his face. That man in the short-sleeved shirt, Fencl
told Napolitano, was an FBI agent.

Napolitano kept his cool and said he didn't know Pistone
but that if he did meet him in the future he would know who
he was and that he worked for the FBI. Fencl also told
Napolitano that he could have a potential problem with his
gangster friends for bringing both undercover agents into Bonanno crime family business. Fencl pulled out his business
card and offered it to Napolitano, just in case he needed it.

"You know better than anybody I can't take this," said
Napolitano. "I know how to get a hold of you if I need to."

The agents left the lounge and were captured on film by
an FBI camera as they crossed Withers Street.

Though he had been cool and collected when Fencl told
him who Pistone was, Napolitano quickly jumped into action after the trio of agents left. His crew members, Ruggiero, John Cerasani, and others were called in for a hasty
meeting and told what Fencl had said. There was disbelief.
On one wiretap a crew member was overheard saying that
the FBI must have kidnapped Brasco (Pistone) and then
forced him to pose with the agents in the picture Fencl had
showed Napolitano.

According to Pistone, Napolitano and his crew kept the
disclosure to themselves and began to look for him, putting
out feelers in Florida and Chicago but came up blank. Pistone was of course off the street and would no longer be
found in the old haunts of his alter ego Donnie Brasco.
Napolitano knew that he had to inform the powers that be
and he made several other calls. One of those calls was to

Massino, another was to Paul Castellano. Rastelli eventually got word in prison.

In the hours immediately after the shocking disclosure that Donnie Brasco, the man he had been pushing for membership in the family, was really an FBI agent, Napolitano needed some time to himself. He did what he always did to escape and think. He went up to the roof where his pigeon coop was and looked out over Withers and Graham streets.

Surveillance photos caught a worried-looking man, his brow creased with deep frown lines, surrounded by pigeons. The winged creatures were the only living things Dominick Napolitano could really trust.

CHAPTER 11

Do It to Me One More Time

Anthony "Fat Tony" Salerno had long been a power in the Genovese crime family. By the summer of 1981, he was getting on in years—he was seventy years old—but still held sway as a major source of loan-sharking money in the garment district and a controlling force behind the crime family's gambling operations in central Harlem. Federal investigators considered him the boss of the Genovese family, although the real power was held by Vincent Gigante. Salerno was a front man, important in his own right, but still just a front.

Salerno traveled around a lot, mainly between New York, Florida, and Las Vegas, places where he had legal and illegal business holdings. He had a large farm near the upstate New York town of Rhinebeck that he escaped to every Friday. But when he was in the city during the week, Salerno could be found at his social club on 115th Street in Manhattan. The Palma Boys Social Club was another one of those nondescript places where mobsters knew they could find their bosses and associates. The origin of the name was obscure, it was possibly an allusion to the Spanish word for *palm* or a bay in Majorca. In nice weather, Salerno, who wore a wide-brimmed hat, would sit outside the club with one of his trademark cigars clamped in his mouth. He walked with a cane for assistance.

After Joseph Pistone had surfaced in his true identity as an FBI agent, bureau officials knew that there was a great incentive for the Mafia families in New York to prevent him from testifying any way they could. Pistone had collected a great deal of evidence against the Bonanno family. The depth of his unprecedented penetration of the mob, his FBI colleagues believed, was an embarrassment to many if not all of the bosses of New York's five families. At least one informant had reported that pictures of Pistone and Edgar T. Robb had been circulated to Mafia families throughout the United States. To let the mob know that Pistone and Robb were federal agents, the FBI decided to talk with leaders of each Mafia family. The object of the talks was simple: Pistone and Robb were federal agents, and any attempt to harm them would bring the wrath of the government down on those who tried.

One of the mobsters approached for a little chat was Salerno. Agents found him at the Palma Boys club, seated in the back at his habitual table. He had on a suit and tie and was smoking one of his ubiquitous cigars. The agents told him they were investigating some mob homicides, notably the deaths of the three Bonanno captains, and that the bureau also didn't want Donnie Brasco (Pistone) harmed.

Salerno was a little perplexed about why the FBI was worried about the disappearance and death of three mobsters. The mob takes care of its own, Salerno told the agents. If the three captains were killed, they probably deserved it, he added.

Though a gruff talker, Salerno understood what the agents were saying about Pistone.

"Nobody is gonna hurt Donnie Brasco," Salerno assured the agents.

Salerno didn't hold the Bonanno crime family in high regard. That became evident after he was heard on a bug placed in the Palma Boys club saying the family was a collection of drug dealers—"junk men" as he called them. So his remarks that the Genovese crowd wouldn't do anything drastic about Pistone seemed a sign to the FBI that the Bonanno family's penetration by Pistone wasn't going to result in any Mafia-wide hunt for the agent. However, it was another story with Benjamin "Lefty Guns" Ruggiero.

When Pistone first made his entrée with the Bonanno family, Ruggiero was in effect his mentor. A gangly man who seemed like Rodney Dangerfield because he was always denied the respect he deserved for being a good soldier for the mob, Ruggiero took Pistone under his wing and taught him the ropes about mob protocol and how to make his way around mobsters. Pistone, through his secret law enforcement connections, was able to generate money for Ruggiero's associates, the most important being Dominick "Sonny Black" Napolitano. It was Napolitano whom Ruggiero decided to align himself with instead of Joseph Massino in the aftermath of the assassination of Carmine Galante. So, when Pistone's undercover identity was uncloaked, it was Ruggiero who felt particularly betrayed.

FBI sources in the mob reported that Ruggiero became obsessed with finding Pistone. One FBI informant said that Ruggiero stated that he was going to find and kill Pistone "if it was the last thing he did." Investigators took the threat more seriously when the same source said that Ruggiero was going to ingenious lengths to find out anything about Pistone that might help locate him. Since Pistone had stayed in a particular Holiday Inn when he visited Florida on undercover business, Ruggiero had contacts who would try to obtain through hotel records the telephone numbers "Donnie Brasco" called, said the source who was only identified as "Source A" in FBI court records. In a more ominous vein, the source said that he had actually seen one such telephone number obtained from a Holiday Inn in Miami Beach where Pistone had stayed. Ruggiero seemed obsessed with the search, and his only mission was to locate "Donnie" said the informant.

Throughout August 1981, Ruggiero worked feverishly trying to find Pistone, the man who had betrayed him. But where was Napolitano and what was he doing? Federal agents had picked up informant information that the powerful Bonanno captain had disappeared and might have been killed. But it was just as possible, investigators thought, that Napolitano had fled to either avoid arrest or the harm he might face from his mob brethren. In August 1981, nobody in law enforcement knew for sure what had happened to Napolitano.

× × ×

Sonny Black Napolitano said he had a meeting to attend and his girlfriend, Judy Brown, didn't press him for details. He gave her some of the jewelry he had—Napolitano favored expensive rings—and left her the keys to his apartment. He took his car keys because he had to drive. It was an evening in August 1981, just a couple of weeks after the Pistone bomb shell had landed on the world of the Mafia.

Napolitano drove himself to the parking lot at Hamilton House, a restaurant in the Bay Ridge section of Brooklyn. Known for its American cuisine until it closed in the 1990s, the Hamilton House was a central meeting place that was convenient to Staten Island because of its nearness to the Verrazano Narrows Bridge.

After parking, Napolitano spotted Frank Lino and Steven "Stevie Beef" Cannone. Lino was a short and stocky gangster who started his life in crime at the age of fifteen when he was a member of the Avenue U Boys, a south Brooklyn gang that did robberies and set up card games for money. A mere three years later, at the age of eighteen, Lino started doing crimes for all five New York Mafia families and finally in

October 1977, he became initiated into the Bonanno family. Cannone was a high-ranked Bonanno member from Elizabeth Street in Little Italy who had done time in a federal penitentiary for narcotics in the 1930s. During the fallout in the crime family when Joseph Bonanno was effectively deposed, Cannone was allied with the Paul Sciacca faction. Considered the consiglieri of the family, Cannone could be found spending his hours at the Toyland Social Club in lower Manhattan.

With Napolitano and Cannone in his car, Lino drove from Hamilton House over the Verrazano to Staten Island. Occasionally, Lino checked his rearview mirror to see if a van was following his car. It was.

Getting off the highway on Staten Island, Lino drove to the house of the father of Ronald Filocomo, a mob associate whose previous employment as a state correctional officer denied him the chance to become a made member of the Bonanno family. Still, Filocomo did what he could for the crime family and on that particular day in August 1981, he allowed his home to be used as a meeting place.

Once they reached Filocomo's house, Lino, Napolitano, and Cannone went to the front door. Frank Coppa, a Bonanno captain whose girth rivaled that of Massino's, let them in. The meeting was to take place in the basement. Lino opened the cellar door. It was the last courtesy Napolitano would ever receive from anybody.

Acting quickly, Lino threw Napolitano down the basement stairs. There was one shot and then somebody's gun jammed. Napolitano, knowing the end was near, didn't want to suffer.

"Hit me one more time and make it good," Lino heard him say.

There was another shot. Then nothing.

How fortunes had changed. Just weeks earlier, after having engineered the killings of the three rival capos—Dominick Trinchera, Philip Giaccone, and Alphonse Indelicato—Napolitano had been riding high. Many considered him the most prominent and powerful captain of the Bonanno family, although he clearly had to jockey for power with Massino. Napolitano had worked up a nice racket in Florida with that newcomer Donnie Brasco at the King's Court Bottle Club and even got to hobnob with Florida's crime boss Santos Trafficante. Napolitano was a force to be reckoned with. Never mind Massino's suspicions about Brasco. He knew the man like a brother.

But in a world where American and Soviet spies had been playing deep penetration games for years, it was relatively easy for an FBI agent like Joseph Pistone to secret himself into a Mafia family. The mob's guiding principle, its raison d'etre, was to make money. To be sure there were rules to follow, ones like the code of silence that gave lip service to the old ways and mores of the Castellammarese. But with money and not the deeper filial loyalty of a common heritage driving the more contemporary gangsters, the smell of quick cash blinded them.

Joseph Massino liked money but he kept his antenna tuned for trouble, be it an informant or undercover agent. Then again Massino was just plain lucky that Pistone never came close to his crew. If he had, if Lefty Guns Ruggiero had decided to join Massino's crew, the man lying dead at the bottom of the basement stairs might well have been the portly caterer from Maspeth instead of the pigeon fancier from Williamsburg.

Frank Lino walked outside the house in Staten Island after the shooting stopped. In the basement, Napolitano's body was being put in a body bag. Lino walked over to a van with sliding doors parked down the street, the one that had followed him from Brooklyn.

It was all done, Lino said to the men in the van.

Lino then put Napolitano's car keys for the vehicle that had been left at Hamilton House in the hands of one of the men in the van, Joseph Massino.

× × ×

One of the things people knew about Lefty Guns Ruggiero was that he liked tropical fish. His small apartment in Little Italy was filled with fish tanks arrayed with all sorts of species he delighted in keeping. But in the summer of 1981, obsessed with finding Pistone, the fish collection probably wasn't the first thing Ruggiero was thinking about.

Charlie Cipolla, another reputed member of the same Bonanno crew with Ruggiero, was also a fish fancier. So, on an August day in 1981, Cipolla suggested out loud that he had a rare fish he thought of giving to Ruggiero. It would have been a nice gesture. Cipolla said it loud enough that not only John Cerasani heard it but that an informant standing nearby did as well. The informant was later identified in court documents as being someone "who continues to operate in an undercover capacity," undoubtedly Raymond Wean.

According to Wean, Cerasani had an ominous reply to Cipolla's musing about a gift for Ruggiero.

"Forget it," Cerasani said. "Lefty is gonna be with fishes. He won't need a pet."

CHAPTER 12

The Gathering Storm

By February 1981, the deep penetration Joseph Pistone had made of the Bonanno crime family had produced enough evidence that federal prosecutors in Manhattan began the secretive and complex task of targeting the upper echelon of the crime family for indictment. It became clear to investigators that the old legend that the Mafia didn't get involved in narcotics was really just a myth. Cocaine and heroin trafficking had become the province of a number of high-ranked mafiosi.

In the Bonanno family, the focus of investigators turned to Alphonse "Sonny Red" Indelicato. He was believed to be one of the family's major cocaine and heroin traffickers and used his contacts in Florida to facilitate the deals. If the FBI needed a strong indication that Indelicato and his two close associates, Dominick Trinchera and Philip Giaccone, might be involved in narcotics, they found a clue during a wedding in 1980 at the Pierre Hotel in Manhattan. One of the reputed bosses of the Milan faction of the Italian Mafia was getting married at St. Patrick's Cathedral in Manhattan and the big bash was surveilled by the FBI. There were lots of pictures taken by agents and the collage of photos seemed like a

Who's Who of organized crime, remembered Charles Rooney. Indelicato, Trinchera, and Giaccone were in attendance as was Salvatore Catalano and a lot of the Sicilians from Brooklyn.

The FBI had just commenced a major heroin investigation involving a curious group of Sicilians who seemed to be in Brooklyn but who had various ties to Bonanno family members. The FBI wasn't sure what the Sicilians were at that point, perhaps a separate clique within the crime family or maybe a distinct family unto themselves. It would take four more years before the FBI would tie the Sicilians into the international heroin trade in a case that would later become known as the Pizza Connection.

But in 1980, whoever the Sicilians were, they accepted the likes of Indelicato and his two friends. Curiously for the FBI, neither Joseph Massino nor Dominick Napolitano were at the wedding reception, a fact that investigators believed indicated that perhaps both men wanted nothing to do with drugs or that some other kind of crime family power play was underway. In any case, federal prosecutors suspected Indelicato was a key player in the narcotics trade and by early 1981 they targeted him for investigation. But with the events of May 5, 1981, when Indelicato, Trinchera, and Giaccone were slaughtered at a social club on Thirteenth Avenue in Brooklyn, federal prosecutors in Manhattan lost their initial target.

However, with the death of Indelicato, investigators quickly shifted their sights to Joseph Massino and Dominick Napolitano and their crews. Both Massino and Napolitano were by August of that year suspected by investigators to have orchestrated the murders of the three captains. In addition, both Massino and Napolitano were believed by federal prosecuters to have been involved in narcotics, as well as extortion and gambling.

Allegations surrounding Massino about drugs proved to be rather ambiguous and amorphous. His brother-in-law,

Salvatore Vitale, later told FBI agents that at some point in the late 1970s, a time when Massino was an up and coming soldier, he instructed him and Duane Leisenheimer to bring a car to Fort Lee, New Jersey. The first town over the George Washington Bridge, Fort Lee has had its share of gangsters living and working within its confines. When Vitale arrived with the car, he spotted Gambino mobster Angelo Ruggiero and Massino nearby. Ruggiero was a known Gambino drug merchant and his appearance with Massino led Vitale to think that perhaps drugs were in the trunk of the car he had just dropped off. He also told the agents that Massino would make trips alone on Saturdays to visit another mobster, something he thought seemed suspicious.

Napolitano, as far as law enforcement was concerned, went missing in August 1981, a fact that led the FBI to think he was either dead (as informants claimed) or had fled to escape indictment or retribution for the Donnie Brasco disaster. Pistone, of course, was off the street. Nevertheless, the federal government's investigation into the New York crime families continued at an unrelenting pace. Joseph Massino was turning out to be a major target.

From offices in Manhattan and Brooklyn, federal prosecutors and FBI agents applied for several court orders for wiretaps in 1981 that targeted key Bonanno crime family locations. While he was alive, taps were placed on the telephones at Napolitano's Motion Lounge. Another tap was also placed on Benjamin Ruggiero's Manhattan telephone, as well as the home telephone of at least one other Manhattan-based family soldier. But it was in late August 1981 that permission was obtained by the FBI to place taps on Massino's home telephone in Howard Beach and his J&S Cake Social Club in Maspeth. The FBI wanted to bug not only Massino but also Vitale.

The affidavit filed in court by FBI agent Edward T. Tucker to get taps placed on Massino's telephone spelled out just how powerful and deadly law enforcement officials considered the Maspeth caterer to be. Tucker said that it had been Benjamin Ruggiero who placed Massino—who is identified in the agent's affidavit as "Messina"—squarely in the planning of the murder of the three captains that May. Massino himself, according to Tucker, was overheard by an informant saying, "We got three of them, but two got away," an apparent reference to the fact that Frank Lino and Bruno Indelicato had not been killed along with Trinchera, Giaccone, and Alphonse Indelicato that fateful night.

Conventional wisdom was that the three captains were killed because they tried to supplant Rastelli's power. But Tucker said that other mobsters had told an undercover agent (presumably Pistone) of another possible motive: Alfonse Indelicato's close affiliation with the Sicilian faction of the crime family had made Massino worried that the Zips might kill him. A preemptive strike thus seemed to be needed.

Apart from his suspected role in the three captains slaughter, Massino was also discovered to have developed a close working relationship with up and coming Gambino family captain John Gotti, said Tucker, referring to intelligence developed from a confidential law enforcement source. A neighbor of Massino in Howard Beach, Gotti had at that time not received the publicity and notoriety that would dog him later in life. He was the boss of a crew of gangsters who had graduated from hijacking to drug dealing and other crimes. Gotti was also a big gambler and that was how Massino became tied to him, said Tucker.

"In May 1981, this Source advised the FBI that Messina and Gotti along with another Gambino Family capo Angelo Ruggiero and two others each owned a percentage of the 'house' in a high stakes dice game run by Gotti on Mott Street in Manhattan," stated Tucker. Mott Street in Manhattan is a main avenue in Chinatown but it also crosses into Little Italy, where lots of Mafiosi lived, worked, and conducted business.

But there was a more bizarre episode reported by Tucker that seemed to show that Gotti and Massino were working together to carry out the murder of the still hiding Bruno Indelicato, the supposedly cocaine-enraged son of the murdered Alphonse. Tucker learned from the same confidential source that Gotti's brother, Gene, and Angelo Ruggiero were overheard relating how they had been driving on a New York City expressway when they were followed by what they thought was a police car.

"When this car pulled up a man inside the car pointed a gun out the window and they [Gene Gotti and Ruggiero] recognized the driver of the car to be Anthony Bruno Indelicato," said Tucker. "Gotti and Ruggiero related that they were able to exit the expressway and get away."

The reason for the roadside encounter, the source told Tucker, was that the killing of Alphonse Indelicato had been approved by Aniello Dellacroce, the underboss of the Gambino crime family and mentor for John Gotti. This made Gambino family members a target for Bruno Indelicato's revenge. As a result, Massino and John Gotti became united in a common effort to find and kill Bruno Indelicato, not only to protect themselves but also Dellacroce, said Tucker, referring to his informant.

Other sources cited by Tucker said that Massino, while he disliked using the telephone to conduct business, would nevertheless sometimes talk on the social club telephone to contact loan-sharking victims about their debts. Vitale would also use the telephone there to call Massino about gambling and loan-sharking, activities the same sources said Massino ran out of J&S Cake Social Club.

As icing on the cake, Tucker said that the FBI pen registers picked up Massino's home telephone making calls to the home of one of Rastelli's brothers, Bonanno street boss Salvatore Ferrugia, as well as John Gotti. In Tucker's view, these calls showed that Massino was a high-ranking Bonanno captain who was loyal to Rastelli. Massino remained, said Tucker, a subject worthy of electronic surveillance.

Judge Eugene Nickerson signed the surveillance authorization on August 27, 1981. Wiretaps were placed on the telephones and a bug was set up inside J&S Cake Social Club. One night a team of about a half-dozen FBI agents led by Patrick Colgan penetrated Massino's social club on Fifty-eighth Road in Maspeth. One agent picked the locks, another decommissioned the alarm, and another planted the bug as Colgan made sure nothing went wrong. The black-bag job took about forty-five minutes to complete. But no sooner was the bug up and running than it stopped functioning.

Bugging devices can be so useful when they work right. But one vulnerability they have is their essential nature of being radio transmitters. A sensitive radio receiver anywhere near a bugging device can pick up the transmission. It just so happened that just a day or two after Colgan and his crew had planted the listening device in Massino's social club that Salvatore Vitale began fiddling with a police scanner. The surveillance-conscious Massino likely had the scanner at J&S Cake to monitor police frequencies. But a sound that Vitale had picked up froze everyone at the club. It sounded like a strange frequency and Massino, who was sitting at a table, became suspicious.

Duane Leisenheimer was in the bathroom and Massino called out to him to clap his hands. Leisenheimer complied and the scanner picked up what sounded like a clap.

Massino now knew his club was bugged and he searched the ceiling until he found the listening device over the area above the card table. Vitale took it out and the surveillance device stopped at that moment.

After being told of the dead bugging apparatus, Colgan's FBI supervisor told him to go back in and retrieve the device.

"How do you expect us to get it out?" Colgan lamented, knowing the difficulty that surrounded the initial planting of the device. The club had a special key-coded alarm system that had allowed the agents only thirty seconds or so to override it.

"I don't care, get it," the supervisor said.

So shortly after lunch one afternoon in the late summer of 1981, Colgan and a partner walked down Fifty-eighth Road and followed Salvatore Vitale through the door of the club. Vitale had been oblivious to their footsteps. One of the other men in the club nervously asked Vitale who was following him. Vitale turned and stared at Colgan and his parnter.

"We are FBI," Colgan told Vitale.

"Fuck you," Vitale answered and took a swing at the agent. (Years later Vitale told a different version, saying he asked what the agent wanted.)

Suddenly, a voice from the backroom called out, "Cool it Sal, it's only Pat."

Massino had recognized his old professional adversary from the hijacking squad and defused the situation.

"I have been expecting you," Massino told Colgan as he gave him the bugging device.

"Joe, it crossed my mind," Colgan said.

Massino asked the agents to have a can a beer and broke out some Budweiser. Colgan, his partner, Massino, and Vitale then sat at the bar and made small talk. The four men sounded like old friends from the neighborhood, asking after each other's family. Colgan couldn't help notice that Massino had gained more girth and had a belly that overhung his belt more than ever. He diplomatically told Massino he looked bigger. Massino complimented Colgan about his recent promotion to supervisor in the FBI. Colgan said he had heard Massino had received a promotion as well.

After finishing the drinks, Colgan slapped a few dollars down on the bar—despite Massino's polite protest—and left with the bugging device. The timing of the discovery of the bug was fortuitous because if there was talk within Massino's club about the murders or anything else of interest to federal agents, the listening device didn't pick it up. Back at FBI headquarters in Manhattan the bug was tested. It worked perfectly.

By the fall of 1981, Massino and Napolitano were being heavily probed for their involvement in the murder of the three captains, as well as for other acts of racketeering through the Bonanno crime family. On November 23, 1981, the first indictment stemming from special Agent Joseph Pistone's penetration of the Bonanno family was announced in U.S. District Court in Manhattan. Six men, Dominick Napolitano, Benjamin Ruggiero, Nicholas Santora, John Cerasani, James Episcopia, and Antonio Tomasulo were accused of participating in the conspiracy as well as in other acts of racketeering involving the Bonanno crime family.

The announcement of the charges on November 24, 1981, was the first indication that the FBI had two undercover agents who had penetrated the crime family. Joseph Pistone and Edgar T. Robb weren't named in the press conference but just the fact that such an infiltration of the Mafia had taken place was big news. Aside from the conspiracy to kill the three captains, the defendants were charged with various narcotics offenses and gambling. It was also disclosed that the group had tried in June 1980 to burglarize the Manhattan apartment of Princess Ashraf Pahlevi, the twin sister of the deposed Shah of Iran. That break-in was bungled when a security guard fired a shot at the would-be intruders.

In a preemptive move designed as much to convince him to become a witness as to save him, federal agents in August 1981, three months before his formal indictment, had arrested Ruggiero. The FBI had known from its informant within the Bonanno family, undoubtedly Raymond Wean, that Ruggiero was targeted for assassination. Since the FBI didn't think Ruggiero would stay in the area if told of the plot against him, he was first arrested for the murder of Alphonse Indelicato, the only one of the three murdered captains whose body had been found. The FBI then told Ruggiero about the threat to his life.

Even his arrest didn't stop Ruggiero's fellow mobsters from trying to plot his demise. During one of Ruggiero's unsuccessful court hearings aimed at his getting bail, Assistant U.S. Attorney Barbara Jones, told the court that an informant told her that Ruggiero would be killed as soon as he got out of jail.

Massino wasn't charged in the Napolitano case even though he was suspected of having taken part in the conspiracy that led to the murders. But by the time the indictment against Napolitano and the others was being unsealed, investigators were conducting an additional investigation of Massino for loan-sharking and narcotics distribution. Separate investigations were also beginning on the other Mafia families as well, probes that would take years to complete. One of those investigations focused on the dealings of the Gambino family and its new, emerging members. Among them was the brash and generally unknown captain John Gotti. A neighbor and friend of Massino's for the better part of a decade, Gotti, who was schooled in the ways of mob life by underboss Aniello Dellacroce, had a crew that counted among its members his brother Eugene Gotti and Angelo Ruggiero.

By November 1981, federal prosecutors had zeroed in on the two Gotti brothers and Ruggiero for their own particular racketeering offenses that included loan-sharking, gambling, narcotics, and murder. Investigators knew that Ruggiero was such an uncontrollable talker that he had earned the nickname on the street of "Quack-Quack," a reference to the quacking of a duck. Since he talked so much, FBI agents got a court order to wiretap Ruggiero's telephone at his home on Eighty-eighth Street in Howard Beach. That tap lasted about a month until Ruggiero moved to a new home in Cedarhurst, Long Island, when agents got a court order to wiretap two phones there.

With subpoenas flying around Howard Beach and the rest of the city on the probe of Massino and the Bonanno family, it was no secret that a major federal investigation was underway. Angelo Ruggiero, a friend and one-time neighbor of Massino, had already been subpoenaed to testify, but under the advice of his lawyer, Michael Coiro, he asserted his privilege against self-incrimination and didn't testify. Once away from the grand jury, however, Ruggiero and Massino talked openly on the telephone about the investigation and the ominous things it portended. The FBI agents were right about Ruggiero, he just didn't know how to control his chatter.

For instance, on November 25, 1981, two days after the announcement of the Napolitano indictment, Ruggiero told Massino about having received the subpoena from "Mrs. Jones," a reference to Barbara Jones, the assistant U.S. attorney in Manhattan who was investigating Napolitano, Massino, and the Bonanno family.

"How the hell did [the agents] throw you into this?" Massino asked Ruggiero. Though both gangsters, Ruggiero had little or no connection to the Bonanno activities, the most notorious being the murders of Trinchera, Giaccone, Indelicato, and—though still unknown to law enforcement— the slaughter of Napolitano.

Massino was clearly getting concerned about the investigation and was overheard wondering if Jones had a subpoena for him as well. It was at this point that Massino asked Ruggiero if it was even wise for him to go home if Jones was getting ready to haul him before the grand jury.

It was during this conversation in November 1981 that Massino hinted that he was entertaining the idea of leaving town. Five of his crime family associates had already been arrested (Napolitano, though charged, was moldering in a mob graveyard). He knew that the investigation was focusing on his connection to the murder of the three captains, crimes that could carry a life sentence if convicted. A sense of dread and panic seemed to be setting in.

Massino told Ruggiero that he wished he could go to sleep and wake up after the approaching Thanksgiving and Christmas holidays. Maybe these troubles would be all over, the panicky mobster said.

"It ain't going to be any better," Ruggiero responded.

× × ×

Subpoenas were everywhere. And there was rumors of more indictments. Furthermore, an FBI agent had penetrated the Bonanno family.

These were the things in early 1982 that added to Massino's sense of discomfort and dread of what could be in store for him. Ruggiero's remarks didn't help him either.

Around the J&S Cake Social Club in Queens, the conversations that took place reflected the troubles. As Vitale later told the FBI, he remembered Massino and mobster Al Embarrato, known by the name "Al Walker" on the street, talking about the Pistone penetration of the crime family. The search for scapegoats didn't stop with the killing of Napolitano. Even though it was Napolitano who had been taken in by Pistone and had pushed the undercover FBI agent for crime family membership, it had been Anthony Mirra who had first unwittingly befriended Pistone.

A bulky man with a reputation for being a killer who was quick with a knife instead of a gun, Mirra was a hothead with anger-management problems who ran some loansharking and gambling operations. As a soldier in the Bonanno family, Mirra reported for a while to a captain named Michael Zaffarano, a pornographer who died of a heart attack during an FBI raid in 1980. Mirra used Pistone as a driver, but after Mirra was arrested and sent to prison for a narcotics charge, Pistone gravitated to Benjamin Ruggiero.

In a snippet of conversation Vitale told FBI agents he

overheard, Massino told Embarrato that Mirra "had to go." Mirra had been released from prison in 1981 for the drug case and was around town again. Some Bonanno members now thought he was an informant, which wasn't a good thing to be called with the FBI playing hardball and building criminal cases all over town.

After Pistone's true identity had become known, Mirra had kept a low profile and had been very hard to reach. "He wasn't meeting with anybody," one mobster said. Embarrato got the job of farming out Mirra's murder and in a case of delegating responsibility passed the order for the hit to Richard Cantarella, who in turn involved Joseph D'Amico, someone Mirra trusted.

On February 12, 1982, as Mirra fumbled for a key to open the security lock of a garage where he kept his gray Volvo, he was shot in the head at near point-blank range by D'Amico. Crime scene photos captured Mirra slumped in the driver's seat, his chin against his chest as if he were taking a nap. A rivulet of blood had trickled out of his right ear and stained his winter coat.

"I was the only one who could get close to him," D'Amico later told investigators.

Any number of suspected informants could have been killed. But no matter how many died, the fact of the matter was that Joseph Massino never shook the feeling of foreboding he had in March 1982. He wanted to get out of town, and fast.

Turning to the fair-haired kid, Duane Leisenheimer, Massino traveled with his driver to the Hamptons. It was in the off-season since the Hamptons didn't get swinging until May at the earliest and the hideaway might provide time to think. Still, Massino and Leisenheimer saw too many people they thought they knew in the beach towns along Long Island's south shore and decided to pull up stakes again and head back to the city.

Vitale remembered getting a call from his brother-in-law

and told to come to Junior Palermo's home on Ocean Parkway in Brooklyn. Palermo was a Colombo crime family soldier who Massino knew. No new charges had been filed against anyone but there were simply too many bad vibes, Massino said. It was time to split.

So Joseph Massino, you are supposed to be a wealthy gangster with the vast resources of the Mafia at your disposal. You know the cops are itching to arrest you. The world is your oyster. Where are you going to go now? Well, it isn't Disneyland, much less Brazil.

"I need a place to go for about thirty days," Massino told Leisenheimer. "What about your parents' house?"

Leisenheimer's family had moved to Pennsylvania's Pocono Mountains area and his mother had a house in the town of Milford. There were plenty of hotels and motels in the area. A careful person could get lost there and stay out of sight. If necessary, Leisenheimer's family could simply be told that his friend Joe was ducking a subpoena.

Leisenheimer later recalled that his father had no problems with his son staying at the family home. But the elder Leisenheimer, his son said, had only a couple of provisos: "Keep the place clean but when I want to go there, you guys got to leave."

So in the face of approaching trouble, Joseph Massino didn't stand around to face the music. But for a guy who spent most of his life in working-class Maspeth, the possibilities Massino saw for life on the lam were not very exotic. He packed up his travel bag and headed west, not to some obscure town or exotic location, but instead to a place made famous for its honeymoon bungalows and heart-shaped bath tubs.

× × ×

Massino's nose for trouble served him well. No sooner had he and Leisenheimer headed for the gentle rolling hills of the Poconos than on March 25, 1982, a federal grand jury in Manhattan indicted Massino and others. It was as bad as he expected. The new charges, actually an expansion of the earlier November 1981 indictment against the other Bonanno members, accused Massino of involvement in the murder of the three captains. There was also a charge against Massino for hijacking.

"Mr. Messina," said one newspaper, "who was labeled in the indictment as a 'capodecina,' or captain, in the crime family, is a fugitive."

With Massino a step ahead of the sheriff, so to speak, and nowhere to be found by the FBI, a bench warrant was issued by a federal judge for his arrest. By then, Massino was quietly spending time at the Milford House, an inn in Pennsylvania. He used the alias "Joe Russo" and on weekends he and Leisenheimer, who used the name "Duane Kelly," went to the younger man's family home in the area.

But living so close to New York and trying to hide out meant you had to be careful. Massino thought he was hiding but he learned that he could run into people he knew when he least expected it. He had hardly been on the lam a month when Massino decided to take a break in the cocktail lounge of a Holiday Inn in Port Jervis. Massino was seated at a table when in walked an old acquaintance named Salvatore Polisi. A mob associate and criminal out of New York, Polisi recognized Massino from some meetings they had in Queens and decided to shake Massino's hand.

"How are you doing?" Polisi asked Massino.

"He was kind of nervous or concerned about me just meeting him," Polisi later remembered about Massino's reaction.

Massino didn't want for much. Vitale, it was later learned by police, would bring him packets of cash and there were occasional visits back to New York City when Massino stayed at the Ocean Parkway, Brooklyn, home of Junior Palermo, a member of the Colombo crime family. When they had to, Bonanno family members made the trip to the

Poconos to caucus with Massino. Vitale made over a dozen trips. John Gotti even made the trip a couple of times, meeting Leisenheimer at the Milford Diner and then being driven to the Leisenheimer family home. On occasion, Leisenheimer drove back to New York and picked up other visitors. This was 1982, before cell phones came into wide use, but Massino was able to stay in telephone contact with Vitale through a system that relied on the use of different telephone numbers that had been reduced to a code.

Cash and calls weren't the only thing Massino got on the lam. In the summer of 1976, Massino was making trips to Dannemora Correctional Facility when he gave a ride to a pretty twenty-two-year-old Bayside High School graduate known as Linda, whose husband happened to be incarcerated there as well. Something then happened. As Linda later told investigators, she began to date Massino on a "personal level," driving with him to the Lewisburg federal prison when he visited Rastelli. Having divorced her husband in 1979, Linda said she kept seeing Massino until their relationship broke off in 1980. Their affair rekindled, Linda told a federal grand jury, in July 1982. With Massino a fugitive, Linda said she visited him in different Pennsylvania motels. She remembered being driven by Leisenheimer for those rendevous during which Massino told her about his indictment for the three captains murder and hijacking.

Given the fugitive status of Massino and the continuous trips being made by crime family members to the Poconos for visits, the question is raised about how much effort the FBI put into looking for him. Massino himself believed that the agents had enough on their hands with the approaching trial of his cohorts for the three captains murder and that he was a low priority. But in fact they were looking.

The FBI believed Vitale was the key in this period to finding Massino and began to pay him unannounced visits and shadowed his movements. For instance, on August 31, 1982, three FBI agents including Charles Rooney stopped by the

J&S Cake Social Club in Maspeth. In the doorway stood Vitale, his business partner Carmine Peluso, and a nervous cook. It wasn't the first time the agents had stopped by.

Rooney did the talking. He flat out told Vitale that if Massino turned himself in the FBI wouldn't make so many visits. After all, Rooney explained, Massino was a fugitive and they were looking for him. If Massino came back and surrendered, there simply wouldn't be a need for the FBI visits.

Vitale, according to an FBI report of the meeting, then did something that seemed strange. He reached into the right pocket of his trousers and pulled out a large wad of cash wrapped in a rubber band, counted it, and then placed the cash in his left pocket.

"Can we talk off the record?" Vitale asked.

"What do you have to say?" one of the other agents asked.

It turned out Vitale had nothing much to say. The agents, he said, were coming on like gangbusters, scaring the poor cook. "He is probably in the back of the shop having a nervous breakdown," Vitale said of the young man.

There wasn't much point to the rest of the encounter and the agents reiterated that they were looking for Massino before getting in their car and driving away. Given the ease Massino apparently had in slipping in and out of the city during his months on the lam, it is likely he was already local in the New York City area when the agents visited Vitale.

But try as they might, the agents simply could never find Massino. They stopped by Massino's home in Howard Beach, usually around holidays such as the Fourth of July, Labor Day, or Memorial Day. They spoke to Massino's wife, Josephine, who told them the obvious: her husband was not around.

Some of Massino's neighbors, knowing about the FBI interest in finding him, began to call in tips, alerting the agents to activity at his homestead or Vitale's actions they thought were suspicious, one law enforcement official said. Based sometimes on those tips, the agents continued to shadow Vitale in the hopes that he would lead them to his brother-in-law. In one instance, a team of agents trailed Vitale one evening as he picked up Massino's wife and two daughters and took them to a house in Queens, said one former FBI agent. Covering both the front and rear exits, the agents knocked on the door and asked to come in, to which Vitale consented, the agent recalled. Massino was nowhere in sight.

Agents also suspected Josephine was visiting her spouse and made a number of attempts to follow her. But either because of her crafty driving or just the vagaries of weekend traffic over the George Washington Bridge, one agent remembered that it was impossible to tail Josephine by car. They never did find her visiting her husband and for all anybody knew she was making visits to New Jersey shopping malls.

As cagey and secretive as he was, Massino almost blew his cover in a trivial but stupid lapse of security. In a Pennsylvania drug store, Massino was caught shoplifting a bottle of aspirin by a sharp-eyed clerk. Seeing how Massino was supposed to be getting restocked with cash by Vitale, it seems strange that he would have to steal such a small, inexpensive item. The store called the police on Massino and Leisenheimer, who happened to be with him. But as luck would have it, Massino used his alias "Joe Russo" and the local police never caught on to the fact that they had a major fugitive in their midst.

Back in New York, and despite Massino's absence, federal prosecutors opened up their showcase trial against the Bonanno crime family members who had been arrested. The centerpiece of the case was to be the testimony of Joseph Pistone in his first big test as a government witness after having spent five years in deep undercover work in the Mafia.

The trial against Benjamin "Lefty Guns" Ruggiero, Anthony "Mr. Fish" Rabito, Nicholas "Nicky" Santora, John "Boobie" Cerasani, and Antonio "Boots" Tomasulo began on July 26, 1982, in the Manhattan federal district court. It was the showcase of mob trials. Never before had a Mafia family been infiltrated by the FBI. Never before had an undercover agent taken the stand in such a fashion after having penetrated a crime family to the extent Joseph Pistone had. No matter what the outcome of the trial, Pistone had made the Bonanno crime family the laughing stock of the Mafia, further condemning it to second-class status in the eyes of all of the other mob families.

It fell to prosecutors Louis Freeh and Barbara Jones, two of the stars of the U.S. Attorney's Office in Manhattan, to present the government's case. Freeh had been an FBI agent before he became a prosecutor and Jones had cut her teeth on a number of successful mob prosecutions, including those against Teamster boss Anthony Provenzano and Pennsylvania mobster Russell Bufalino. Together, they were a formidable pair.

It was Freeh who addressed the jury of four men and eight women in the government's opening statement and first described for the panel that the case was historic because it involved an undercover FBI agent who used the name "Donnie Brasco" and played the role of loyal mob soldier to move up the ranks of the Bonanno crime family.

"Brasco became such a trusted member of this crew," Freeh said, referring to the cadre of Napolitano and Ruggiero, that they "promised to propose him for membership in the Bonanno family."

Freeh and Jones believed that if Brasco's true identity as Joseph Pistone became known, he would be endangered. According to informants, a $500,000 contract had been placed on his head, and security was a concern for the government. The prosecutors asked Judge Robert W. Sweet to allow the agent to use his undercover name when testifying as a way of further protecting him from mob retribution. But

Sweet ruled that such a request would violate the rights of the defendants to confront and cross-examine their accuser. As a compromise, Sweet said that Pistone, as well as fellow agent Edgar T. Robb, didn't have to reveal any personal information such as addresses or the names of their family members.

In his opening statement, Freeh sketched out the main allegations and told the jury the Bonanno family was led by Philip Rastelli, who survived a power struggle with Carmine Galante, the captain murdered in 1979. Most of the jurors must have known about Galante's murder since it was front-page news all over town when it happened in 1979. But the murders that mattered in the case, Freeh said, was the May 1981 killing of the three Bonanno captains. Secret tapes made by Brasco, he said, would be crucial pieces of evidence pointing to the defendants' alleged roles in the slayings.

When it came time for their opening statements, however, the attorneys for the defendants told jurors that it was actually a man not in the courtroom—"Joseph Messina"—whom they described as a rival captain, who had ordered the killings in the case. Massino could hide in Pennsylvania, but that didn't mean his name would stay out of the case.

Joseph Pistone would be the marquee witness in what was at that time the biggest Mafia trial to hit New York City in years. But one of the first crucial government witnesses to take the stand would turn out to be none other than Joseph Massino's old hijacking associate: Raymond Wean. Life hadn't been good to the fifty-one-year-old Wean. After bouncing around with Massino and getting the short end of the stick when it came to sharing the loot from their days as truck thieves, Wean told the jury how after "roughly 200 crimes" and numerous convictions that he needed a break. After a felony charge in Nassau County, Wean decided to cooperate with the FBI and become an informant, he stated.

After he decided to cooperate with the government, Wean

hung around Dominick Napolitano's club on Graham Avenue in Brooklyn and related that he saw and heard a lot of things. He mentioned how Massino and Napolitano came up with the audacious plan to rob the Manhattan home of Princess Ashraf Pahlevi, a sister of the late Shah of Iran, in June 1980. The gangsters believed jewelry, art work, and the contents of safes in the house at 29 Beekman Place in Manhattan would be a mother lode of valuables.

"It seemed like a piece of cake to us," Wean said of the robbery plan, which he told the jury also involved John Cerasani, one of the six men on trial in the courtroom.

It may have seemed like a piece of cake, but the planned heist didn't go off well. Wean testified that he and Cerasani were let into the townhouse by posing as delivery men carrying a case containing an air conditioner. A gullible security guard let the pair in and Wean said he suddenly drew out a pistol.

"Don't move!" Wean shouted out.

The startled guard threw up his hand and in the process jarred the gun's trigger. A shot was fired, wounding Wean in the hand. A panicky Wean said his group of robbers thought the guard had been shot (he had not) and fled through the streets of the East Side.

Judge Sweet would only allow Wean, who by then was in the federal witness protection program, to testify in limited fashion about the disappearance of Napolitano. Outside of the presence of the jury, Wean recalled that after Napolitano disappeared in August 1981 that even in the Motion Lounge, which had been the missing captain's headquarters, no one would mention his name. Then something more ominous happened, a sure sign that Napolitano was dead, said Wean. The pigeon coop, long Napolitano's refuge and the focus of his sport of bird racing, was dismantled. The birds were individually strangled by hand, informants later told the FBI. To Wean, the destruction of the pigeon coop was a clear sign that Napolitano was "no longer alive."

With the jury present, Wean referred to Napolitano's disappearence and his pigeon coop being taken down off the roof of the Motion Lounge. Though he said he never saw Napolitano again, Wean didn't say he thought the man was dead. Wean recounted that it was John Cerasani who appeared to take over the Bonanno crew that had been run by Napolitano.

It wasn't just with Massino and Napolitano that Wean got close to the Bonanno family. While he was imprisoned in the federal jail in lower Manhattan after his 1976 hijacking conviction, he earned the job of trustee from correctional officials. Selected because of their good behavior, trustees are able to perform tasks and leave the jail under supervision to carry out manual tasks such as picking up mail and provisions. While in the Manhattan detention facility in 1978, Wean said he met Carmine Galante, who happened to be incarcerated for an alleged parole violation. Wean took care of the Bonanno captain.

"Cigars, booze, cigarettes, or anything he wanted," Wean smuggled in to the facility for Galante.

The long-awaited testimony of Joseph Pistone finally began on August 3, 1982. An athletically trim man with thinning hair, Pistone was the center of attention as he walked through a rear entrance into Judge Sweet's courtroom. At last, the man who had infiltrated the Mafia in one of the most daring assignments in FBI history was getting his day in court. His appearance would not be disappointing.

For five days Pistone testified about his life with the Bonanno crime family and the way he infiltrated it. After setting the table with preliminaries, Pistone was then guided by prosecutor Jones through the events that surrounded the killing of the three captains, the main racketeering charge facing Rabito, Ruggiero, and Santora. It became clear from his testimony that Pistone had no direct knowledge of the killings, nor was he involved in any of the planning discussions. Instead, using his recollection and audio recordings he secretly made with Ruggiero and the missing Napolitano, Pistone told the jury how he learned why the men were killed. In so doing, he implicated Ruggiero, Napolitano, and Santora, as well as the fugitive Massino, in the slaughter.

It was defendant Nicholas Santora, Pistone testified, who told him how Dominick Trinchera was blasted apart by a shotgun.

"Nicky said you should have seen when they shot him— fifty pounds of his stomach went flying," Pistone said.

Ruggiero had also said that Trinchera's body was so heavy—he weighed close to 300 pounds—that it took a stronger Cerasani to move it, according to Pistone.

"He was surprised how strong Boobie [Cerasani] was because he moved it," testified Pistone.

Though he was in Florida when the killings took place, Pistone recalled that Napolitano had called him to come to a meeting back in Brooklyn at the Motion Lounge. After flying back to LaGuardia on May 14, nine days after the murders, Pistone said he wired himself up with a small transmitting device and went directly to the club, which was also known as "Charlie's Lounge."

Once inside the club, Pistone said, he went into a backroom with Napolitano, where the Bonanno captain sat down with him at a card table and spoke to him.

"Sonny and I sat down at the card table and Sonny said to me, 'We took care of those three guys, they're gone,' and he asked me if I knew anything about Miami and I said 'Yeah,' and I asked why," Pistone recalled.

"'Because Bruno got away,'" Napolitano replied.

Napolitano was talking about Bruno Indelicato, the son of the slain Alphonse Indelicato. The younger Indelicato was widely reputed to have a big cocaine habit and traveling in the Miami area.

"So I asked him, you know, 'What do you want me to do down there?'" Pistone said, referring to Miami.

Napolitano's response was direct.

"And he said, 'I want you to go down and look for him, and if you find him, hit him.' And he said, 'Be careful, because when he's coked up, he's crazy.'"

Earlier, Pistone told the jury that it was Ruggiero who had told him that the Mafia Commission as far back as April 1981 had assured the Bonanno family that Rastelli would be recognized as the boss. An earlier attempt to assassinate Indelicato, which had been called off, had been arranged by Napolitano and Massino.

"At one point in the conversation Lefty said that the thing that had happened the prior week [attempted assassination], put together by Sonny Black and Joey Messina— Because of what they put together, the Commission had assured them that Rusty Rastelli would be the absolute boss of the family."

The Sicilians, or Zips, Pistone said, were according to Ruggiero to come over to the side of Massino.

Ruggiero also had some unkind words about Massino because of the fact that Indelicato's body had surfaced shortly after the murders.

"That was a screw-up," Ruggiero said. "Joey Messina was supposed to get rid of that body."

The effect of Pistone's testimony about the murders was to implicate Massino, Napolitano, and Ruggiero in the killings through circumstantial evidence. There was of course more evidence he gave as the prosecution attempted to tie the defendants into narcotics distribution and gambling. For instance, Pistone said that on May 15, 1981, he arranged with Napolitano and Cerasani to purchase some Quaaludes for distribution in Florida. Samples were given to him, Pistone said, by Santora and Cerasani at a local car service run by Tomasulo up the street from the Motion Lounge. Pistone took the samples and delivered them to fellow agent Patrick Colgan. Ruggiero was picked up on a wiretap about a week later talking with Pistone about the quality and price of the pills, telling Pistone to let him know when he was ready for a larger sale.

Evidence about gambling was also presented to the jury and included Pistone relating how he brought $2,500 up from Florida at the request of Napolitano to cover losses suffered during a tough weekend of sports betting. Tomasulo, said Pistone, had been introduced to him as being a partner in Napolitano's gambling ring. Ray Wean also testified that he had seen Tomasulo reviewing bets with Santora and Cerasani a number of times. Coded conversations between Tomasulo and Santora that had been intercepted by the FBI were analyzed by prosecution experts who said they showed both men were involved in a numbers operation.

The defense attorneys had their turn with Pistone and attempted to discredit him by showing he was involved in drug dealing and had once proposed a murder of a mobster. It was Robert Koppelman, who was representing Ruggieo, who tried to show wrongdoing on Pistone's part when he was playing his undercover role. In what struck trial observers as polite responses, Pistone parried each of Koppelman's insinuations with denials and explanations.

"I never thought of doing anything illegal, sir," Pistone said.

When Koppelman said that Pistone had "twisted the truth" for years while undercover, he asked the agent if he was doing the same on the witness stand.

"That is incorrect," Pistone said. He said he lied only with individuals he was investigating to enhance his credibility with them.

Cerasani was represented by Manhattan attorney David Breitbart, who had leapt to prominence after representing the one-time Harlem drug kingpin Leroy "Nicky" Barnes. Brietbart's advocacy had earned three acquittals for Barnes although a fourth trial led to a conviction—and life in prison for the drug dealer. With an in-your-face method of questioning, Breitbart had a habit of facing a hostile witness, hands in trouser pockets, and pepper them with persistent, embarrassing questions that sometimes elicited angry responses.

In defending Cerasani, Breitbart had asked a lot of questions that brought up Massino. Through Breitbart's questioning, Massino, although he was absent from the trial, had a presence in the case. However, it was just that tactic that began to anger some of Massino's allies who had been watching the progress of the case. They didn't care much for Breitbart's tactics. So, one August afternoon after the trial had finished for the day, Massino's ever loyal brother-in-law, Salvatore Vitale, accompanied by James Tartaglione, paid a visit to Breitbart's office off Broadway in lower Manhattan.

Vitale didn't mince any words. Stop mentioning Massino's name, he told Breitbart. Stop mentioning Massino's name or he, Vitale, would throw Breitbart out the window, Massino's brother-in-law later told the FBI. Though he was not tall in stature, Breitbart had martial arts training, and while taken aback by Vitale's remark, he told him to cool off. Nothing he said in court could ever be used against Massino, Breitbart replied. Though it was a strange meeting, the irony of it all would play out years later when it would be Breitbart to whom Massino turned for legal help.

On August 25, 1982, the jury began its deliberation after two full days of summations and hours of final instructions from Sweet. The prosecution admitted that Pistone and his testimony were crucial to the case while the defense attorneys said that the government had spent millions of dollars on a farcical case that nabbed "minnows."

Robert Koppelman, Ruggiero's attorney, said that there wasn't one witness who testified with any firsthand knowledge of the crimes, particularly the murder of the three captains in May 1981. Breitbart, in his closing statement on behalf of Cerasani, called Pistone a liar and said Wean, Massino's old hijack buddy from Maspeth, was "evil incarnate."

Three days later the verdict was in: Ruggiero, Santora, and Tomasulo were convicted of the racketeering conspiracy charge, which accused them of being involved in affairs of the Bonanno crime family. Specifically, the jury found Ruggiero and Santora guilty of conspiracy in the murders of Trinchera, Giaccone, and Indelicato. Tomasulo was convicted of conspiracy to distribute Quaaludes and conspiracy to conduct illegal gambling. Anthony Rabito was acquitted of the main conspiracy count but convicted of a drug offense. All would receive prison sentences. Part of Santora's conviction was later overturned.

John Cerasani, the reputed crime family soldier who Ray Wean provided evidence against, was acquitted of everything, including the charge he took part in the abortive robbery of the home of the sister of the former Shah of Iran. When the verdict was announced, the convicted men embraced Cerasani, who was free to walk out of the courtroom. The other defendants were taken away by federal marshals.

On August 12, 1982, about two weeks before the verdict, Police Officer Edward Mosher of the 122nd Precinct in Staten Island responded to a call. A man passing through the wooded area near the intersection of South Avenue and Bridge Street came across a hospital body bag that contained human remains. The corpse was in an advance stage of decomposition and Mosher's report contained what had to be a big understatement: "Suspicious death! No arrest."

Investigators weren't sure if the corpse was that of a man or woman. The right arm had fallen away from the body and some of the fingers were missing, possibly from animal activity. The body bag contained the words "Bellevue Hospital Mortuary."

Back at the morgue the corpse was so decomposed that the doctor doing the autopsy noted many times in his report that organs had shrunken or rotted away. The body was in a state of adiposcere, meaning much of its tissues had congealed into a mass of fatty tissue. The eyes were sunken so that there was no color to the irises. An x-ray determined that there were bullet fragments in the brain, although that organ was also severely decomposed. The fragments, con-

sisting of a bullet and the metal jacket that had once surrounded it, were recovered from the skull. There was a bullet
hole in the left rear of the skull and since there didn't appear
to be any other fatal injuries the coroner's report said that
death was from a fatal gunshot wound to the head. Forensic
specialists at the city medical examiner's office labored for
weeks, studying dental records, doing x-rays, and making all
kinds of studies.

With a body in such poor condition, forensic experts had
to rely on dental comparisons to make an identification. Although one or two teeth seemed to be missing postmortem,
there was still enough left. On November 10, 1982, the Office of the Chief Medical Examiner announced that the body
found in Staten Island was identified as being that of Dominick Napolitano, who had been missing for over a year.

The discovery of Napolitano was an eerie foreshadowing
of Ruggiero's fate at sentencing five days later. Judge Sweet
gave him forty years in prison, robbing Ruggiero of any
hope that he would live life as a free person outside of a cell;
instead, he would be relegated to spending his days making
futile pleas to the court for a reduction of his sentence.
Maybe his old friend Sonny Black got the better deal.

CHAPTER 13

Murder on the Lam

From his haven in the Poconos, Joseph Massino followed the machinations of the New York City trials and saw that Joseph Pistone was deadly as a centerpiece of the government's case. Raymond Wean, his old buddy from the hijacking days in Maspeth, was more problematic since the defendant he testified against, John Cerasani, was the only person who was acquitted and walked away a free man.

Had Massino gone to trial along with the others, he would have been playing a crap shoot. It was true that Massino was charged with conspiracy in the murder of the three captains, rather than with the actual participation to kill them. But a conviction on the conspiracy would have subjected Massino to a possible conviction for racketeering, which turned out to be the fate of Benjamin Ruggiero and Nicholas Santora and resulted in substantial prison sentences. As Salvatore Vitale later told investigators, Massino figured he had a better chance of beating the case if he didn't go on trial with the others. It was a strange bit of intuition on Massino's part, but it turned out to be not too far from the mark.

Massino stayed on the lam, shuffling around the Poconos and making trips back and forth to New York City for well over a year after Ruggiero and the others were convicted. If there was any big business to attend to, if a "piece of work" needed to be arranged, the leaders of the Bonanno family knew where they could find Massino. In turn, he knew how to call on them.

× × ×

Cesare Bonventre was born in the mob. Having grown up in the Mafia breeding ground in Sicily known as the city of Castellammare del Golfo, Bonventre was blooded to the life of La Cosa Nostra by virtue of his uncle, John Bonventre, the underboss of Joseph Bonanno. When a number of ambitious young Castellammarese took up Carmine Galante's advice and immigrated to Brooklyn, Cesare Bonventre was one of them. He became a fixture among the Sicilians in the cafés on Knickerbocker Avenue, and by the late 1970s he became a close associate of Galante.

There was something about Bonventre that made him stand out from the other Castellammarese and ethnic Italians of the Bonanno family. Unlike the other pasta and pastry loving wiseguys with the high body mass indexes, Bonventre was tall and lean, almost athletic. While the other Bonanno confederates looked like fashion disasters, Bonventre, with his stylish clothing, aviator sunglasses, and European man's purse, reeked of Italian couture and made him look like a Continental lady killer.

Cesare Bonventre had also been lucky. The day Galante was gunned down in Bushwick, it was Bonventre and Baldassare Amato who were supposed to be bodyguards for the slain mafioso. Neither Bonventre nor Amato were hurt in the assassination of Galante, although others nearby were either killed or wounded. The fact that both men escaped unscathed seemed to be a sure sign that the Sicilian faction of the Bonanno family, of which they were members, had gone along with the hit.

Fleeing the crime scene, Bonventre and Amato headed for the hills only to resurface a couple of weeks later in the company of a lawyer who escorted them into the office of Brooklyn District Attorney Eugene Gold. The two Galante bodyguards answered questions from investigators about the murder. But there seemed to be little to tie them to the killers, so they were let go and were never charged—at least with Galante's killing. Not long after that, Bonventre, at the age of twenty-eight, became a Bonanno captain, the youngest of that rank in the family. Amato earned his stripes as a soldier.

Bonventre and Amato had other family business to take care of. In the early 1980s, they and other Sicilians became part of a large-scale international heroin importation ring. The conspiracy was grounded in both Italy and the United States. Sicilians, both in Brooklyn and back in Sicily, were involved in the refinement and shipping of the heroin to the United States, where pizza parlors served as key meeting places and venues for some of the money transactions surrounding the narcotics trafficking.

On February 2, 1980, about six months after Galante was murdered, the FBI began an investigation of the Bonanno family, and Charles Rooney, an experienced agent who had been doing white-collar crime investigations for the agency out of its Rego Park office, was assigned the case. It was not an easy job. The FBI had done a lot of surveillances of the crime family, particularly at the Toyland Social Club, and Joseph Pistone was well entrenched in his undercover role as Donnie Brasco. But piecing together a major heroin case would take more than just sitting in surveillance vans or waiting for Pistone, who was not a made member of the Mafia and had virtually no interaction with the Sicilian wing of the crime family, to report back what the mobsters allowed themselves to tell him.

So, for three years Rooney and the other agents undertook the arduous task of first identifying the Sicilian players in the heroin connection. They did it by intensive surveillances all over the New York and New Jersey metropolitan area. The spying discerned that one Sicilian in particular, Salvatore Catalano, a major figure in the Bonanno crime family, was central to the heroin ring. Catalano had become the boss of the family for about a week but couldn't hold the job since he had trouble communicating with the rest of the family and had already been made in Italy. Concerning the latter, per American Mafia code, he could not be a boss because he hadn't been made a member of the American Mafia.

The surveillance by Rooney and the other case agents never put Catalano in close proximity to Joe Massino. In fact, Massino was conspicuously absent from major Sicilian functions like weddings and funerals, a likely indication that he kept himself apart (or was deliberately kept apart) from the heroin trade, regardless of what Vitale later told the FBI.

By 1984, after the FBI had placed key wiretaps on the Sicilian traffickers, they were charged in a spectacular case that became known as the "Pizza Connection." The April 9, 1984, news conference announcing the arrests brought U.S. Attorney General William French Smith, FBI Director William Webster, and Manhattan U.S. Attorney Rudolph Giuliani together for the announcement that the Sicilian drug ring had brought in over $1.5 billion in heroin into the country over a five-year period. Reporters covering the story later said that the name originated after they prodded Giuliani to use the term *Pizza Connection* and the moniker stuck.

The FBI used a massive 300-plus-page criminal complaint, drafted by Rooney, to initiate the case in which he named Catalano, Bonventre, Amato, Sicilian mafioso Gaetano Badalamenti, and over a dozen other men as defendants. Like the complaint, the Pizza Connection trial would be a monster affair, spanning eighteen months in Manhattan's federal court. But Cesare Bonventre would never live to see it.

× × ×

The New York boys of the Bonanno crime family had plenty of access to Joseph Massino while he was hiding out in Pennsylvania. In early 1984, a group of Massino's friends made the trip. Salvatore Vitale was among them. He later told the FBI that he was accompanied by two other men, Louis "Ha Ha" Attanasio and James Tartaglione. Attanasio earned his particular moniker not because he was a good joke teller but, so the story goes, he laughed when he heard someone in the underworld died. Neither Vitale nor Tartaglione, a gangly, bespectacled man with a boney face, were actually made members of the crime family. But Attanasio was and bore the rank of acting captain.

When Massino had such visits and wanted to keep too many people from knowing his business, he went on a solitary "walk-and-talk" with one person of his choice. Vitale said that his brother-in-law took a brief constitutional with Attanasio as he and Tartaglione watched.

Massino never told Vitale what he talked about on that walk. But Attanasio did, and according to Vitale it wasn't good news.

"We are going to kill Cesare and I need you to help set it up," said Attanasio, according to Vitale.

Why did Bonventre have to die? The FBI came up with two key theories. One centered on speculation that he had offended someone, possibly in another crime family, with poor-quality heroin. Another assumed that he had gained too much power too quickly and because he was so ruthless he was viewed as a threat to boss Philip Rastelli and his supporters such as Massino.

Whatever the reason, Vitale said he worked in earnest to set up Bonventre. Because Rastelli was released from prison in April 1984 after serving his term for extortion in the lunch wagon case, Vitale enlisted the crime boss in the plot. According to Vitale, he told Bonventre a fabricated story that Rastelli wanted to meet him at a diner in Queens. A car was needed for the hit and Vitale turned to the fair-haired Duane Leisenheimer, who promptly commandeered a stolen car.

As planned by Vitale, the killing of Bonventre was to take place in a garage in Queens located near the intersection of Fifty-seventh Street and Metropolitan Avenue. The day of the killing, Bonventre parked his car at the corner of Flushing and Metropolitan avenues and sat in the front seat of the stolen car being driven by Vitale. Louis Attanasio sat in the backseat. The prearranged signal for the actual killing, Vitale told the FBI, was to be his remark, "It looks good to me."

A few blocks later, with Bonventre settled into the front seat, Vitale started to make a turn on to Fifty-seventh Street where the garage was located.

"It looks good to me," Vitale said.

Bonventre might have thought the remark referred to the way Vitale negotiated the turn into the garage. On hearing the signal, Attanasio, according to Vitale's later testimony in federal court, reached into his boot, pulled out a gun, and fired two shots into the back of the handsome Bonventre's head before the car entered the garage.

Incredibly, though wounded grievously, Bonventre struggled. He tried to put his foot on the gas, perhaps in a futile gesture to crash the car and take his assassins with him. It didn't work; Vitale was able to drive the car into the garage when he saw Leisenheimer open the door to the building.

Next, Leisenheimer opened the car door and a dying Bonventre fell out, flopping and heaving like a dying fish. Vitale said to investigators that he and Attanasio also got out of the car and walked around to the opened vehicle door. It was then, Vitale told the FBI and also testified in Brooklyn federal court, that Attanasio pumped two more shots into Bonventre.

It was done. Bonventre's body was placed in the trunk of the car that had delivered him to his death and driven to the Clinton Diner. It was now Gabriel Infanti's turn to do the dirty work. Meeting Vitale at the diner, Infanti had the job of disposing of the body and the vehicle. Infanti had specific instructions that the body was not to be found. He assured Vitale it would disappear forever. In fact, a week later a proud Infanti told Vitale that Bonventre had been chopped up and buried.

Well, forever lasted about two weeks. On April 16, 1984, New Jersey law enforcement officials were called to a warehouse in Garfield. Inside, they found two fifty-five-gallon drums packed with grisly contents. One drum contained a human torso with the head. The other contained the legs. Further investigation determined that the corpse had first been taken to nearby Wallington, where it was placed in a vat of adhesives before the dismemberment took place.

Police told reporters that the dismembering operation wasn't successful and that the remains were finally moved to the Garfield warehouse. After three weeks of forensic investigation the body was identified as being that of the thirty-three-year-old Cesare Bonventre. His body had been discovered ten days after Rooney and the other FBI agents in the Pizza Connection case had scoured New York City to serve him an arrest warrant.

Vitale had to tell Massino that Bonventre's remains had been found. Aside from disappointment in Infanti, Vitale recalled that Massino became concerned that Infanti had lied about burying the corpse. It was certainly not a good way for Infanti to get in the good graces of Massino, who despite being on the lam was the most powerful person in the crime family

"The guy fucked up," Infanti told Vitale, referring to yet another person who had been tasked with the job of disposing of the remains. A tough-talking Infanti assured Vitale that he would take care of the man who botched the burial. But who would take care of Infanti?

CHAPTER 14

Return

With wiretaps all around him and investigators breathing down his neck, Gambino captain Angelo Ruggiero had enough problems in the spring of 1984. But when he called his attorney, Jon Pollok, one of the heavy hitters in the defense bar who took on the defense of Mafia figures, it was to ask a favor for someone else.

A friend of his, Ruggiero explained to Pollok, had a situation in which he needed some advice. Ruggiero brought around to Pollok's Manhattan office on Madison Avenue a copy of the March 25, 1982, indictment involving Joseph Massino, the one that accused Massino, Benjamin Ruggiero, and the others of racketeering and involvement in the murder of the three captains. What did Pollok think of the case?

Pollok had never met Massino or even heard of him until that point. But looking at the indictment, Pollok saw something in it that made him think it was poorly drafted and possibly beatable in court. There didn't appear to be a single substantive act of racketeering attributable to Massino that had occurred within five years of the indictment, the attorney remembered some years later. In plain English, for Massino to be convicted of being part of the racketeering enterprise known as the Bonanno crime family, he had to be convicted of two acts of racketeering within the five years preceding the grand jury issuing the indictment. Pollok didn't see enough to make that case against Massino and said as much to Ruggiero.

"Would you like to take a ride?" Ruggiero asked his lawyer.

Pollok, a cautious man, had some trepidation about the cloak-and-dagger stuff, and his first reaction to the request was something like, "What are you crazy?" But his client insisted.

A few days later, Pollok recalled, he was driven by a man whose name he doesn't recall over the George Washington Bridge into New Jersey, where he was blindfolded. Pollok was a New Jersey resident, and even though he was blindfolded he knew from the direction of the car's continuing travel and the feel of the road that he was going west along Interstate 80. The only thing to the west along the road was the Delaware Water Gap and Pennsylvania. Soon, the car made a right turn and a half-hour later the car arrived where Pollok knew they had been going all along: rural Pennsylvania.

The car drove into a vacation bungalow area. Though it was late spring, there weren't a lot of people in the area. Inside one of the buildings was Massino, "a fat guy," as Pollok recalled. Massino said he wanted to know from Pollok what he thought about the case and whether he could mount a defense. Pollok shared with Massino the earlier assessment he had made. But being an officer of the court Pollok knew he had to convince Massino to return to New York and not remain a fugitive. Pollok had done a good sales job on Massino because a short time later, a matter of a few days it seemed, the fugitive gangster communicated to Pollok that he wanted to come back and for the attorney to see about bail.

Back in New York, Pollok and his partner, Jeffrey Hoffman, got to work on Massino's surrender. Their first call,

Pollok remembered, was to Assistant U.S. Attorney Louis Freeh.

"I want to bring in Joe Massino, let's talk bail," Pollok told Freeh.

The prosecutor, who would later go on to head the FBI, was tough and couldn't be talked into agreeing to give Massino bail. Bring him back and then we can talk about bail was Freeh's position.

"Can I see the boss?" Pollok recalled saying, referring to Barbara Jones, who had tried the 1982 case against Ruggiero and the others with Freeh.

As professional adversaries, Pollok and Jones had known each other for years and had come to appreciate each other's abilities. Now head of the criminal section of the Manhattan U.S. Attorney's Office, Jones had a great deal of power. Though it took some negotiation, Pollok said that he worked out what he thought was a "reasonable" bail package for Massino of $350,000 bond cosigned by his wife, Josephine, and secured by their marital home and two apartments Massino owned. The missing gangster was coming home.

News of Massino's imminent return leaked out to his cronies, but oddly enough not to the FBI. In fact, special Agent Patrick Marshall and his colleagues continued to prowl New York City in search of the elusive Joseph Massino. It was a job that was getting old fast since the agents were hitting nothing but dry holes. Finally, in late June Marshall visited Gabriel Infanti, who was still smarting over the botched disposal of Bonventre's body, and had the usual chat about needing to find Massino.

"Don't worry, I hear he is coming back," Infanti told Marshall.

Finally, on the morning of July 7, 1984, Salvatore Vitale drove Massino to Pollok's office on Madison Avenue. From there, Massino, Jeffrey Hoffman, and Jon Pollok took a cab to Manhattan's U.S. District Courthouse on Foley Square and walked up the long granite staircase to surrender. The time was 9:00 A.M., and in the company of the lawyers, Massino looked like anybody with business to do inside. Unlike Joseph Bonanno's surrender some twenty years earlier after he had been on the lam, Massino's return would not be taking anyone in the U.S. Attorney's Office by surprise. At around 9:40 that morning, Assistant U.S. Attorney Barbara Jones got a call from the courthouse to notify her that her quarry had arrived.

"Miss Jones, what is the history here?" asked Magistrate Sharon E. Grubin after Massino's case was called in the courtroom.

If she took the question literally, Jones could have spent hours relating the history of the Bonanno crime family and the role Massino was believed to have played. But she kept it short and sweet, telling Grubin that Massino had been indicted in March 1982.

"He was never arrested and subsequent fugitive investigation failed to locate him," Jones said. "Within the last two weeks Mister Hoffman and Mister Pollok, lawyers for Mister Messina, contacted the government and advised us that he did wish to appear before the court and surrender to stand charges."

By waiting, Massino had put himself in a better position for trial and he knew that. Had he stood trial with the other defendants in 1982, he risked being pulled into a vortex created by the presence of the others. Sometimes just sitting around the same table with your codefendants may create a poor inference about you in the minds of jurors. Massino was accused of involvement in the conspiracy to murder the three captains. Tape recordings introduced at trial contained the voices of Benjamin Ruggiero and Dominick Napolitano talking in conspiratorial tones and in substance to an undercover FBI agent about the killings. Massino's name was mentioned in the recordings, but he himself was not overheard saying anything incriminating. Since no mobster had testified about the killings, the case was a circumstantial one at best and more so for Massino, who kept his distance from Joseph Pistone's body recorder.

There was also the potential flaw in the indictment that Pollok had picked up on. Racketeering law had been steadily evolving since the famous 1970 RICO statute, formally known as the Racketeer-Influenced and Corruption Organizations Act. Prosecutors had been using it with some success against the mob, but it still presented problems on occasion and it wasn't unheard of for indictments to be thrown out or convictions reversed on appeal.

But such problems wouldn't come to light for many months. As Jones explained, part of the negotiations with the lawyers involved a bail recommendation that prosecutors had become comfortable with. The government agreed that Massino would be released on a $350,000 bond secured by the three properties. Appraisals had shown the amount of equity was enough to secure the bail package.

But a puzzled Grubin, considering Massino's very recent history of being in the wind, said to Hoffman, "It is somewhat unusual to release a defendant on [a personal recognizance bond] who has been a fugitive for two years."

Hoffman explained that the Massino family was putting its home on the line, a place where the defendant, his wife, and children had lived for over ten years. No matter what the charges, there were also some fine points about Massino's record to consider.

One point was that the forty-two-year-old Massino had no prior convictions of any kind. Another factor was that while Massino was charged with a racketeering conspiracy involving three murders, he was not charged with actually committing the homicides, said the attorney. The only actual substantive crimes charged against Massino in the indictment centered on two hijacking allegations. In one count,

Massino was accused of stealing a load of tuna fish, the other involved "dry goods," said Hoffman, referring to the 1975 Hemingway truck hijacking. That had been the case that Massino was able to beat in court after his statements to the FBI were thrown out by a federal judge.

The recitation of the case history by Jones and Hoffman seemed to convince Grubin that Massino could have bail. But she had a duty as a federal magistrate to lay it on the line and tell Massino and his wife what would happen if he ever skipped town again.

"Is his wife in the courtroom," asked Grubin. "Have her step forward, please."

Josephine Massino approached Grubin and answered "I understand" when the magistrate told her that if her spouse didn't show up in court each and every time he was supposed to that she would owe the government $350,000 and in the process possibly lose her house.

"Do you believe that he will show up in court when he is supposed to?" asked Grubin.

"Yes, I do," Josephine Massino answered.

"And will you help him to do that?"

"Yes, I will."

As the paperwork was prepared to secure the bond, Grubin next turned to Massino and told him that if he failed to show up when needed in court he could be prosecuted for bail jumping. That was a separate offense that carried a five-year prison term.

"Do you understand that?" Grubin asked.

"Yes, your honor," answered Massino.

After entering a not guilty plea, Massino, Josephine, and the lawyers waited around lower Manhattan for a session later in the day with Judge Robert W. Sweet. It was Sweet who had handled the trial of Massino's codefendants in 1982 and had sentenced them to prison terms ranging from fifteen years in the case of Ruggiero and Nicholas Santora to four years to a minor low-level defendant who pled guilty to a robbery conspiracy. A soft-spoken jurist, Sweet was quite familiar with the facts in the case after sitting through the earlier trial. Now, he faced a reprise of the case that would develop some very unexpected turns.

CHAPTER 15

Horatio Alger of the Mob

After he was released on bail, Joseph Massino made a line straight to his old club on Fifty-eighth Road in Maspeth. His brother-in-law, Salvatore Vitale, and business associate, Carmine Peluso, had kept the place, J&S Cake Social Club, in good order so that when Massino returned he was able to hold court just like he used to. There were no restrictions on who he could see while on bail, so a lot of Bonanno family cronies made the obligatory visit to the club where Massino held court.

About a day or two after Massino showed up, FBI agent Patrick Marshall also stopped by. The visit was strictly business. There was a lot of grand jury action brewing and federal prosecutors used the FBI to serve a variety of legal papers to their mob quarry. Massino had been overheard on a number of wiretaps placed in the telephones of his friend Angelo Ruggiero of the Gambino crime family. Under the federal wiretap statute, a person whose voice was captured on the surveillance had to be served with a notice of interception. These were fairly routine and Massino, ever the gentleman, took the document from Marshall with no hassles.

But a few hours later that same day, Marshall returned with yet another legal document. This time it was a subpoena for Louis "Ha Ha" Attanasio. Curiously, Marshall noticed that the door to the club was locked. Usually, social clubs have open doors but now that J&S Cake Social Club appeared closed, Marshall knocked on the door several times. The agent knew Massino, Attanasio, and several others were inside because he had watched the building from a location down the street. Marshall knocked again. Finally, a curious Attanasio unlocked the door and was served with the subpoena.

Perhaps he was spooked by the fact that so many of his mob cronies were together with him. Maybe he believed the federal government had changed its mind and wanted to revoke his bail and send him to jail. Whatever the reason, while Marshall was speaking to Attanasio, Massino and his friends had bolted out the backdoor of the club and into the adjourning yard that housed another Massino business. Massino, ever the cautious one, apparently didn't want to lose his freedom. So, Massino did what he showed a penchant for whenever trouble brewed: he ran.

Of course, the Bonanno family was having nothing but trouble at this point. Philip Rastelli had been out of prison since earlier in the year, and he desparately wanted to assert himself with the ruling Commission. Rastelli felt he was the boss of his family, and he wanted a role on the Commission, a position no one in his family had since the debacle with Joseph Bonanno back in the 1960s. The problem was that the family's troubles, notably the penetration by FBI undercover agent Joseph Pistone, as well as the rampant drug dealing that had been publicly revealed in the Pizza Connection case, made other mob bosses look on the Bonanno group as a bunch of crazy relatives.

Though he wanted to be on the Commission, Rastelli had a lot of opposition. This was made clear in a number of bugged conversations of Anthony "Fat Tony" Salerno, the street boss of the Genovese crime family, when he held court in early 1984 at his Palma Boys Social Club in East Harlem.

At one point, Salerno recounted a conversation he had with Gambino boss Paul Castellano about Rastelli.

"I said to Paul, '[inaudible] that's the boss if the Family wants him. But, as far as the Commission, he cannot be on it,'" said Salerno.

"I told the Commission," Salerno continued, 'Ah, ah, hey, listen this guy [inaudible] wants to be the Boss. He can be the Boss as far as I'm concerned,' I said, 'but he cannot be on the Commission.'"

Rastelli was lobbying members of the Commission, including Castellano, in an effort to get the Bonanno family's seat back on the ruling body as late as May 1984. But Salerno would have none of it and said he would veto it if pushed to a vote. The Bonanno's family narcotics trafficking also bothered Salerno.

"There are too many junk guys," said Salerno in a May 22, 1984, conversation in the club. "They got a crew of eighty guys like that."

So Rastelli, now free from prison after serving time for extortion in the lunch wagon case, was considered the Bonanno boss. Of course, there would be no chair for him on the Commission. But it was Massino who was the preeminent captain and considered by many in the crime family to be running the show as the intelligence information about the murder of Cesare Bonventre had made clear. Vitale and others later told the FBI that it was Massino who had put the plan for that killing into motion.

Though he was free on bail, Massino remained in the sights of law enforcement precisely because he had become a major player in the Bonanno family. The family, as the 1982 Bonanno trial and the Pizza Connection indictments showed, had become a key target of law enforcement. Events would later show that the FBI and local prosecutors were spending a lot of energy and time on the other crime families. But it was the Bonnano family that was bearing most of the heat in these early stages. Since Massino was a power in the family, it was inevitable that he would attract his own problems, no matter how careful he tried to be. With his family's home on the line with the bail package arranged by his lawyers, Massino couldn't just cut and run.

Almost a year after he returned from being on the lam, Massino was hit with another federal indictment. It was a serious case of labor racketeering, an activity the mob had perfected over decades. A Brooklyn federal grand jury charged that Massino, Rastelli, his brother, Carmine Rastelli, and fourteen other defendants used Teamsters Local 814, which covered the moving and warehouse industries, to shakedown moving and storage companies in the city. It was a lengthy indictment that covered sixty-four counts and alleged that members of the Bonnano crime family, Local 814 officers, and moving company officials took part in a racketeering scheme that started in 1964 and stretched into 1985.

The scheme alleged in the indictment showed a lot of chutzpah for the mob. Among the racketeering activities charged was that the moving companies rigged bids on contracts to move a number of government offices. Those rigged bids involved inflated charges and the irony was that one case involved the moving in 1979 of the FBI office in Manhattan, which had been in the area of Sixty-ninth Street, to the big federal building known as Federal Plaza. The cost of the FBI move was inflated by $5,000, not a princely sum by any means but still a crime, prosecutors charged, particularly because it was shared with members of the Bonnano crime family.

There were other big names said to have been victimized by the scheme. The New York Coliseum, the city's main convention and exhibition venue at the time, had to pay some of the defendants $5,000, while the New York Islanders had to put up an unspecified amount as well for labor peace, the indictment charged.

Massino was arrested on June 14, 1985 in the moving industry case by his old adversary Pat Marshall of the FBI. At first, the arrest went without incident since Massino was his old gentlemanly self when he was taken into custody at his Howard Beach home. Marshall was driving and Massino sat in the backseat flanked by another agent. The vehicle was stuck in some neighborhood traffic when Marshall spotted another car pull up behind. A man jumped out of the car and went up to the side of the FBI car where Massino was sitting. Marshall recognized him as John Carneglia, a Gambino crime family member who lived nearby.

"Step away from the vehicle," a worried Marshall called out to Carneglia. The FBI agent had no idea what Carneglia was going to do.

However, Carneglia had no hostile intentions and instead asked Massino if he was okay and if he could do anything for him, like call a lawyer. Massino seemed to reassure Carngelia, and his neighbor stepped away from the car, allowing Marshall to drive away.

Massino languished in the local federal lockup in Brooklyn for about a week before Jeffrey Hoffman, one of the attorneys who had successfully argued for bail a year earlier when Massino returned to the city, was able to post another bond.

Besides the racketeering count, the indictment accused Massino of taking part in fourteen payoffs from moving companies, one sportswear company, and a furniture installer. Those were all done, the indictment charged, in violation of federal labor law. Prosecutors said that Philip Rastelli, even though he was in prison during some of time period covered by the indictment, sent orders through his brothers, particularly Carmine, to union and company officials involved in the payoff scheme.

The trial in the moving case got underway in April 1986 with an unusual request by the defense. The twelve defendants who went on trial—the five other defendants would eventually enter guilty pleas—convinced the judge, Charles B. Sifton, that they should have separate tables in the well of the court. That was needed, defense attorneys said, to make the point to the jury that the defendants were entitled to separate consideration by the jury. So, Massino, Rastelli, and the others who elected to go to trial forked over a combined total of $1,800 to rent tables and chairs. The trial was expected to last about two months.

However, Rastelli got sick and collapsed three times during the nearly month-long jury selection process. Though he was supposed to be a big Mafia boss, Rastelli appeared to be a bit of a nervous and physical wreck. He sat at his defense table and often quivered, sometimes covering his face with his hands, as Assistant U.S. Attorney Laura Brevetti told jurors in her opening statements how the Bonanno family helped carve up the $250 million a year moving and storage industy.

But it was more than Brevetti's rhetoric that had Rastelli shaking. For a man who was only out of prison for about two years, the future was not looking very promising for Rastelli. Two months before the Brooklyn indictment came down, Rastelli was named as a defendant in a separate federal indictment that became known as the Commission case. In a bold stroke on February 26, 1985, the FBI and federal prosecutors in the office of Manhattan U.S. Attorney Rudolph Giuliani announced the indictment of several major Mafia leaders, including members of the ruling Cosa Nostra Commission. Named as defendants along with Rastelli, the head of the Bonanno family, were Gambino boss Paul Castellano; Aniello Dellacroce, Gambino underboss; Anthony Salerno, the street boss of the Genovese family; Lucchese boss Anthony "Tony Ducks" Corallo; Carmine "the Snake" Persico; and a handful of other defendants, including Bonanno captain Anthony "Bruno" Indelicato.

Essentially, four key New York members of the Commission—Castellano, Salerno, Corallo, and Persico—were now

Joseph Massino, circa 1975. (Photo courtesy U.S. Attorney's Office, Eastern District of New York)

Joseph Massino, January 2003. (Photo courtesy U.S. Attorney's Office, Eastern District of New York)

Vincent Basciano, a.k.a "Vinny Gorgeous" and "Vinny from the Bronx," reputed acting boss of the Bonanno family from the time of Massino's arrest in January 2003 until late 2004, when Vinny himself was arrested. (Photo courtesy U.S. Attorney's Office, Eastern District of New York)

A rare photo of Barry Weinberg, former parking lot entrepreneur. Weinberg, who was a business partner in parking lot ventures with some Bonanno members and their relatives, was the victim of an extortion attempt by high-ranking members of the family. (Photo courtesy U.S. Attorney's Office, Eastern District of New York)

Michael Mancuso, reputed acting boss of the Bonanno crime family from late 2004 until early 2006, when he was arrested. (Photo courtesy U.S. Attorney's Office, Eastern District of New York)

Salvatore "Good Looking Sal" Vitale, January 2003, Bonanno underboss and Massino's brother-in-law. (Photo courtesy U.S. Attorney's Office, Eastern District of New York)

James "Big Louie" Tartaglione, Bonanno captain. (Photo courtesy U.S. Attorney's Office, Eastern District of New York)

Anthony Graziano, Bonanno captain. (Photo courtesy U.S. Attorney's Office, Eastern District of New York)

Richard "Shellack Head" Cantarella, Bonanno captain. (Photo courtesy U.S. Attorney's Office, Eastern District of New York)

Frank Coppa. He was the first Bonanno captain to agree to cooperate with prosecutors after he was indicted in October 2002. (Photo courtesy U.S. Attorney's Office, Eastern District of New York)

Duane "Goldie" Leisenheimer. A close associate of Massino's, Leisenheimer traveled with him while he was on the lam between 1982 and 1984. (Photo courtesy U.S. Attorney's Office, Eastern District of New York)

Baldo Amato, Bonanno captain. (Photo courtesy U.S. Attorney's Office, Eastern District of New York)

Frank Lino, Bonanno captain. He escorted the three captains to the Brooklyn social club where they were killed. (Photo courtesy U.S. Attorney's Office, Eastern District of New York)

Philip Giaccone, one of three captains killed in 1981. (Photo courtesy U.S. Attorney's Office, Eastern District of New York)

Dominick Trinchera, another of three captains killed in 1981. (Photo courtesy U.S. Attorney's Office, Eastern District of New York)

Gerlando Sciascia, a Bonanno captain who was killed in 1999. (Photo courtesy U.S. Attorney's Office, Eastern District of New York)

Vito Rizzuto, a Bonanno soldier from Canada who was accused of the murder of the three captains. (Photo courtesy U.S. Attorney's Office, Eastern District of New York)

Joseph Massino, 1977, outside Toyland Social Club on the Lower East Side of Manhattan. (Photo courtesy U.S. Attorney's Office, Eastern District of New York)

Joseph Massino outside Toyland Social Club, circa 1977, with former Bonanno family underboss Nicholas Marangello, the late Alfred Embarrato, and Carmine Francese. (Photo courtesy U.S. Attorney's Office, Eastern District of New York)

Surveillance photo of Frank Lino and the late Bonanno crime family member Gabriel Infanti. Infanti was killed on Massino's orders. (Photo courtesy U.S. Attorney's Office, Eastern District of New York)

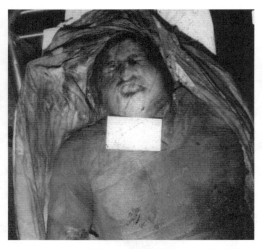

Autopsy photo of Alphonse Indelicato, the third Bonanno captain murdered in May 1981. (Photo courtesy U.S. Attorney's Office, Eastern District of New York)

FBI agent Joseph Pistone (*second from left*), who penetrated the Bonanno crime family as "Donnie Brasco," poses with fellow agents shortly before the men he befriended in the crime family were told of his true identity. The time was late July 1981. (Photo courtesy U.S. Attorney's Office, Eastern District of New York)

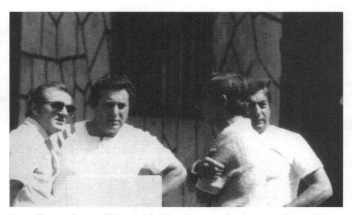

Surveillance photo of Dominick Napolitano and other members of his crew outside the Motion Lounge in Williamsburg minutes after FBI agents told him about Joseph Pistone's true identity as an undercover FBI agent. (Photo courtesy U.S. Attorney's Office, Eastern District of New York)

Telephoto surveillance shot of Dominick Napolitano on top of the Motion Lounge building in Williamsburg, feeding his pigeons and thinking about the serious repercussions from the revelation that his crew was infiltrated by undercover FBI agent Joseph Pistone. (Photo courtesy U.S. Attorney's Office, Eastern District of New York)

Surveillance photo of Bonanno underboss Salvatore Vitale with Anthony Spero and Vincent Aloi. (Photo courtesy U.S. Attorney's Office, Eastern District of New York)

Joseph Massino (*far right*) with his wife, Josephine, and brother-in-law, Salvatore Vitale, at a social event, circa 1999. (Photo courtesy U.S. Attorney's Office, Eastern District of New York)

Josephine Massino (*in strapless gown*) with her two sisters at the same social function depicted in the photo above. Her husband, Joseph, is seen in the background, talking with Bonanno soldier Louis Restivo. (Photo courtesy U.S. Attorney's Office, Eastern District of New York)

Joseph Massino with Frank Coppa while both men vacationed with their wives in the south of France. (Photo courtesy U.S. Attorney's Office, Eastern District of New York)

Crime scene photo of Gerlando Sciascia after he was found shot to death on a Bronx street on March 18, 1999. Massino has admitted ordering the murder. (Photo courtesy U.S. Attorney's Office, Eastern District of New York)

Crime scene photo of the decomposed body of Dominick Napolitano when it was recovered on Staten Island in August 1982. Massino was convicted of ordering the murder. (Photo courtesy U.S. Attorney's Office, Eastern District of New York)

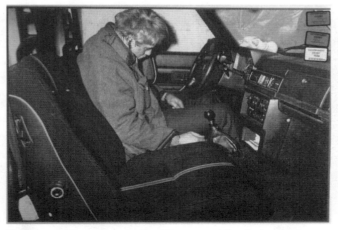

Crime scene photo of the body of Bonanno soldier Anthony Mirra. Massino was convicted of passing on the order to have Mirra killed. (Photo courtesy U.S. Attorney's Office, Eastern District of New York)

The now-shuttered CasaBlanca, the Massino-owned Italian restaurant where Massino held high-level mob meetings and planned murders between the antipasto and the shrimp oreganato. (Author photo)

under indictment. On a chart used by Giuliani and FBI Director William Webster at a news conference announcing the case, Rastelli was listed as the fifth Commission member from New York, although secretly taped conversations from a year earlier indicated that the Bonanno boss was not allowed to sit on the ruling body. Another chart showed "Joseph Messina," although not indicted in the Commission case, as being a significant Bonanno family member.

Giuliani later said he came up with the idea of prosecuting the Commission as a racketeering enterprise after reading Joseph Bonanno's book *Man of Honor*, published in 1983. Bonanno talked at length about the Commission, and to Giuliani that ruling body was a racketeering organization, a criminal enterprise, involved in a variety of activities that would make its members criminally liable.

Mafia members didn't like Bonanno's book and were turned off by the celebrity it gained the deposed boss. They also hated him for so openly betraying the code of silence and speaking about the secrets of mob life.

"I was shocked," said reputed Lucchese member Salvatore Avellino in a bugged conversation on March 1983, right after Bonanno gave an interview to Mike Wallace on *60 Minutes*.

"What is he trying to prove," Avellino said, "that he's a Man of Honor? But he's admitting—he, he actually admitted that he has a Fam, that he was the boss of a Family."

The Commission case wouldn't go on trial until September 1986, but in the meantime Rastelli and Massino had their hands full with the moving industry case. The key government witness turned out to be a relative of Rastelli's through marriage. He was Anthony Louis Giliberti, a sixty-two-year-old former business agent and vice president of Local 814, the local whose members came from the moving and storage industry.

Giliberti, by his own admission during his testimony, was something of a viper. A brother-in-law of Carmine Rastelli,

Giliberti said that Philip Rastelli tried to gain control of Local 814 as far back as 1964 but lost out in a power play by some other "bigwigs in organized crime." A guy who talked in street lingo, Giliberti described how he would threaten to "break the shoes" of a shakedown target. Court records also showed that while he took part in collecting payoffs from employers, money that was used as a Christmas "slush fund," Giliberti was not above a little larceny among his fellow thieves. Sifton found, court records show, that in 1979 Giliberti began pocketing some portions of the moneys he collected and sometimes kept all of it. It was not a good practice to follow with the kinds of acquaintances Giliberti had.

Although it wasn't mentioned at trial, Giliberti was the victim of an attempted assassination in July 1982. He was shot nine times in front of his Queens home and suspicion fell on Massino, who had earlier smacked Giliberti in the face in a confrontation on the street. Investigators developed information that Massino was angry with Giliberti because the union official had disobeyed his order not to involve Raymond Wean in any illegal activities because of suspicion—which proved correct—that Wean was an informant.

Giliberti survived the assassination attempt and was placed in the federal witness protection program. At the trial, his testimony was devastating to the defendants, particularly Rastelli. Giliberti told the jury that Rastelli, knowing he was going to prison in the lunch wagon extortion case, told him in 1976 what to do.

"Philly explained to me I was his eyes and ears in the union," Giliberti testified. "He said, 'I'm leaving you in charge of the store. If you have any problems go to Nick [Marangello].'"

Any payoff money was to go to Rastelli's brother, Marty.

Philip Rastelli collapsed a few more times in court, incidents that invariably led to recesses and delayed progress in the trial. But his swooning, apparently caused by problems with medications he was taking, didn't do Rastelli or his codefendants any good. On October 15, 1986, the jury convicted Rastelli of twenty-four counts of labor racketeering and acquitted him of nine. Also convicted were Nicholas Marangello, the former Bonanno underboss, some former Local 814 officials, and Carmine Rastelli. Massino was convicted of being associated with a racketeering enterprise and playing a role in accepting labor payoffs even though he was neither an employer nor union official.

Massino and Rastelli were immediately jailed after the verdicts. For Rastelli, it would be a return to life behind bars that defined much of his adulthood. For Massino, jail was a new experience in what had so far been a charmed life in which he had avoided prison. Sentencing on January 16, 1987, saw Sifton give out stiff terms of twelve years to Rastelli, ten years to Massino, eight years to Marangello, and six years to Carmine Rastelli.

The prison terms, particularly for Philip Rastelli who was ailing, were serious. But they were nothing next to the ones handed down earlier that week in the Manhattan federal court. In October 1986, the heads of the Genovese, Lucchese, and Colombo families, as well as several underlings, were convicted on various racketeering charges in the Commission case. The only reason the Gambino family was spared was that Paul Castellano had been assassinated in December 1985 and never stood trial along with the other bosses for being part of the Commission. Each of the remaining bosses—Anthony Salerno, Carmine Persico, and Anthony Corallo—were sentenced to 100-year prison terms.

Rastelli dodged a bullet in the Commission case because although he was indicted in the Manhattan action he was severed because of the Brooklyn trial. Then, in a move that raised some eyebrows, prosecutors dropped the Commission charges against Rastelli for "reasons of judicial economy."

In terms of the Mafia, the Department of Justice was clearly on a roll. In the space of a month in late 1986, the heads of four of the five Mafia families were convicted of major racketeering crimes. A number of their subordinates, a group that included Massino, were also convicted. The headlines and quotes following that development told of the doom of the mob, an obituary that had been written before but that now seemed more truthful then ever.

"The verdict reached today has resulted in dismantling the ruling council of La Cosa Nostra," crowed Manhattan U.S. Attorney Rudolph Giuliani after the Commission verdict.

Other experts predicted that many mafiosi would shun the spotlight and that law enforcement would continue to target up and coming leaders. Without the power of the Commission available to settle disputes, more mob violence on the streets was expected.

With the results of years of investigations to go on, federal prosecutors and the FBI continued pressing cases. Both Joseph Massino and his old friend John Gotti, the only Mafia boss still out on the street, faced another onslaught of prosecutions. In Massino's case, there was the old indictment that he tried to flee in 1982. But after he returned in 1984, Massino had to face the music.

But Massino's second racketeering trial, already delayed when he fled in 1982, was not going to be an easy ride for either the government or the defendant. For a start, the government kept going to the grand jury and had it amend the original 1982 charges to the point where they added hijacking charges that included the 1975 Hemingway trucking case and a conspiracy to rob the Galerie Des Monnaies. The prosecution also beefed up the indictment with more murder allegations, adding a count to cover the conspiracy to murder Massino's old cigarette smuggling friend Joseph Pastore. The grand jury also added someone new to the case: Massino's brother-in-law Salvatore Vitale. The ever loyal Vitale was charged with obstruction of justice, involvement in hijackings, and a conspiracy to use hijacked goods. For good measure, Vitale was also charged with racketeering conspiracy.

Massino's lawyers attacked the new, so-called superseding, indictment on the grounds that the FBI agents screwed up in the way they handled surveillance tapes that prosecutors intended to use in the trial. The tapes in question were obtained from telephone wire-taps and bugs that targeted Gambino crime family captain Angelo Ruggiero from late 1981 through July 1982. While Massino wasn't the target of the surveillance, he was overheard on telephone taps, particularly musing openly to Ruggiero about hiding out until the investigation blew over. Vitale was overheard as well not only on some telephone taps but also through a bug in Ruggiero's Long Island home talking about a hijack incident in which he claimed his brother-in-law took a driver "right out of the truck" and then had Ray Wean drive the load.

"Joey was the boss" in the hijacks, Vitale told Ruggiero.

When Ruggiero questioned Vitale about what he and Massino had done with Wean, Vitale answered "nothing really serious," referring to a load of tuna fish and bicycles.

It turned out that the superseding indictment included the stolen tuna fish load Vitale didn't think was so serious. Court records also show that Vitale and Ruggiero talked about a plot to murder Benjamin "Lefy Guns" Ruggiero, who at the time in 1982 was incarcerated in a federal jail in lower Manhattan. Vitale said that Massino wasn't worried about Ruggiero but did want to "get to Wean," who was also housed in the same jail.

The tapes could be troublesome, so the defense lawyers went after them, asking Judge Sweet to suppress the recordings and seeking to have the indictment thrown out. Vitale also asked to be tried separately from Massino. The main argument advanced by the attorneys for Massino and Vitale about the tapes was that the government had failed to seal the surveillance recordings immediately as required by law. Court records show that the FBI agents did seal some of the recordings promptly—within a day—at the expiration date of the various court orders authorizing the surveillance. But one set of tapes in particular, made at Ruggiero's home, had a problem. The month-long court order permitting the bugging expired on July 7, 1982. But the tapes were not sealed until July 22, a gap of fifteen days.

The FBI was forced to admit that the delay came about because of a serious breach of security surrounding the Ruggiero investigation. On July 6, 1982, the FBI had learned that Ruggiero had received confidential information used by the agency to get court permission to plant the various bugs. Court records revealed that an FBI agent left a copy of confidential documents in a bar not far from his office in Rego Park. Somehow the material got to Ruggiero and the FBI started an investigation to find out the source of the leak. That investigation, federal investigators said, took time.

Judge Sweet didn't buy the FBI excuse. On April 12, 1985, he found that the agency "consciously chose" to pursue an investigation that really was "unrelated" to the act of sealing the tapes. He ruled that prosecutors could not use the 110 reels of tapes affected by the fifteen-day delay in sealing, recordings that captured Vitale talking with Ruggiero. However, Sweet said the other tapes covered by earlier court orders, those that captured Massino and Vitale talking with Ruggiero, could be used. The other defense requests were denied by Sweet.

Giuliani's office decided to appeal Sweet's ruling and took the suppression of the tapes to the U.S. Court of Appeals for the Second Circuit. It was a smart move. The higher court thought that Sweet's ruling was too harsh and believed instead that there might be legitimate manpower reasons, such as in the case of the leak investigation, for there to be delays in sealing. On February 21, 1986, Sweet's ruling on the tapes was reversed and the evidence could be used at trial if needed.

The favorable ruling for the government prompted the defense to face the future with some realism. The govern-

ment had been on a roll with Mafia cases and the man who
was going to try Massino was Assistant U.S. Attorney
Michael Chertoff, who had just come off a spectacular win
in the Commission trial. He was assisted by Helen Gredd.
Massino was represented by Sam Dawson, a former federal
prosecutor from Brooklyn who had a reputation for being a
skillful cross-examiner. Vitale was defended by Bruce Cutler, a former assistant district attorney from Brooklyn who
had rapidly risen to prominence defending Massino's old
friend, Gambino boss John Gotti.

Dawson and Cutler, chastened by the appeals court ruling
and hoping to avoid a trial that involved evidence that had
been used earlier to great success by the government, started
plea negotiations with Chertoff. As Cutler later remembered,
Dawson met him in the cafeteria of the federal court house
at 40 Centre Street and said he had a deal.

"I worked it out," Dawson told Cutler.

"It sounded like a good deal too," Cutler said during an
interview for this book (Dawson died of cancer in 1991).
Massino didn't have to admit to any Mafia membership and
while he had to plead guilty to racketeering, the only crime
he had to admit to in his plea was hijacking. The conspiracy
to murder the three captains would be dropped. Though the
prison sentence in the deal would be for twenty years, the
sentence would run concurrent with Massino's ten-year term
for labor racketeering, which according to Cutler would
wind up giving Massino four more years, allowing him to be
released in 1996 instead of 1992.

Cutler said his client Vitale would only have to face a
five-year prison term for what he jokingly called "felonious
moppery." Since the sentences predated 1987 changes in the
federal sentencing laws, Vitale could be out in about three
years.

But Cutler said there was a catch. The government
wanted Massino to make a statement when he entered his
plea that he was involved in the conspiracy to murder Do-

minick Trinchera, Philip Giaccone, and Alphonse Indelicato, the three captains. Massino refused, so the case went to trial.

By the time Massino's trial for the murder of the three captains was set to begin, he had already been in the local federal jail for over a year following his conviction in the Local 814 labor racketeering case. It had been nearly three years since he had surrendered to face the indictment. A big man used to a rich diet, Massino lost a lot of weight in jail. When the murder conspiracy case finally opened on April 28, 1987, Massino had to borrow a suit from a slimmer friend to dress for court. That more svelte buddy, it turned out, was Angelo Ruggiero, a chubby mafioso to be sure but nothing like the 300-pound girth that Massino sported.

"This case is about money and it is about murder," Chertoff told jurors in his opening statement. "It is the biography of a man who made his life in crime and that man is Joey Massino."

Chertoff said that Massino had risen to become one of the powers in the Bonanno crime family and labeled him "the Horatio Alger of the Mafia." The deaths of the three captains was rooted in a struggle within the Bonanno family for power and Massino was part of the conspiracy that led to their deaths.

When his turn came, Dawson told the jury that they would acquit Massino because there simply wasn't evidence that the defendant had done anything wrong. Jurors may not like Massino's lifestyle and it was true that he wasn't a saint, said Dawson. But the key witness about the murder conspiracy, FBI agent Joseph Pistone, hadn't even met Massino.

Vitale was not accused of being part of the murder conspiracy, but he had a closeness through marriage and friendship with Massino that could be looked on with disfavor by the jury. Cutler didn't shy away from Vitale's linkage to his brother-in-law.

"Not only does he love Joe Massino, not only is he related to Joe Massino through marriage, but he is proud of it and the evidence will show that," said Cutler.

The case contained numerous charges related to hijackings and who better to testify about that than Massino's old hijacking crony Ray Wean. Although he was not a member of organized crime, Wean told the jury about things that implicated Massino in the Mafia. For instance, Wean said that while he was a trustee at the federal jail in Manhattan in the late 1970s he helped and did favors for Carmine Galante at Massino's insistence.

Wean also testified that as soon as he got bail in early 1981 on the Nassau County robbery case—with some help by the FBI—he went to Massino's J&S Cake Social Club and asked his old friend if there were any "scores coming down." Massino didn't have anything, Wean said, but offered him use of a house in Pennsylvania if he needed a place to stay. Still, Massino did talk about a stolen tuna fish load he had handled with Wean.

To prove the Joseph Pastore murder was linked to Massino, the prosecution brought in the testimony of Salvatore Polisi. It was Polisi, a career criminal, who had run into Massino at the Port Jervis Holiday Inn while the Maspeth mobster was on the lam. Polisi testified that in early 1976, at the request of mobster Dominick Cataldo, that he "went to find a grave site for the man that was to be murdered." Polisi said he found the site and reported back to Cataldo during a night at the bar in the Pan American Motel in Flushing. Seated at the table with Cataldo, Polisi said, were Massino and his friend "Tootie" Franzese.

At that point in the testimony, Dawson objected and Sweet excused the jury. Outside the presence of the jury, Gredd asked Polisi if Cataldo shared his information about the grave site with anyone else. "To Franzese and Massino," Polisi answered.

Gredd told Sweet that it appeared that Cataldo was "reporting" to Massino. But Sweet was not so sure.

"In fact, what he said is that this was the conversation at the table and Massino sat there," said Sweet. "He said Massino said nothing."

In a curious piece of testimony, the old girlfriend of Joseph "Doo Doo" Pastore was called to testify about the way he had become frightened in May 1976. Gloria Jean Young said she immediately dropped out of Pastore's life and did not know why he was found murdered that month. Clearly, Pastore was facing a problem. But while Chertoff said in court that investigators believed Massino had a role in the killing, there was never any firm proof introduced that he was involved.

Reprising his role in the earlier trial, which centered on the murder of the three captains, undercover agent Joseph Pistone again took the witness stand in Massino's case. A lot of Pistone's testimony repeated what he had stated in the 1982 trial, which recounted his covert penetration of the crime family and the close relationship he developed with Sonny Black Napolitano and Lefty Guns Ruggiero. Both Napolitano and Ruggiero, according to Pistone's testimony, were intimately involved with the killing of the three captains. But when it came to Massino, the evidence was highly circumstantial. Pistone was able to recollect a conversation he had with Ruggiero about the way Massino had screwed up the disposal of the bodies of the three murdered captains. Things had been so slipshod and hastily done that Alphonse Indelicato's corpse was found in the vacant lot in Queens three weeks after the killings.

Pistone's testimony, while circumstantial, could be seen as implicating Massino in the murder conspiracy. After all, wouldn't the other members of the conspiracy have to entrust such a crucial job—the disposal of the bodies—to a person who was also part of the plot? That was essentially what Assistant U.S. Attorney Helen Gredd argued to the jury in her summation.

"Lefty didn't give Pistone all the details of how the three murders were planned or carried out but he confirmed that Joe Massino was a part of that plan, by telling Pistone about something that Massino had agreed to take care of but had screwed up, getting rid of Sonny Red's body," Gredd stressed to the jury.

But Dawson brought up the fine point that when Sonny Black Napolitano recounted to Pistone who was involved in the murders, Massino's name was never mentioned.

"Not a single mention all day of Joseph Massino being happy about it, being a participant in it, having planned it, being interested in it. Not a single mention of Joseph Massino," noted Dawson.

The verdict took many by surprise. It was also a bit confusing. On June 3, 1987, the jury found that Massino had not conspired in the murder of the three captains. Apparently, Pistone's testimony didn't carry enough weight. Massino was also acquitted of the conspiracies to murder Pastore and Bruno Indelicato, the son of slain capo Alphonse. But the jurors found that he and Vitale were guilty of hijack- and theft-related acts: Massino for the 1975 Hemingway tractor-trailer heist and for possession of stolen tuna fish and frozen shrimp; Vitale for possession of the tuna fish and shrimp. That should have been enough to convict both of the racketeering conspiracy charges.

But there had been a legal twist to the case, one first spotted by Jon Pollok, the lawyer who negotiated Massino's surrender in 1984. It appeared that the hijacking charges, the only charges for which Massino and Vitale were convicted, involved events that took place over five years before the indictment. Because of that, Judge Sweet had to ask the jury to consider a special question: Did the racketeering enterprise continue beyond October 1979? The date was important because it represented the date in time that was more than five years from the date of the third superseding indictment in the case in October 1984. If the jury found that conspiracy continued beyond October 1979, the panel then had to consider whether Vitale and Massino were part of it.

According to court records, it took the jury less than twenty minutes to come to a decision about the special verdict form. No, the jurors decided, the racketeering conspiracy was not shown to continue beyond October 1979. Massino and Vitale were off the hook. They had been acquitted on a legal technicality.

The verdict showed that a combination of luck and stealth, as well as some superb defense lawyering, had worked in Massino's favor. Even with Ray Wean having evidence that Massino told him that Pastore was "gone," even with Pistone's detailed testimony and his tapes of mobsters talking about the murder of the three captains, the jury had reasonable doubt about Massino conspiring to kill anyone.

The problem was that there was no direct evidence, no testimony of a witness who participated in any of the killings, that linked Massino to a murder conspiracy. Massino, as was his cautious nature, had been fairly discrete in his conversations with the witnesses who did testify. The jury was then left with a very incomplete and ambiguous portrayal of his activities. It all failed to convince the jury that Massino was involved in the murders.

Massino's courtroom victory was a lesson for the prosecution, as well as for any investigator who thought of targeting the Mafia leader. They had better have their ducks in a row and the strongest case possible if they wanted to get a conviction. Any less would be just too damned unpredictable.

After the special verdict was announced, there were handshakes all around the defense table. Massino was taken back to the local federal jail since he was serving a prison sentence on the Teamster case. Vitale was free to leave the courthouse. In Massino's absence, he had all kinds of business of a family sort to deal with.

CHAPTER 16

By the Numbers

"What do you think is going on?" asked FBI Director Louis Freeh.

Though he was based in Washington, D.C., Freeh kept abreast of crime news out of New York City, where he had worked as a federal prosecutor in the 1980s. That morning, March 20, 1999, the Manhattan tabloids had reports about the killing of a Bonanno crime family captain named Gerlando "George" Sciascia on a Bronx street. His face was bloodied from three shots to the head and his left eye was shot out.

Freeh, who had led some of the big prosecutions of the crime family in the 1980s, had a meteoric rise in his career that led to his appointment by President Bill Clinton to the directorship of the FBI in 1993. But he never lost his interest in the Bonanno group. The killing of Sciascia, a major family member out of Canada, was a sign that something big had happened. So Freeh called his trusted friend, Charles Rooney, special agent in charge of the Chicago office of the FBI, to brainstorm.

Rooney had studied the Bonanno crime family for years and had an encyclopedic knowledge of the group, as well as an indelible memory. He had put together the Pizza Connection case and had known all the players in the family. He especially knew the ways of Joseph Massino. He had a quick answer for Freeh about Sciascia's death.

"This is Joey cleaning house," said Rooney.

What Rooney meant was that Massino was continuing what the investigator believed was a long process of killing off anyone who might be able to implicate him in the 1981 murder of the three captains or any other homicides for that matter. A surveillance picture taken on May 6, 1981, at a Bronx motel, the day after Dominick Trinchera, Philip Giaccone, and Alphonse Indelicato had been killed, showed Massino with three other men: Vito Rizzuto, a key Bonanno captain from Canada and a suspected shooter in the killing of the three captains, Gianni Liggamari, a mafioso from New Jersey, and Sciascia.

There were other theories to be sure that would emerge about the Sciascia killing. Among them would be the fact that Sciascia had spoken his mind about the drug use of Anthony Graziano, an old Bonanno captain who Massino had a soft spot for. But to Rooney's way of thinking, a lot of high-ranked mobsters like Massino got paranoid about their crimes. Massino in particular was overly sensitive about breaches in security and tried to foresee who might be a turncoat. So it made sense, Rooney believed, that Massino was trying to cover his tracks in the three captains homicide.

"You just get a sixth sense of it," Rooney later said. "You just learn how they think."

The motel picture and the strange deaths of some of the mobsters depicted in it pulled it all together in Rooney's mind about the mob homicides that had been cropping up. He felt Massino had to be involved and said as much to Freeh. After serving the majority of his ten-year sentence for labor racketeering, Massino had been paroled in 1992. Even before Massino walked out of prison, the Bonanno captains held a meeting and elected him the new boss after Philip

Rastelli died in 1991. To Rooney and a lot of organized crime experts in the FBI, Massino was now the boss to watch. He wouldn't be an easy target.

Back in the New York FBI office, supervisor John Stubing didn't need any convincing that Joseph Massino was a hard guy to build a case around. A career agent, Stubing took over as acting head of squad C10 in November 1995, a job that became permanent in April 1996. Stubing oversaw investigations that targeted both the Bonanno and DeCavalcante crime families and he knew from experience that Massino was a crafty adversary who studied the ways of his law enforcement foes.

"Massino knew how to insulate himself from the day-to-day activities," Stubing recalled. "He knew how to play the game."

Not long after he took over as squad supervisor, Stubing paid a surprise visit to Massino at a company he had on Long Island known as King Caterers. It was an outfit he and Salvatore Vitale had taken an interest in during the early 1990s to, as law enforcement officials believed, protect the owner from extortion by another crime family. In return, Vitale and Massino took home salaries and benefits.

At King Caterers, Stubing had a friendly chat with Massino and quickly recognized that the mobster had a lot on the ball. Massino seemed to remember every time he had been watched by law enforcement and had a good memory of his past racketeering case. To Stubing, who had seen the stunning victory the Maspeth gangster had pulled off in his 1987 murder conspiracy trial, Massino was a mafioso who represented the toughest quarry out of the old mob tradition. He had some simple watch words: keep your mouth shut and take care of your own problems.

Building on mob intelligence mined in the 1970s and 1980s, the FBI in New York had kept the Bonanno family in its sights. Even though Massino had been in prison from 1987 until 1992, FBI agents had plenty of targets in the family. Setting up cameras in 1991 outside a social club run by Sal Vitale in an alley adjacent to 69-64 Grand Avenue in Maspeth, agents photographed not only Vitale but also Bonanno captains Louis Restivo, Anthony Urso, Michael Cardiello, and the ill-fated Gerlando Sciascia. Vitale, who was Massino's underboss, was effectively an acting boss of the crime family during his brother-in-law's absence, so his Queens club was a focal point for the Bonanno leadership.

The Maspeth investigation became known by the code name "Grand Finale." Aware of the possibility of bugging devices in the club, Vitale and the others appeared to make calls from a pay telephone outside the nearby Maspeth Public Library. The FBI spotted that maneuver and got a court order for a tap on that line.

The Grand Finale case didn't lead to anything big. In reality, the Bonanno squad had a lot on its plate because around the time of the Grand Avenue social club probe the Colombo crime family got into a bloody internecine feud and Stubing's squad had responsibility for that problem as well. When Massino finally got out of prison in 1992, he resorted to his cautious methods of operation, insulating himself and avoiding weddings, funerals, and other events where he might be photographed by the police. He was also careful about what he said over the telephone. The penetration by Pistone was also fresh on Massino's mind and he was extra cautious about possible informants. It was a kind of wiliness that Stubing knew would make Massino a tough investigative target.

Traditional methods of investigation, Stubing reckoned, seemed obsolete against Massino. The Bonanno boss had studied law enforcement methods—he carefully watched car mirrors to spot surveillance vehicles—and he knew how federal agencies tried to build a racketeering case. Informants said that Massino decreed that gambling couldn't take place in any building he owned out of fear that the federal government might try to seize the property. But since money was at the root of organized crime activity, Stubing and his staff believed they had to follow the cash if they had any hope of nabbing Massino.

"I knew that nothing else was going to work against this guy," Stubing remembered some years later.

A forensic accounting approach, in which investigators delved into the source of money generated by mobsters and their associates, had been of some success in other cases, particularly intricate fraud schemes. The Bonanno squad had subpoened a lot of financial records of crime family members and associates. But Stubing didn't have enough background to crunch those kinds of numbers. He had to look for people who could work with financial records, so he made the unusual request to his superiors to have agents who were accountants assigned to study an organized crime family. Stubing learned that there were two new agents in New York who might be just what he needed.

× × ×

When Special Agent Kimberly McCaffrey's beeper went off, she saw the call back number was that of her supervisor in the Manhattan FBI office. He had good news. After months of drudgery as a new agent doing surveillance work, McCaffrey had been assigned to the C10 squad. She was to report to work immediately. It was early March 1999 when McCaffrey walked into the squad office at Twenty-six Federal Plaza for the first time. Gerlando Sciascia still had about a couple of weeks to live.

McCaffrey hadn't started out in life aiming to be an FBI agent. Her first real passion had been gymnastics, which she began doing at her suburban New Jersey Catholic school. A petite woman, McCaffrey took to the sport easily and excelled in high school–level competition, although she was sidelined for a while after dislocating her elbows on the uneven bars. The injuries didn't deter McCaffrey from competing in the sport at Towson State University in Maryland. But in January 1994, while representing Towson in competition, McCaffrey had another accident, this time blowing out a knee during a floor exercise. Sports wouldn't be in her future, at least not at the level demanded by competitive gymnastics. McCaffrey focused on something that would give her a steady job: accounting. Being an FBI agent wasn't on her mind at all.

Unlike McCaffrey, Jeffrey Sallet had always wanted to be a G-man. He had studied accounting in college, with the FBI as his long-range career goal. Grounded in the world of balance sheets, Sallet liked certitude. But he wasn't a nerdy guy with a plastic pocket protector who never took chances. He liked to ski and had what could be said to be an eclectic taste in music. When Sallet worked at the firms of Arthur Andersen and Ernst & Young, his mentor was a former FBI agent who introduced him to the world of forensic accounting. With a little prodding from his mentor, Sallet joined the FBI in July 1997 at the age of twenty-seven, a little less than a year before McCaffrey, who signed on at the age of twenty-five. In FBI life, they were both just kids.

Sallet had already been on the Bonanno squad a few months when McCaffrey came on board. By the time both young agents were together, the situation with the New York Mafia had changed enormously since the days Joseph Pistone was posing as a wiseguy. Four of the five mob families had been targeted so often by investigators that a lot of the old household names—Gotti, Persico, and Colombo—were either incarcerated or dead. Their replacements had, as in the case of the Lucchese crime family, turned government witness or were under indictment. A lot of the old rackets such as the concrete industry, the garment district, and the waterfront had been seriously constricted by continued investigations.

The Bonanno family had also taken its share of hits and for years had been the laughing stock of La Cosa Nostra because of Pistone's penetration. That breach of mob secrecy in the Brasco affair, as well as the family's profligate drug trafficking shown in the Pizza Connection case, had deprived it of a seat on the ruling Commission. The Bonanno family had also gone through a period of about two decades when its leaders such as Philip Rastelli and Joseph Massino were incarcerated. Though both men ran the affairs of the family by communicating through intermediaries and ruling committees, it was still a cumbersome arrangement. The committees sometimes went off and ordered homicides without the bosses' knowledge.

But in a curious way, the earlier problems that befell the Bonanno family provided some insulation from law enforcement scrutiny. Stubing noted to his young agents that by not having a seat on the Commission, the Bonanno family was not part of the concrete conspiracy that was at the center of the 1986 Commission trial or the so-called Windows case, involving allegations of crimes in the window replacement industry. As a result, the Bonanno family had to adapt and change to find new rackets. One lucrative area turned out to be Wall Street, where stock fraud schemes became the specialty of captains Frank Coppa, Frank Lino, and some of their other associates.

Aside from plowing new territory with the financial crimes, the Bonanno group also kept a hand in drug dealing. It was no longer the secretive world of heroin trafficking of the Pizza Connection days, but the more run-of-the-mill crack-cocaine business. Working out of a group of cafés and coffee shops in Queens and Brooklyn, a couple crews of crime family associates ran distribution operations.

Prosecutors suspected that the cocaine trade in Brooklyn was run by associates of Anthony Spero, a Bonanno captain with a social club on Bath Avenue. In Queens, federal investigators stumbled across Baldassare Amato, who had been convicted years ago in the Pizza Connection case but never seemed to learn his lesson. Amato appeared to be the mentor to a bunch of mob associates who based themselves out of a café in Ridgewood known as Café Giannini. The "Giannini Crew" robbed some gambling operations in other clubs and also became involved in drug dealing, according to investigators.

James Walden, a prosecutor in the Brooklyn U.S. Attorney's Office, secured a number of indictments against Amato, Spero, and their associates. Both Spero and Amato had been spotted by FBI agents meeting in Queens with Massino. Years later, Walden said revenues from drug dealing might have gotten as high up the crime family chain as Spero. He thought it plausible that Massino, who had warned Frank Lino about drug dealing, may have taken a cut of the money as tribute, even if he knew it was narcotics cash.

Though convicted of racketeering, Spero decided not to cooperate with the government, so he never implicated Massino. It might have been possible to use information from the Spero-Amato prosecutions to eventually build a case against Massino. But some prosecutors knowledgeable about those investigations said that could have taken years of constant surveillance, wiretaps, and other time-consuming methods. In the meantime, the Bonanno family would have been run by a leadership that remained intact.

Instead, Stubing sat down with Sallet and McCaffrey and gave them a history of the Bonanno family and its main players. The supervisor had one clear direction for his young agents: Don't focus immediately on the big boss; instead, find the people around him. Find the weak links. It was the time-honored domino theory of investigation: get one important criminal to cooperate and that might lead up the food chain to the kingpin.

In terms of Massino, Stubing told his agents, the ultimate key would be his brother-in-law, Salvatore Vitale, the crime family underboss. Since he had been initiated into the Mafia in the 1980s, Vitale had been a close confidante of Massino and his eyes and ears while in prison. It was a relationship made more complex by the fact that Vitale had essentially been raised by Massino's wife, Josephine. Later, it was Vitale who served as a surrogate father to Massino's daughters in the crime boss's absence. Vitale was the "swing man" in the Bonanno family regarding Massino.

"I told Jeff and Kim that if you can't get one without the other, you are going to lose," recalled Stubing.

Fortified by Stubing's lectures on the crime family, Sallet and McCaffrey contacted Assistant U.S. Attorney Ruth Nordenbrook over at the federal prosecutors' offices in Brooklyn. With wide-rimmed glasses, black outfits, and black hair, which she often wore pulled back, Nordenbrook looked as much like a college literature professor as she did a federal prosecutor. She had joined the office in the late 1970s and earned her early mark doing some of the first credit card fraud cases. By the 1990s, she had picked up a number of organized crime cases that found her prosecuting several Bonanno family members. One of them was Anthony Graziano, a Bonanno captain who plead guilty to tax crimes.

But what really earned Nordenbrook some notoriety was her philosophy that the wives of mafiosi shouldn't be immune from prosecution if they took part in crimes, with or without their husbands. It had been something of an unwritten rule that the wives were off limits to prosecutors, that their spouses would take the fall. But Nordenbrook didn't like playing by that mob rule and chafed when some of her colleagues in law enforcement wanted to. She lived up to her ideals by prosecuting Marie Attanasio, the wife of Louis "Ha Ha" Attanasio, for tax fraud in 1984, a case that ended with an acquittal. Years later, she prosecuted loan shark John Zancocchio and later went after his wife, Lana, the daughter of Anthony Graziano, getting her convicted for tax evasion.

With Nordenbrook's insights as guidance, Sallet and McCaffrey started the FBI part of the investigation into the finances of the Bonanno administration. Armed with subpoena power through Nordenbrook's role as investigating prosecutor, Sallet and McCaffrey started looking at the particular finances of Massino and Vitale. Nordenbrook's supervisor over at the U.S. Attorney's Office in Brooklyn was Mark Feldman, a career prosecutor who saw the value of a detailed financial probe and kept the two agents focused on their objective despite the desire of other investigators to focus on the murders in the crime family. Although they weren't coming up with hard evidence of crimes being committed by the two brothers-in-law, the agents did start to notice some intriguing relationships.

One of the things that jumped out was that Josephine Massino was discovered to have an interest in a number of parking lots in Manhattan. Though she had been a housewife for most of her life, Josephine Massino had business relationships with her brother, Salvatore; his wife, Diana; Loretta Castelli, who was the wife of crime captain Richard Cantarella; and others. The agents surmised that Massino might be the real power behind his wife's presence in those partnerships, but on the face of it there didn't appear to be anything wrong with the finances of those companies.

But after plowing through myriad financial records, Sallet and McCaffrey found a new name that kept appearing again and again as the recipient of a number of checks. It was the name of Barry Weinberg, a Queens man who had an interest in a number of parking ventures around the city. Checks uncovered by the agents showed a number of payments, sometimes for as much as $16,666, going to Weinberg.

Who was Barry Weinberg? He was a nervous, stoop-shouldered, and chain-smoking entrepreneur. Surveillance had revealed that Weinberg, who lived in Queens, would often meet with Richard Cantarella in Little Italy at restaurants like the Dixie Rose Café and DaNico. Their relationship at that point was not clear. But in reviewing Weinberg's finances with the Internal Revenue Service, Sallet and McCaffrey discovered evidence that he was involved in tax evasion—lots of it. One official said that he had income of $14 million for several years, money that he appeared to evade paying taxes on in grand scale. On January 9, 2001, Weinberg was arrested and brought by the agents to a small office in downtown Manhattan. After puffing his way through innumerable cigarettes, Weinberg quickly decided that the agents had a very strong case against him. So he did what many would do. He decided to cooperate with the FBI. He also went one step further: he also agreed to wear a recording device.

Weinberg soon made recordings of a number of Bonanno family members and associates. His list of targets was pretty impressive: Frank Coppa, Richard Cantarella, and his son Paul, as well as Joseph "Mouk" D'Amico. Not everyone recorded on over eighty tapes made by Weinberg was caught committing a crime. But Coppa, an old friend of Massino's, and Richard Cantarella, the tapes showed, were milking Weinberg for cash in what appeared to be an extortion scheme.

Coppa, who had traveled with Massino and his wife to Europe, was a portly man who had a head for business. Starting out in his working life as a grocery clerk, he went on to jobs in the waterfront and trucking. At the age of nineteen, he had his first arrest for the attempted burglary of a clothing store. He had been inducted into the Mafia in 1977 at a ceremony presided over by Carmine Galante. Investigators believed that had he led a law-abiding life, Coppa could have made a fortune legitimately. Instead, he became entangled in a number of frauds over the years, including some involving the stock market. He had blood on his hands as well, having been present the night Sonny Black Napolitano was killed.

Coppa was also the target of an assassination attempt in the late 1970s when a bomb detonated in his vehicle outside a Bagel Nosh store. Coppa believed the culprit was a mobster by the name of Tony Coglitore, who had been swindled out of about $8,000 by Coppa. Commercial arbitration in Mafia stock scams aren't the normal way such disputes are settled. After Coppa, who was then a Bonanno soldier, was injured in the explosion, he spoke with his captain, Matteo Valvo, who said he could seek retaliation. Coppa later said he had Gambino soldier Eddie Lino and another man try to kill Coglitore.

Weinberg continued to tape Coppa and the others for several months. Nordenbrook and her two agents believed there was enough evidence to support both an extortion charge and a charge of money laundering against Cantarella. As they also focused on Salvatore Vitale's finances, they came up with leads that showed that he had infiltrated the branch of a Long Island bank. Vitale had moved from Queens in the 1990s and settled with his wife in the town of Dix Hills, not far from the Farmingdale office of King Caterers, the business where he had a no-show job with Massino. Vitale targeted the branch of a local bank but had been sloppy in his scam, drawing the attention of the FBI and setting himself up for an indictment.

However, everything Sallet and McCaffrey were working on suddenly took a backseat beginning on the morning of September 11, 2001. Both agents were at the federal courthouse in Foley Square in downtown Manhattan as case agents for a trial when just blocks away American Airlines Flight 11 plowed into the North Tower of the World Trade Center.

The terrorist attacks that day brought about the mobilization of U.S. law enforcement. The FBI and other federal agencies dragooned every available person to assist in the recovery at ground zero. Joining scores of other investigators in the Hades-like setting left by the destruction of the Twin Towers, Sallet and McCaffrey helped scour the site for two days searching for the black boxes of the two airlines used by the terrorists.

With September 11, the priorities of law enforcement at

every level shifted. Gone were the old assignments. New York City put cops on heightened security duty at bridges, tunnels, airports, and other public venues, even baseball parks. Prosecution of quality of life crimes like prostitution fell by the wayside as police struggled to meet the demands of protecting the city. At the FBI, agents were quickly shifted into counter-terrorism investigations and away from traditional areas like organized crime. After rummaging through ground zero, Sallet was reassigned to Washington, D.C., where he was part of a team of agents that spent six months probing the finances of the hijackers.

McCaffrey briefly worked on the September 11 investigation but was kept at Twenty-six Federal Plaza where, despite the massive deployment of agents on terrorism cases, she kept the Bonanno crime family investigation alive. She would have continued to have Weinberg prowling the streets of Little Italy with his body wire, but there were signs that the nervous informant was wearing out his welcome with the mob. Cantarella seemed suspicious of the businessman and even said as much to Vitale, who offered help if Cantarella wanted to kill Weinberg. The worst thing that happened was that Cantarella told Weinberg not to come around the various restaurants in Little Italy where they had dined. That was enough to have McCaffrey, Stubing, and Sallet, who was still in touch with the Bonanno investigation while working on the terrorism probe, decide to pull Weinberg from the street in December 2001.

But as one avenue of investigation shut down another opened up. The Weinberg tapes and other evidence indicated that Massino and Cantarella were involved in crimes and pointed to a man named Agostino Scozzari as a possible source of information. Scozzari was a German businessman of Italian ethnicity who had emigrated after he had made a lot of money in Europe in the scaffolding business. Because of his Italian heritage, Scozzari gravitated to the Little Italy area of Manhattan and opened up a restaurant. In the close

202 *Anthony M. DeStefano*

environs of Mulberry Street, Scozzari became associated with Cantarella. Scozzari was never arrested, but Sallet and McCaffrey persuaded him to cooperate in their investigation.

Scozzari's incentive to cooperate would never be revealed. Regardless, in December 2001 Scozzari started wearing a recording device and made over twenty tapes of talks he had with Cantarella. The recordings indicated that Cantarella had introduced Scozzari to Massino, telling the informant it was Massino, who was called "Joe" on the tape, who helped him become a Mafia member in the early 1990s.

Cantarella was also overheard on tape complaining to Scozzari about the newspaper publicity Massino had received after the death in June 2002 of Gambino boss John Gotti from cancer. That kind of publicity, which painted Massino as being the big Mafia boss in town, could only draw law enforcement attention for Massino, he said.

"What the paper is saying is that Joe is the big guy now," Cantarella said. "That's not good. You know what I mean? That's not good. That's not good."

Cantarella, who went by the moniker of "Shellack Head" because of his high-coiffed, slick hairstyle, was facing some serious problems beyond his financial picture. He and some others in the crime family and their relatives held no-show jobs at the *New York Post* in the delivery and distribution area. Among them was Al Embarrato, Cantarella's uncle, a *Post* delivery foreman and an old mobster who was seen by the FBI over the years hanging out at the Toyland Social Club and other places frequented by the crime family. The mobsters ran loan-sharking and other rackets out of the *Post* facility on South Street in lower Manhattan.

By 1992, Manhattan District Attorney Robert Morgenthau got a state grand jury to indict Cantarella, the eighty-two-year-old Embarrato, and several others, including the *Post*'s delivery supervisor Robert Perrino. Two *Post* executives admitted to Morgenthau's staff during the course of the probe that they had a role in fraudulently inflating daily circulation figures by about 50,000 phantom copies to get more money from advertisers. Both executives plead guilty to labor law violations in exchange for helping prosecutors with the case. In 1994, Cantarella pled guilty in the state case.

During their probe, state investigators looked for Perrino, a relative of imprisoned Bonanno consiglieri Nicholas Marangello, when they raided his home with a search warrant. But while they found about $100,000 in cash and several weapons, Perrino was missing.

Nordenbrook and the agents secured a search warrant for Cantarella's home and in August 2002 took boxes of financial records from his home in Staten Island. The materials showed that Cantarella and his family, as well as Josephine Massino and her brother, Salvatore Vitale, were involved in parking lot ventures. It was Cantarella's wife, Loretta Castelli, who sometimes had a 50 percent interest in the businesses, although prosecutors believed she simply served as her husband's nominee. The search also revealed a safe containing a list of Cantarella's crew members. His telephone address book was also taken by FBI agents and not surprisingly it was found to contain the names and numbers of Massino and his wife, Josephine, as well as Vitale, who was listed as "Sal Handsome."

In October 2002, Nordenbrook, who was now partnered with Assistant U.S. Attorney Greg Andres in the Bonanno investigation, secured indictments of Coppa, Cantarella, his wife, and thirty-one-year-old son Paul, as well as several other Bonanno family members and associates. Among them was Anthony Graziano, the foul-tempered captain the late Gerlando Sciascia thought was a druggie and who was charged with racketeering. It was the opening salvo of the probe into the financial hierarchy of the crime family.

The extortion charges were serious enough, but Cantarella faced a worse problem. The grand jury had accused him of taking part in the murder of *Post* delivery supervisor Robert

Perrino. A suspect in the labor racketeering probe at the newspaper carried out by Morgenthau's office, Perrino disappeared on the night of May 5, 1992, after leaving the home of his daughter on Long Island. His body had never been found. Murder in aid of racketeering carried a penalty of life in prison without parole for Cantarella should he go to trial and be convicted.

The charges also put Coppa in a deep predicament. His various Wall Street scams had earned him a conviction for stock fraud and in July 2002 he was serving a stiff seven-year prison term. The October 2002 charges of extortion involved the beleaguered Weinberg and could earn Coppa another several years, since he would be a repeat offender with a big criminal history. Such extra time would be added to what he was already serving on the stock swindle. On top of that, he faced a fine of $1 million, which would have been on top of the $5 million he had to pay back to his Wall Street victims.

Frank Coppa had some serious thinking to do. At the age of sixty-one and suffering from a heart condition, he did not like prison. In fact, in 1992 when he had done another stint in jail, he had cried about doing time because, as he later said, "I had left my family." He may have been a con man and thief for most of his life, but Coppa didn't like to pay the price if his landlord was the Bureau of Prisons.

But caught Coppa was, and he knew it. There was evidence uncovered by Sallet and McCaffrey that he had told Weinberg that only he, Coppa, could be his broker for the parking lot deals. He had taken the oath of omerta in front of Carmine Galante and he knew that betrayal of the code of silence meant death. Well, it could mean death if the mob ever got to you. Coppa knew that the federal government had a witness protection program. He also knew that deals could be made, even if you were a killer like Sammy "the Bull" Gravano, who claimed to have helped kill nineteen people but later got out of prison in less than five years after helping convict John Gotti. Like Gravano, a lot of mafiosi turned their backs on omerta and salvaged what they could of their lives.

Coppa didn't want to die in prison. He also wanted to be close to his wife and family. The portly mobster made his own calculation. Omerta may have worked for Joseph Bonanno and the older Sicilians, but nobody believed in that anymore. Coppa, the man with a head for numbers and betrayal, decided his future wasn't with La Cosa Nostra. It certainly wasn't with Joe Massino. Now, life was all about self-preservation and family of a different sort.

It took about two weeks for Coppa to contact his attorney to tell prosecutors he wanted to make a deal. The first step was a "proffer," a session in which Coppa told the FBI what he knew. Proffer sessions are common in criminal cases. They afford prosecutors a chance to see what information a potential informant really has while the informant is not in danger of being prosecuted for what is mentioned in the session, assuming he is truthful.

In Coppa's case, he talked for ten days straight. But because Nordenbrook had prosecuted some Mafia women and even once threatened to prosecute his sister, Coppa didn't want her around to hear what he had to say.

"I was told he hated me because I did the women," Nordenbrook later recalled. Nordenbrook protested about the way Coppa was trying to dictate the terms of his proffer session. But at least one FBI official saw no harm in playing up to Coppa's sense of Mafia ethics. Nordenbrook felt she didn't have to apologize for her pursuit of Mafia wives and other women. In her view, it was unacceptable that mafiosi could try to shelter their income and ill-gotten gains with their women. But she also realized that no one of Coppa's stature in the Bonanno crime family had ever turned into a cooperating witness before. So Nordenbrook decided not to make a big stink and possibly spoil Coppa's decision to flip. She stayed away from his proffer sessions.

So it was with Greg Andres, as well as with Sallet and McCaffrey, that Coppa talked. He told them what he knew about Joseph Massino and life in the mob.

The deal that Coppa worked out with the federal government depended on his cooperation with the Bonanno investigation. If he helped prosecutors, Coppa would get a letter from the government that spelled out his cooperation to the judge who had sentenced him. Coppa was also promised, assuming he cooperated to the government's liking, that prosecutors would make a motion to the court, known as a Rule 35 motion, to get his sentence reduced. It would be up to the judge to decide how much of a reduction Coppa would get. His wife and one son who wasn't involved in crime would be relocated by the government. Lastly, Coppa wouldn't have to testify against his other son, Frank Jr., who he told investigators was a member of organized crime.

Coppa's decision to turn into a witness for the prosecution, a decision directly precipitated by his indictment that came from Sallet and McCaffrey's financial sleuthing, was a very big deal for a number of reasons. Coppa had been close to Massino—although not as close as Vitale had been—and he knew about the crime boss's illegal financial dealings, particularly in the area of loan-sharking. Since he passed up thousands of dollars a month in tribute to Massino, Coppa was in a position to help investigators build a tax evasion and money laundering charge against the Bonanno boss.

But there was some much more powerful stuff Coppa possessed in his memory. Though he didn't kill a lot of people himself, Coppa was a font of information about several homicides. Better yet for the investigation, Coppa could implicate Massino—sometimes directly, sometimes circumstantially—in mob murders. Among them were the killing of the three captains and Dominick Napolitano, homicides that had become the Holy Grail of the investigation.

Richard Cantarella might have been a big boy in the Bonanno crime family. After his induction into the life of La

Cosa Nostra in 1990, he began dining with Massino weekly at his J&S Cake Social Club and got promoted quickly to the rank of acting captain. He made a lot of money through his shakedown of Weinberg, the parking lot ventures, and other rackets. He got his hands dirty with murder. Before his indictment, Sallet and McCaffrey had approached him about cooperating, but he didn't budge and even told Massino about the FBI attempt to turn him.

But when things got rough, Cantarella wasn't a true believer or stand-up guy. Though brought into the life of crime by his uncle Al Embarrato, the rule of omerta meant nothing to Cantarella. As soon as he was indicted in October 2002, Cantarella figured cooperation was his way out of trouble, his ace in the hole. "In my mind I knew I was cooperating," Cantarella later said.

Cantarella's deal with prosecutors involved the same kinds of general conditions and promises worked out for Coppa. There would be a letter to the judge who would sentence him extolling his cooperation with the prosecution and asking for a sentence reduction. But the deal didn't involve his son or his wife. They had to work out their own plea bargains.

So in the space of a few weeks in late 2002, the government's squeeze play on the Bonanno crime family showed results that no one had anticipated would have happened so fast. Two significant captains in the crime family had agreed to cooperate. Coppa and Cantarella had a lot to offer because they both had intimate knowledge about several mob homicides. Both were men who Joseph Massino trusted and had relied on to run the crime family at different times. But in the end they waved the white flag of surrender as soon as the first salvo was fired by the government. That kind of news was not good for Joe Massino. He had been so wrong about them.

CHAPTER 17

Ghosts

"Criminal cause for arraignment, United States versus Joseph Massino, Salvatore Vitale, and Daniel Mongelli, docket number zero-two cr three-zero-seven," the woman court clerk announced. "Please state your appearances."

A few hours after the news conference ended announcing his arrest on January 9, 2003, Joseph Massino and his codefendants were brought across the East River into federal court in Brooklyn before a federal magistrate judge. The six-story courthouse was opened in 1961 on Cadman Plaza, a park by the Brooklyn anchorage of the Brooklyn Bridge.

Though woefully in need of more space (a new fourteen-story replacement building was going up next door), the Eastern District Courthouse had a spacious ceremonial courtroom on the second floor. It was there that arraignments, initial court appearances for those charged in which they invariably enter pleas of not guilty, took place. Massino entered the courtroom shortly after lunchtime. His case was one of a number of criminal matters on the calendar.

The first to speak was Greg Andres, the assistant U.S. attorney in charge of the Massino case. A lean man with the narrow eyes of a panther on the hunt, Andres told the attending magistrate, Joan Azrack, that he was representing the government and was accompanied by Ruth Nordenbrook.

Though it had been Nordenbrook, one of the veteran federal prosecutors in Brooklyn, who had shepherded the efforts of FBI agents Sallet and McCaffrey, the bureaucracy in which she worked had its own machinations and power plays. For one reason or another, Andres, at least twenty years' Nordenbrook's junior, had been given the job of prosecuting Massino. The Bonanno investigation had been a source of tension between various prosecutors in the office in terms of the approach that would work best. Nordenbrook believed the financial probe targeting the hierarchy of the crime family was the best way to go. Others thought the case should focus on murders and racketeering. Andres ultimately saw the wisdom of using the financial probe to get witnesses who could then help make a larger murder investigation. Supervisor Mark Feldman had kept a steady hand on the tiller and kept his team focused on the financial probe. In the end, Andres's superiors gave him the nod to be the lead prosecutor. When it came time to arraign Massino in court, Nordenbrook, without any noticeable discomfort, took a second seat to Andres.

Massino's old friend and lawyer Matthew Mari of Manhattan appeared on his behalf. Mari's links to the Bonanno crime family were more than just professional. Though himself not involved in anything illegal, it had been Mari's father, Frank, who had been for a short time the boss of the crime family. His father's notoriety was a cross Matthew Mari would have to bear for the rest of his life. A reputed hit man, Frank Mari was picked to run the Bonanno clan in a May 1969 meeting of crime family captains in a restaurant in Manhattan. His major credential for the job it seemed was that he had been able to survive the so-called Banana War of the mid-1960s.

Frank Mari disappeared not long after he was named boss, and his son went on to become a criminal lawyer who represented some of his father's old associates, as well as other defendants in criminal cases. Grainy surveillance photos had even shown the younger Mari attending some social events with the mobsters. As the afternoon wore on, Mari's previous representation of Bonanno family members would become an issue.

Representing Vitale were John Mitchell, a veteran defense attorney from Manhattan who also specialized in criminal appeals, and Sheldon Eisenberger. Mongelli was represented by Gerald Marrone. After the attorney introductions ended, Azrack got straight to work.

"Alright, Mister Massino, have you viewed the charges with your attorney?" the magistrate asked.

"Yes," Massino responded in his characteristic husky voice.

"Do you understand what you are being charged with?" Azrack asked.

"Yes," Massino again responded.

Looking at Mari, Azrack asked if he wanted to enter a plea on his client's behalf.

"Yes," said Mari. "Not guilty."

"Mister Vitale, where are you?" Azrack said, looking around for Massino's brother-in-law.

"Right here your honor," responded Vitale.

"What plea do you want to enter?"

"Not guilty," answered Vitale.

Mongelli also entered a not guilty plea, and Azrack then turned to the issue of bail. It was at this point that Andres told the court what the news media and defense attorneys already knew: that bail was going to be a remote possibility.

"The government will be asking for detention for each of the defendants on dangerousness grounds," said Andres. "They are each charged with murder or murder conspiracy."

As happened in cases against crime bosses, federal prosecutors put together a long letter and a thick legal memorandum of law spelling out just why Massino should not be given bail. Anyone familiar with the workings of the criminal justice system knows bail is a method of ensuring the courts that a defendant will appear for future proceedings and stay within the jurisdiction of the court, which in Brooklyn also meant Staten Island and the surrounding counties of Queens, Nassau, and Suffolk. Usually, a defendant executes a bond by paying around 10 percent of the bail amount set by the magistrate. Sometimes real estate or other property like stocks and bonds are used to secure the bond.

With changes in the law in 1984, federal courts had become much tougher places for major criminal suspects such as mob bosses and drug gang leaders to get bail. The Bail Reform Act allowed judges (and magistrates) to order a suspect detained, which means held without bail, if the person was found to be a danger to the community or a risk to flee the jurisdiction. Though critics would maintain that the bail act provisions could be used as a form of preventive detention or punishment without trial, the U.S. Supreme Court had upheld it.

There were four factors that the court needed to consider whether to detain a suspect: the nature of the crimes charged, the history and character of the defendant, the seriousness of the danger posed to the community if the defendant was released on bail, and evidence of guilt. On each of these factors, Greg Andres said in his letter to Azrack, Massino was a loser and should be held without bail. Andres spelled out in his memo to the court that Massino had to be held without bail because he was dangerous in a way that few other crime bosses were.

A former Peace Corp volunteer from the New York City area who spent his time in the hot and semiarid West African nation of Benin, Andres now had what could be the biggest case of his life. It was the kind of prosecution that was a major stepping stone in the career of an aggressive and imaginative young attorney like Andres. He had been an aspiring player in the ranks of the office for a few years and got his big turn at bat when he was tapped as the lead in the Bonanno family investigation.

"Massino, who himself has a violent criminal history, heads a violent criminal enterprise which totals more than one-hundred soldiers, men who have pledged to commit acts of violence for the Bonanno family," Andres stated in his memorandum. "That Massino himself has been involved in serious acts of violence, including the charge murder and several others, makes the case for detention overwhelming."

Though he was only charged with one murder, Andres made clear that Massino would eventually be facing more accusations that he took part in other gangland hits. There was a witness, Andres revealed without disclosing anyone's name, who would prove that Massino once said he was involved in seven murders, all with Vitale. That remark showed that FBI agent Kim McCaffrey had been right about Massino being implicated in a number of murders. It just wouldn't be listed in the indictment Andres had in his hand this particular day.

Andres also had behind him the weight of some higher rulings from appellate courts, which said that just by holding a leadership position in a crime family meant that a suspect was dangerous. It didn't even matter, some judges said, that a defendant might not have committed any acts of violence. A leadership role in the mob put a person in a position where society couldn't be protected by even the toughest of bail measures.

There was no question, Andres argued, that Massino was the Bonanno boss. He said that not only would witnesses say as much but also that Massino had been seen over the years—despite his consciousness of surveillance—in the company of John Gotti and most of the upper echelon of the Bonanno crime family. Bolstering that argument, the prosecutor dredged up the tape-recorded remark an indiscreet Cantarella had made to an informant five months earlier about how Massino ensured that he would become a Mafia member. The same draconian denial of bail also applied, courts had ruled, to acting bosses, captains, soldiers, and associates. In other words, if Massino was not going to get bail, underlings like Frank Lino, Vitale, and Mongelli couldn't count on going home either.

The memorandum made clear that not even Clarence Darrow, let alone Matthew Mari, would have any success in getting Massino sprung from jail. Though Andres and Nordenbrook's memo asking that Massino, Vitale, and Mongelli not have bail was filled with all sorts of accusations, the issue was not to be argued on this particular afternoon. The defense attorneys agreed to their clients being held for the moment with the possibility that they could apply for bail—admittedly a remote possibility—at a later date.

Andres, Mari, and the other defense attorneys argued their positions about bail to Azrack in a courtroom where the dark wood paneled walls were lined with large oil portraits and photographs of past and present federal judges who had sat in the district. The earliest image was that of muttonchopped Charles Benedict, the first judge for the Eastern District appointed by President Abraham Lincoln in 1865, a month before he was killed by John Wilkes Booth. It was a room where many ghosts lurked. If his spiritual antenna were tuned, Joseph Massino would have sensed the maligned presence of one of those who had once preceded him in the courtroom. It was Philip Rastelli, the wizened mob politician who had once sat shaking with apprehension as he faced arraignment on his own racketeering charges in 1986.

"I didn't do nothing!" an ailing Rastelli once blurted out as he was bundled off into an ambulance after his court appearance. He recovered and went on to be convicted of racketeering.

Though he became a shadow of the powerful mobster he once was, Rastelli proved to be the bridge with the past. In the fractious interregnum between elder Mafia statesman Joseph Bonanno, for whom the family was named after, and the twenty-first century, it was Rastelli who helped provide stability and link the crime family's past to the future. That future, investigators said on January 9, 2003, was embodied in Joseph Massino, the one-time lunch wagon operator who Rastelli mentored and baptized with the blood of many fallen rivals.

If there was any one person who Massino could point to as the person tying him to the legacy of the Bonanno crime family and ensuring him his title as boss, it was Rastelli. Then, too, if he wanted to feel some self-pity as he waited for his arraignment to end, Massino could have looked to Rastelli as the root of his problems. For it was Rastelli who not only took Massino under his wing but also anointed him as an emissary of death, the conduit through which the orders for many a mob murder was passed. The mob polices itself through brute force—murder when necessary—and among the ghosts were those of many in the Mafia whose executions would come back to haunt Massino.

Massino wouldn't shake or cry out like Rastelli had once done, not even when Azrack denied him bail, which she would do eventually. After Azrack talked with the attorneys over scheduling and future court dates, Andres raised the issue of why he thought Mari couldn't stay on the case. The prosecutor's main concern was that Massino's attorney had a number of conflicts of interest. The Brooklyn federal prosecutor's office was painfully aware of how the existence of legal conflicts could hurt their cases. In 2000, an appeals court reversed one of the high-profile convictions of former police officer Charles Schwarz in the sodomy attack by police on Haitian immigrant Abner Louima because Schwarz's attorney at his first trial had an "unwaivable" conflict of interest. Since then, the Brooklyn U.S. Attorney's Office seemed to take great pains in raising potential conflicts with defense attorneys before cases progressed very far. Mari had his own special issues.

"I have discussed this with Mister Mari," Andres explained to Azrack. "He has a variety of conflicts, actual conflicts, with respect to his representation of Mister Massino. Among other things he represented at one time one of the murder victims in the indictment, Robert Perrino. He has represented other members and associates of the Bonanno crime family."

"Based on some published reports that I may have actually represented someone who could be a witness in this case," Mari interjected, "I have discussed that with Mister Massino and, uh, its his present intention to retain other counsel prior to, prior to the next court date."

The arraignment was essentially finished, but as had been seen in so many Mafia cases, particularly those with elderly or overweight defendants, medical issues always loomed. The Mafia was aging and court appearances were like medical consults. Before anyone was able leave the courtroom, Azrack acted like an assistant in a doctor's office.

After Azrack was told that Massino had diabetes, she had her courtroom clerk hand over some medication forms to the Bonanno boss's lawyer.

"Is it just for diabetes, just diabetes?" Azrack asked Massino.

"Sugar diabetes, that is it your honor," answered Massino, using an archaic term for his illness.

Vitale then piped up that he had a heart attack at age thirty-one and was on medication as well. So, for the next few minutes, Massino and Vitale filled out forms with their attorneys about the various medications they needed. Massino told Mari that he took Glucophage and Avandi, two medications that were used to control his type-2 diabetes. Overweight, a big eater, and living a sedentary life, Massino had been diabetic for years. Having been rousted from his home over eight hours earlier, Massino's medication schedule was all screwed up so he had Mari ask Azrack if he could take one of his pills. He was supposed to take Glucophage up to three times a day.

"Yes, he should take one now," said Azrack.

Mob bosses instill fear in many, but age also makes them prime candidates for the geriatric ward. Amid the whispers of the lawyers and the bustle of the courtroom crowd, the only other sound was the rattle of the Glucophage pills, sounding like candy Chiclets, as Massino dispensed his dosage from a plastic bottle.

CHAPTER 18

All in the Family

She just had to know.

The life Joseph Massino had lived for most of his forty-year marriage couldn't have been a secret to his wife, Josephine. There were just too many arrests, too much time spent away in prison, too many newspaper headlines, too many solicitous dropoffs of cash at the house by men who were deferential to him for Josephine to think that Joseph was any candidate for sainthood.

It would be easy to condemn wives like Josephine Massino for staying with a mafioso husband and not leaving him and renouncing his way of life. But she was a woman of many deeply seated loyalties, including the Sicilian quality of fealty to family and the Catholic tradition that marriage was to last no matter what. Her brother, Salvatore Vitale, had also become part of the Life, as the gangs lifestyle was called, and was another psychological involvement that complicated things. Then again, her husband had done pretty good in his lines of work, legal and illegal. He had provided.

So, on the morning of January 9, 2003, at the house on Eighty-fourth Street in Howard Beach, Josephine Massino told her daughters what they had come to expect and dread for many months. Their father was arrested. It was that simple. They could wait to see if by some long shot he would make bail that day. Of course, he wouldn't.

So Josephine Massino had to face things alone again. Counting Joseph Massino's time in prison and his years on the lam in Pennsylvania, his wife had been without a spouse in the house for about ten years. Some people, especially the wives of those killed in Bonanno family bloodbaths, could care less about her loneliness. At least she knew where her husband was. Some of the crime family victims were lying in unmarked graves, dissolved by lye, in places no one remembered.

Things promised to get worse for Massino's wife. The federal government had a potent tool with the racketeering law because it could not only prosecute mafiosi but also go after their assets. The theory behind the law of "forfeiture," as the government grab bag was called, was that criminals shouldn't be able to profit from their crimes. Usually, in big mob cases prosecutors would list assets of a defendant they believed were the wages of crimes and that a criminal had no right to keep. In Massino's case, the government wanted to seize not only the house he and Josephine had lived in for two decades but also his mother's house in Maspeth and several properties held in Josephine's name in Florida and New York, as well as her deceased parents' house in Queens.

Some of the buildings listed in the indictment were rental properties from which Josephine derived income. But prosecutors saw it as simply a way that Massino sheltered his assets, figuring that if he was prosecuted the government wouldn't be able to take property held in his wife's name. It didn't matter. Greg Andres was going after any Massino buildings the FBI could find.

For Joanne Massino, the indictment led not only to the jailing of her father but also of the man who had become a surrogate parent: uncle Sal Vitale. As in the case of her mother, the arrest for Joanne symbolized another episode of abandonment. It was compounded by the fact that Vitale, a man who had been a source of stability as she grew up as a teenager, was also gone now. Her older sister, Adeline, later said she was overwhelmed by the charges and simply couldn't believe them. She sometimes chuckled about her naiveté. How could her father be at all of those Mafia meetings like the newspapers said? He traveled everywhere with his wife and even brought his grandchildren along.

Joanne seemed wiser to ways of the Life. Joanne had been plugged into street talk in Howard Beach and knew that chubby Frank Coppa had turned into a government witness in late 2002. She even told her uncle, Sal Vitale, the news when she and her mother visited him while he was under house arrest for the Long Island case. It was the kind of news that made Josephine Massino and her daughters realize that it was just a matter of time before the FBI cars would prowl the neighborhood looking for Joseph Massino.

There was a ritual at the federal Metropolitan Detention Center in Brooklyn whenever a high-profile defendant was incarcerated. It was a parade of lawyers that was like a Sunset Park Mardi Gras. Massino, like New York's major crime boss, was a good client to have because his case would draw news coverage and he could pay his fees. What more could a defense attorney ask for?

As soon as Massino was brought into the jail facility, some of the big criminal defense attorneys trooped in to see him. It was basically an audition for lawyers, who told Massino why they might be the best person to handle his defense for the fees they required. The sessions were good for Massino because if nothing else they kept him out of his cell and allowed him to spend his time in the lawyer conference rooms having some human contact. If he was really lucky, the attorneys would have remembered to bring him candy and sweets from the jail house vending machines.

Attorney David Breitbart was a known quality to Joseph

Massino. For a short period of time before Massino's 1987 trial, Breitbart actually represented him until a scheduling problem forced Massino to hire Sam Dawson. A former high school teacher, Breitbart had carved out his own niche as a defense attorney known for his skill at cross-examination. He started defending drug cases in the 1970s and among his more infamous clients was Leroy "Nicky" Barnes, the king of Harlem heroin. Breitbart had won a number of mistrials for Barnes until the drug dealer was finally convicted in 1978 and sentenced to life in federal prison.

Breitbart's creed was that all witnesses can be vulnerable on cross-examination and it is a defense attorney's job to probe persistently to find the contradictions, inconsistencies, and embarrassing facts that would destroy the person's credibility as a prosecution witness. Breitbart was short in stature but he exuded a self-confidence and was not easily rattled, qualities that could infuriate his opponents in the backbiting world of criminal defense work. He was also something of a moody loner in the gossipy legal fraternity of the city.

Massino put out a call for Breitbart, who had actually put in a notice of appearance in the case. Once he got to the federal jail, however, Breitbart saw that a number of his legal brethren were on the list ahead of him to try to sign up the mob boss as a client.

"You know, I put in a notice of appearance in this case," Breitbart said to one of the other attorneys trying to entice Massino as a client.

"We will see about that," the lawyer responded.

In the end, Breitbart had a major advantage. He had already represented John Cerasani in the 1982 Bonanno racketeering trial. That was a case in which the murder of the three captains was charged as a conspiracy. As a result, Breitbart was familiar with a lot of the institutional history of the Bonanno crime family as it came out in that trial. He was also familiar with the testimony and witnesses, factors that just might play into Massino's trial. There was something else. Cerasani was the only defendant acquitted of all the charges at that trial. Massino put Breitbart on the case.

Things were rough for the Massino family with the arrests. But more shocking news was lined up like a freight train, ready to run over Joseph Massino, his wife, and daughters.

The day Massino was arrested, his wife heard from her doctor and discovered that she had uterine cancer. Surgery had to be performed. Terrific. There was no way Josephine Massino was going to tell her husband that, she recalled later. She wanted to keep as much of the bad news from him as she could. But there were other things that could never be kept quiet.

In the past two years, things had not been good between Diana and Salvatore Vitale. His house arrest on the 2001 indictment allowed Vitale to go to work, but he had to be home by 6:00 P.M. Vitale was allowed to take his wife out to dinner three nights a week. The probation officer just required Vitale to fax over the name of the restaurant. Still, the stress of home detention and the legal problems aggravated what was already a pressure-filled Vitale marriage. The couple had separated and there were all kinds of stories about Vitale's girlfriend. When her husband got arrested in the bank case in 2001, Diana complained that Massino's family didn't show any concern and never visited, a remark that prompted a visit by Adeline and her husband.

After the January 2003 arrest, Diana Vitale looked to Josephine Massino and her daughters for emotional support—and vice versa. Telephone calls became more frequent between the women. They now faced a common predicament with the two men in custody. At one point in late February, one of Vitale's sons called up Josephine to simply say he loved her. She was deeply touched.

A day later there was nothing.

Joanne Massino remembered making some calls to her aunt Diana's house on Long Island, and her messages got no response. It wasn't just the Massino family phone calls that weren't being returned. Other relatives and friends had tried as well. An elderly aunt quizzed her niece, Joanne.

"What is going on? I haven't heard from Diana," the aunt said.

On February 28, nearly two months after the Massino indictment, defense attorney John Mitchell checked his fax machine in his Manhattan law office. Mitchell, one of a cadre of well-known defense attorneys who specialized in organized crime cases, had been retained to represent Sal Vitale in the Bonanno case. Noticing a document in the receiving tray of the machine, Mitchell picked it up and read. The message said tersely that Vitale had a new lawyer, a fellow named Bradley Simon. The fax had actually come from Simon and he asked Mitchell to send over the Vitale case files and thanked him in advance for his cooperation.

Defendants switch lawyers all the time. But Simon was among a group of attorneys who sometimes represented clients who had decided to help law enforcement after being arrested. Some defense attorneys viewed the actions of such "cooperating attorneys," as one lawyer called them, as being unworthy of wearing the mantle of defense lawyer. But there was really nothing ethically wrong with the practice and defendants who went over to Team America, as the government was called, needed skilled legal help in negotiating deals and protecting their interests.

The fact the Vitale had Simon as a lawyer was a clear indication to Mitchell that his former client had decided to cooperate. This was the worst possible news for Massino because while Frank Coppa and Richard Cantarella, the other turncoats, didn't know everything Massino might have been done, Vitale had been an aide-de-camp to his brother-in-law. Vitale knew much of the institutional history of the Bonanno family and knew many more of Massino's dark secrets: the murders he played a role in and the illicit profits he raked in. Massino was definitely in trouble.

Mitchell made a call to Breitbart. The lawyer then told Massino, who made a jail house telephone call to tell Josephine.

Betrayal. Now the Massino case was more than just another mob whodunit. It was a story that Shakespeare would have loved.

Massino had been leery of his brother-in-law from the first hours they were locked up together and believed he might have become an informant as soon as he believed the metal handcuffs on his wrists. Both men had been taken to different federal jails: Massino to Brooklyn and Vitale to Manhattan.

"Where is my brother-in-law?" Massino asked the guards in the holding area. When he didn't see Vitale, he suspected he might have turned cooperator. At that point, Massino's suspicions had been premature, but not by much.

On Eighty-fourth Street in Howard Beach, the Massino women felt the traitorous action of Vitale deeply.

"It was like a building coming down on my head," Josephine Massino recalled later.

The relationship Josephine had developed with her brother since childhood was one that intensified the emotions she felt with his decision to turn on her husband. Within her Sicilian immigrant family, it had fallen on Josephine to raise Vitale since her parents were constantly working to provide for all four siblings. It was natural then for their relationship to be special and for Josephine to be protective of Salvatore. In her study of brother and sister relationships, author Francine Klagsbrun states that older sisters always manage to be protective and caring of their younger brothers. In an Italian family with only Salvatore to carry on the family name, the need for his sisters to protect him and in the process spoil him must have been a task implicitly communicated to them by their parents.

So by turning on Massino, Vitale was turning on his closest sister, the one person in the family with whom he had developed a special bond of caring and trust. The severing of that bond, on top of the financial and legal jeopardy it created for Josephine, made her brother's decision to turn on Massino all the more traumatic.

Joanne Massino didn't have those deep familial ties to Vitale. But her uncle had nonetheless played a special role in her life. He had become a second father. She had been a freshman in high school when her father went on the lam and Vitale played the role of surrogate father. When Joanne was ready for her Sweet Sixteen party, it was Vitale who made the arrangements for a catering hall and danced with his niece to the sounds of the syrupy Luther Vandross song "Always and Forever." The teenaged Joanne was so taken with the way Vitale stepped up for her that whenever the song played on the radio, she would call him to say which station he should tune to. They even had a special beeper code—"143"—which meant "I love you."

But now the sweetness was gone, and replaced by venom. Learning of Vitale's decision to turn against her father, Joanne cursed her uncle. Rushing through her home in Howard Beach, she opened drawers and photo albums to gather up as many pictures of Vitale as she could find. First communion pictures, weddings, the Sweet Sixteen party, Thanksgiving, Christmas—she ripped them to shreds and then dumped them in the trash. She kept one photo of Vitale's four sons and one day was poised to get rid of it as well. Her mother was reluctant to have it discarded. No, Josephine said with a wistful look as she held the picture in her hand. Don't discard it, she implored her daughter. In the end, Josephine took it home. It was likely to be one of the only images she would ever retain of her nephews being together.

Adeline Massino didn't have the same kind of close connection to her uncle Sal as her sister. Adeline was about twenty years old and seriously dating when her father went on the lam, so she likely didn't have the same kind of emotional need for a father figure as her sister. A psychology major in her college days, Adeline had become increasingly uncomfortable with her uncle Sal. There was something she didn't trust about him. He seemed too full of himself. His preening, his vanity, his fixation on being a boss man, turned her against him. But even if she only had vague knowledge and suspicion about her father's life, Adeline Massino knew that her uncle's decision to testify was trouble.

Actually, Vitale's decision to turn was a no-brainer for him. He had resented Massino for years, since the mid-1990s. His brother-in-law may have given him the title of underboss, but he assigned him no captains and kept him on a short leash. Vitale felt emasculated. He had always been the big boy in his own family, growing up in an Italian household with three doting sisters who spoiled him rotten and made him the center of attention. With Massino he was disrespected and belittled. What was worse was that the deprecation came at the hand of a man who had married his sister.

Vitale was unable to even get Christmas gifts from the family captains. In mob parlance, he had been put "on the shelf." Of course, Massino had his reasons. Vitale wasn't liked by the other Bonanno family members and his brother-in-law told him that. Some wondered out loud that the only thing keeping Vitale alive was the fact that he was related to Massino by marriage.

The isolation he felt in 2001 from Josephine and her daughters was something Vitale blamed on Massino. Those who study brother-sister relationships say the bonds that develop can sometimes lead to powerful undercurrents where the spouse of one sibling may be viewed as an adversary by the other sibling. This kind of resentment just might have been at the core of the hatred Vitale developed for Massino. But if it was, Vitale never acknowledged it.

Proffers agreements are known as "Queen for a Day" letters, a reference to the 1950s television show where ordinary housewives were lavished with gifts and attention for one day in their life. In Vitale's case, he spent over a week proffering to prosecutor Andres, telling him what he knew about Massino, the Bonanno crime family, and the various murders. Cesare Bonventre, Alphonse Indelicato, Dominick Trinchera, Philip Giaccone, and Gabriel Infanti—they were victims Vitale put squarely around Massino's neck in the early days of March 2003.

Jeffrey Sallet and Kimberly McCaffrey, as well as fellow agents Nora Conley and James McGoey, sat mesmerized as Vitale told them stories of how the Bonanno crime family worked. This was the real deal, the history of the crime family fleshed out by someone who had lived through a good part of it. He talked about Massino's loan-sharking, gambling, and arsons. Vitale also talked about his own crimes, which included the murders everybody in law enforcement thought Massino played a hand in but could never prove. It was nice to have somebody like Vitale fill in the details of the mob hits. But suddenly that caused an unexpected problem.

On March 7, 2003, as he was being debriefed by the FBI agents, Vitale started to tell them about the slaughter in the Bronx of Gerlando Sciascia. The agents clammed up and suddenly closed their notebooks. That killing was a potential death penalty murder they told Vitale. They couldn't talk to him about it unless the Department of Justice agreed to exclude Vitale from the death penalty as an option. Seeing the wisdom of keeping a key witness in the fold, Washington agreed to cut Vitale out of the death penalty calculation.

Free of the embargo caused by the death penalty concerns, Vitale continued to talk to the agents. He did so for a good part of the next year. Some of the information amounted to mob gossip, such as how reputed mob associate Sandro Aiosa had a reputation for being a "liar and a cheat." He told the agents who was up and who was down in the Bonanno family, gave the agents lists of names of members in all the crime families, and even provided the names of deceased gangsters to fill in gaps in the FBI crime family lists. Did anybody realize that the Mafia had a prohibition about performing oral sex on a woman and then talking about it? According to Vitale, one Bonanno associate who had been proposed for membership was scratched from consideration because he had been overheard discussing cunnilingus. Another, John Arcaro, was inducted as a courtesy before his death in April 2001, according to Vitale.

Under Mafia rules, the five families could induct new members to replace those who had passed away. It was a way of keeping the status quo. But according to Vitale, he played a little scam. On a few occasions he made up the names of deceased Bonanno soldiers to pad the membership roles and allow the family to induct more members than the rules allowed.

At least once Massino played the role of marriage broker, Vitale said, approving the nuptials of one Bonanno soldier to a woman who was once engaged to a Lucchese soldier. It seemed the Lucchese crime family didn't want the wedding to go off. But Massino said it could, according to Vitale.

But it was with more substantial stuff that Vitale enthralled the agents, stories of big Mafia meetings where legendary mob bosses sat down with him and Massino. Around 2000 a lot of those meetings involved what La Cosa Nostra was going to do about the wayward and dissolute Colombo crime family. The family had been riddled with turncoats and informants, as well as bloodied by continuous warfare. The mob bosses considered a number of moves, some of them drastic. Some called for dissolving the Colombo group and dividing up the members among the other Mafia families. It was a plan that was rejected, Vitale said, because the other families wouldn't want to take on men they didn't know.

Another plan, not much different than the first, was to put all the Colombo family member names in a hat and have the four other crime families draw the names they would take into their family, he said. Some even considered not recognizing the Colombo group at all but thought doing so would show too much disrespect for Carmine Persico, the old family boss who was serving a life sentence, said Vitale.

These meetings sometimes got to be catty and backbiting affairs. One time Peter Gotti, who was the acting boss of the Gambino crime family, was asked why his imprisoned brother John didn't step down as head of that family. Peter Gotti, obviously angry, responded by asking why didn't Vincent "the Chin" Gigante, who was also in prison, step down as boss of the Genovese family, said Vitale. The response from another Genovese member at the meeting was that Gigante would be getting out of prison one day—something that wouldn't be happening for John Gotti.

Vitale also told the agents some intriguing bits. He said that at one point he and Massino had chatted in Howard Beach with Gotti's son, known as John Jr. The subject of the conversation was Thomas Uva, who with his wife, Rosemary, were believed to be burglarizing mob social clubs all over the city. A lot of mobsters wanted the Uvas dead and the Mafia families put an "open contract" out on them, meaning anyone could collect on it. The younger Gotti remarked "we took care of it" when the couple was discussed, said Vitale. Thomas and Rosemary Uva were shot dead on a Queens street on Christmas Eve 1992. For years, investigators suspected Junior Gotti might have played some role, but he was never charged, and he always denied any involvement.

The bad state of affairs of the mob was often on the agenda at such meetings. Vitale said that at one sitdown session with Peter Gotti, acting Colombo boss Vincent Aloi, and reputed Genovese captain Barney Bellomo, he asked for permission to induct fifteen new members into the Bonanno family. In response, Nicholas "Little Nicky" Corozzo of the Gambino family asked "Where are you going to find fifteen new members?" Peter Gotti jumped in and said that it was not the time to make new members because of the continuing pressure of law enforcement.

As fascinating as such inside talk about the Mafia was, Vitale's real value to the FBI agents listening to him was the hard details he had about the murders. In the murder of the three captains on May 5, 1981, Massino just wasn't involved in the planning of the hit, he was actually present the moment the slaughter took place, Vitale told the agents. In the pandemonium that occurred during the shooting, Vitale said he didn't get a chance to fire his gun and saw a terrified Frank Lino flee through a door he had been assigned to guard. Vitale said he stayed around to clean up the bodies with Dominick "Sonny Black" Napolitano and others, placing the corpses in drop clothes and then following a van that drove the gruesome cargo to Howard Beach.

Vitale's information about the three captains was dynamite for the prosecution. It was the first direct evidence of an eye witness and participant to implicate Massino in the planning and execution of the slayings. Previously, the evidence was indirect and circumstantial. Even taped remarks that Massino had screwed up in disposing of the bodies had not been enough to win a conviction, as the 1987 trial showed.

Sonny Black Napolitano's murder was also laid at the feet of Massino by Vitale. After it became known in July 1981 that undercover agent Joseph Pistone had penetrated the Bonanno family, an angry Massino, walking with Vitale in Howard Beach, said that if he had to go to jail because of Pistone, it would be Napolitano who would get a "receipt," meaning be killed. Vitale told the agents that after picking up a stolen van one day from Duane Leisenheimer, he drove Massino and Steven Cannone to a house in Staten Island. It was during the drive, said Vitale, that Massino said that Napolitano was going to be killed that very night. The three men waited in the van outside the Staten Island house until a man, who Vitale identified as Bobby Lino Sr., came out and said, "It was all done."

Throughout March 2003, Vitale told the FBI agents about both his and Massino's involvement in a total of ten murders: Alphonse Indelicato, Dominick Trinchera, Philip Giaccone, Dominick Napolitano, Anthony Mirra, Cesare Bonventre, Gerlando Sciascia, Gabriel Infante, Joseph Pastore, and Vito Borelli. He also tied Massino into a conspiracy to murder union official Anthony Giliberti. Vitale confessed to playing a role in conspiracies to murder two other men and involvement in two actual murders that didn't involve Massino.

As a mobster, Vitale had done a lot of work. Now he was doing it for the FBI. Vitale told special Agents Sallet, McCaffrey, Conley, and McGoey about his life of crime, implicating Massino and a lot of other Bonanno brethren in crimes that ranged over two decades. There were even times he talked about his sister, Josephine. Had he not insisted in his negotiations with prosecutors that nothing he told them could be ever used against her, she might have found herself in trouble as well. Vitale told the FBI that while Massino was incarcerated he visited his sister and turned over cash to her that represented her husband's share of loan-sharking and gambling profits.

After Vitale decided to cooperate, there was a stampede of other Bonanno members to sign on to the prosecution's team. Frank Lino, who had been arrested with Massino in January, felt vulnerable. It had been Vitale, while he was part of the ruling committee of the family, who had Lino carry out some homicides.

"When he cooperated, there was no way I was going to win anymore," Lino said later. "He was giving all the orders to do all the killings when he was there."

So after nearly three months in jail—most of it in solitary confinement—Lino decided he wanted to cooperate. On April 4, 2003, a little over a month after word had leaked out about Vitale's turncoat status, Lino told Andres he wanted to make a deal.

But even before Vitale and Lino there was "Big Louie."

The tall, gangly Big Louie was really James Tartaglione, a mobster who had earned his stripes in the 1980s. His thick glasses and bony face made him look like a high school under-achiever who didn't have the mind or inclination to do much in life but work in a grocery store. But Tartaglione was well liked by Massino and had done his own pieces of work for the Bonanno family.

Yet, there came a point in Tartaglione's life when he tired of the mob. He had been convicted earlier in the decade and decided to spend his time in Florida. Massino had been troubled by too many Bonanno members taking a break and moving out of state. He tried to pull Tartaglione back but the newly minted Floridian resisted. He had a great life in the Sunshine State and wanted to retire there, spend time with his family, and peacefully watch the sun set.

The indictments in New York had Tartaglione worried. It was just a matter of time before other informants began placing him at the scene of murders. Tartaglione had been outside the door of the Brooklyn social club when the three captains were slain in May 1981. In 1984, Vitale had asked him to help out in the murder of Cesare Bonventre. It was Tartaglione who pulled a squirming, mortally wounded Bonventre out of the car in a garage. Tartaglione had been involved in loan-sharking, arson, and gambling. He had some baggage to be concerned about.

Still on probation for his earlier federal conviction, Tartaglione had always remembered the woman prosecutor in Brooklyn who he came to respect. She was younger than he was, but like him her graying hair showed her seasoning. When his daughter thought she had breast cancer, the woman had passed along to Tartaglione the name of a med-ical specialist who could help. (No cancer was detected.) The prosecutor was Ruth Nordenbrook, and through his Florida probation officer Tartaglione reached out to her shortly after Massino had been indicted.

Some of Nordenbrook's associates in the Brooklyn U.S.

Attorney's Office had figured that her patient manner and bonding with Tartaglione, even though she had prosecuted him, would somehow pay off.

"He thought I dealt with him fairly," Nordenbrook later recalled.

One incident in particular solidified Tartaglione's respect for the middle-aged prosecutor. Tartaglione was due in court one day on the federal case Nordenbrook had brought. But when his daughter collapsed in the doctor's office, Tartaglione naturally missed his court date. Normally, when a defendant who is out on bail doesn't show up in court, it could be grounds for a contempt citation and a charge of bail jumping. But Nordenbrook didn't insist on any such action and for that Tartaglione was grateful.

So, despite some resistance from at least one FBI supervisor, Nordenbrook flew to Florida with fellow prosecutor Greg Andres and convinced Tartaglione to sign a cooperation agreement.

The odd thing about Tartaglione's decision was that he didn't wait for an indictment to make his decision. True, he might have eventually been charged based on what the other turncoats said. But since he was free and living outside a jail cell, Tartaglione was the one cooperator who could circulate freely among his criminal confederates.

The FBI immediately saw the usefulness of Tartaglione's freedom and convinced him to begin wearing a wire as he met with key Bonanno crime family members and others. Now, not only did the federal government have witnesses like Vitale, Coppa, and Lino, they actually had a made member of the crime family making tapes. It was another coup for the government that had exceeded anyone's expectations.

From January 2003 until January 2004, Tartaglione taped over forty-five conversations with Bonanno captains Vincent Basciano, Anthony Urso, the crime family's acting boss while Massino was in custody, Joseph Cammarano, acting underboss, and others. Federal prosecutors have released only small portions of the recordings, but they reveal that many of those conversing with Tartaglione talked openly about the way the Bonanno family was trying to adjust to the pressure from the arrests and prosecutions.

It was during this chaotic period that Cammarano was recorded telling Tartaglione to move back from Florida "to show strength." Meetings of the Bonanno family administration found mobsters talking about trying to locate the families of turncoats and to induct new members to build up strength. Since legal troubles were causing Massino big legal bills, the crime family decreed what prosecutors called a monthly "tax" of $100 for each member to pay into a war chest.

In one snippet of a recording of a September 2003 crime family meeting that was widely circulated in court documents, Urso was heard speaking about killing the families of turncoats.

"This has got to stop," said Urso. "Fuck it, he can do it, I can do it. This is how they should have played, and they might have done this before you turned, we wipe your family out."

"Why should the rats' kids be happy, where my kids or your kids should suffer because I'm away for life. If you take one kid, I hate to say it, and do what you gotta do, they'll fucking think twice," said Urso.

Cammarano cautioned Urso, court records show, that such a bloody strategy of retribution would only bring on more law enforcement pressure. It might also reflect poorly on Massino, added Cammarano.

What Tartaglione was thinking when he heard Urso's rant about the family of informants, all the while he was secretly recording him, was never disclosed. But his recordings, as well as the evidence given by Vitale, Coppa, Lino, and other turncoats, gave the FBI a field day. In May 2003, a federal grand jury in Brooklyn indicted Massino on more murder charges, accusing him of killing Anthony Mirra for the

Joseph Pistone–FBI infiltration of the Bonanno family. Frank Lino, who was already talking to prosecutors, was indicted for the 1990 murder of Louis Tuzzio, the man killed as a favor to John Gotti.

A glowing news release from the Brooklyn U.S. Attorney's Office stated the latest tally: "To date, both the Bonanno family boss and under have been charged, as well as six captains, two acting captains, eight soldiers and twelve associates. With the 2001 conviction of Bonanno family consiglieri Anthony Spero, all three members of the Bonanno family administration have now been charged with, or convicted of, murder, and all potentially face life imprisonment."

Because of concerns about the families of turncoat mobsters like Vitale, Tartaglione, and the others, federal prosecutors resorted to courthouse cloak-and-dagger operations. It was unwise, investigators reasoned, for guilty pleas of cooperators like Vitale to be taken in the downtown Brooklyn federal courthouse. Secret guilty pleas, with courtrooms sealed off and spectators not allowed, happened all the time. But the Bonanno investigation was fraught with too many perils. Officials feared that if word leaked out that a particular person was pleading guilty with a cooperation agreement, the individual's family members might be in peril. Comments of the kind Urso made to Tartaglione only reinforced those fears.

So, on particular days when a Bonanno turncoat was pleading guilty, Judge Nicholas Garaufis, who had been picked by random selection to handle the cases involving the crime family, disappeared from his chambers on Cadman Plaza East in Brooklyn. Garaufis had been active in Queens County politics and had once served as counsel to Borough President Claire Shulman, the woman who replaced the corruption-tainted Donald Manes, who committed suicide in early 1986 during the city Parking Violations Bureau scandal. After stints as a private lawyer in Bayside and as an assistant attorney general in New York state, Garaufis went on to become counsel to the Federal Aviation Administration. He was nominated to be a federal judge in 2000 by President Bill Clinton. An affable man of Greek ethnicity, Garaufis was press savvy and prided himself on open courtrooms. But sometimes necessity required secrecy.

On certain days, Garaufis would walk over to the nearby Marriott Hotel on Adams Street. There, he would go to a suite that had been booked by federal prosecutors and on entering he would find FBI agents, a court stenographer, and various assistant U.S. attorneys. Also in the room was a defendant who had decided to cooperate with the government and his attorney. Garaufis would preside in the room as the cooperator pled guilty to various crimes and admitted that he had signed an agreement to testify at any trial. For added security, Garaufis sometimes drove to one of a number of hotels near LaGuardia Airport in his home borough of Queens, where other cooperators were taken to enter their guilty pleas.

Despite these precautions, word of who had decided to cooperate leaked out anyway. By then, there had been more indictments. August 20, 2003, saw another news release revealing that Massino was charged with three more homicides: the killing of Cesare Bonventre in 1984, of Gabriel Infante in 1987, and of Gerlando Sciascia, whose death in 1999 had piqued the interest of FBI Director Louis Freeh.

Some new defendants were also added to the ever growing list of Bonanno family members under arrest. Two reputed Bronx members of the family, captain Patrick "Patty from the Bronx" DeFilippo and soldier John Joseph Spirito, were charged with taking part in the Sciascia killing while Massino was vacationing in Mexico with Josephine. (That kind of detail was something Vitale knew and apparently was a key source of what was alleged in the indictment.) It was Spirito, a tough guy with the thick, bony face of a prize fighter, who was accused of picking up the ill-fated Sciascia and then dumping his body in a Bronx street to make it look like the Canadian gangster was killed by drug dealers.

Defendants awaiting trial without bail often hold joint defense meetings in jail. After the Sciascia indictment, Massino, Spirito, DeFilippo, and other defendants held joint defense meetings at the Brooklyn federal detention center to plot strategy with their lawyers. Massino sat at the head of the table in the jail conference room, a posture that seemed to say he was in charge. He usually had two sandwiches brought in from the vending machines, and if he didn't think the cheese was warm enough he had one of his underlings microwave it again.

Murray Richman, a well-known criminal defense from the Bronx, was representing Spirito and made it clear to any one who was present that he didn't like these jail house meetings. Richman had a simple rule that one out of four people would turn informant, ruining the defense strategizing. Massino thought differently.

"Not my guys," said Massino, referring to Spirito and De-Filippo.

But Massino was ignoring the obvious. Turncoats had already occurred in his ranks—Coppa, Vitale, Lino, and Tartaglione had already become cooperating witnesses. They had put Massino in a bind for five homicides. There was also something else for him to worry about.

FEDS MULL WHACKING MOBSTER, said the *Daily News* headline for a 388-word story on page nine in its August 21, 2003, edition. The item said that for the Sciascia murder, Massino, DeFilippo, and Spirito could face the death penalty. "If U.S. Attorney General John Ashcroft authorizes Brooklyn prosecutors to seek capital punishment, it would mark the first time an alleged boss of a New York crime family faced possible execution by the government," the story by reporter John Marzulli stated.

On Eighty-fourth Street in Howard Beach, Joanne Massino was sleeping late. Since her divorce, she hadn't worked much, but in the summer months she had a full-time job of sorts figuring out things to do with her son and daughter. The children would write to their grandfather at the Brooklyn federal jail but really didn't know the full import of what had been happening. Their mother kept the worst of the news from them.

Up the stairs of Joanne's two-story modern home, built on land she had been given by her mother, came her ten-year-old daughter. The child was going to treat her mom to breakfast in bed and the morning newspaper, which was rolled up and held fast with a rubber band. Joanne thanked her daughter and still in bed opened up the paper. The item on page nine gave her a start. She was puzzled by what she read. New indictment? Death penalty? Joanne hadn't heard of the new charges. But the words "death penalty" caused her further incomprehension.

"With five made members of the Bonanno crime family now cooperating with the feds—including underboss Sal Vitale—the hits keep on coming for Massino," Marzulli noted.

Seeing her uncle's name and reading it in the same story about the prospect of her father being executed, all thanks to Sal Vitale, sparked another rage in Joanne. Then she cried hysterically.

CHAPTER 19

"Let's Bring In the Jury"

The charges against the Bonanno crime family kept coming.

On January 20, 2004, just a year after Massino had been charged, a Brooklyn federal grand jury returned another set of indictments as a result of evidence provided by turncoats Salvatore Vitale, James Tartaglione, Frank Lino, and Frank Coppa. This time, the government was aiming at cleaning house in a big way.

Among those charged in this indictment were Anthony Urso and Joseph Cammarano, the two men who had been taped by Tartaglione musing about executing the families of turncoats. Urso was identified as the acting Bonanno boss now that Massino was incarcerated, while Cammarano was his underboss since Vitale was out of the picture.

Cutting its way through the Bonanno hierarchy, the grand jury also indicted over two dozen other members and associates. The catch was impressive. Charged with various acts of racketeering were such illustrious names as Vito Rizzuto, the Canadian soldier suspected of being one of the assassins who jumped out of the closet during the murder of the three captains in 1981. Other key captains charged were Louis Attanasio, a suspect in the 1984 slaying of Cesare Bonventre and restaurant owner Louis Restivo on charges he played a role in the killings of Gabriel Infanti and crime family associate Anthony Tomasulo.

All together, eight captains or acting captains, thirteen soldiers, and four associates of the crime family were charged. The consequences for the Bonanno family were ominous.

"Since March 2002, the government has prosecuted more than 70 members and associates of the Bonanno family," crowed the government news release. "Today, virtually the entire family leadership of the Bonanno family has been incapacitated, with only a few family captains remaining unindicted."

From one of the most insulated crime families that Joseph Massino boasted had never had a major turncoat, the Bonanno family had seen six of its made members, including the underboss, agree to cooperate with the prosecution. Massino had once decreed that the family name should be changed from Bonanno to Massino because the old patriarch, Joseph Bonanno, had disgraced his legacy by writing a book that exposed some La Cosa Nostra secrets. Bonanno died in 2002. But had he seen the way "This Thing of Ours" had become tattered, he might have sued Massino for sullying his old family name.

The indictment cut like a scythe through the Bonanno family and there was a rush of people to take guilty pleas and hope for a break on sentencing. Vitale, Lino, and the other turncoats had made their deals with the government. So did Daniel Mongello, one of the other soldiers nabbed in the January 2003 roundup. So many gangsters worked out guilty pleas that by May 2004 there was only one person left standing who was going to go to trial: Joseph Massino.

× × ×

The trial of Joseph Massino was preceded by nearly a month of jury selection. Normally, it takes about a day or two to select a jury to hear a run-of-the-mill criminal case in

Brooklyn federal district court. But in big cases, particularly where there are allegations of organized crime, the whole process takes much longer. Massino's trial was no exception. To weed out bias or people who couldn't fairly decide the fate of the defendant, potential jurors had to answer detailed questionnaires about everything from their reading habits to whether they or family members had ever been victims of a crime. After the questionnaires were perused by prosecutors and defense attorneys, the people in the jury pool were called into court and individually questioned about some of the answers they had given. Depending on what was said by the potential jurors, they were either dismissed from further consideration or told to stand by.

Mafia cases in the Brooklyn federal court also invariably use anonymous juries. The practice of using such panels had come into vogue during the big mob trials of the 1970s and 1980s, when courts feared that Cosa Nostra defendants might try to bribe, influence, or intimidate juries. There was good reason to believe that could happen since John Gotti's minions were found to have done it twice, once during his 1986 trial in Brooklyn and another time in 1990, when he was on trial in Manhattan on state charges. Both times he was acquitted.

So, in Massino's case the approximately 200 potential jurors who trooped into the Cadman Plaza courthouse in early May 2004 had already been given numerical designations to use on their jury questionnaires. Their identities were known by only a small group of court personnel, even though there was no indication that Massino was thinking about trying to meddle with the jurors.

The questioning revealed some who had obvious bias against Massino, like the man who said he thought the Howard Beach gangster looked like Tony Soprano, the lead character played by actor James Gandolfini in *The Sopranos* show on HBO. Another man said he didn't think loan-sharking was a crime since borrowers in the Hispanic community, where usury was common, knew that high interest rates went with such loans.

On May 19, 2004, after three weeks of questioning, the prosecutors and defense attorneys officially agreed on a panel of twelve regular jurors—four men and eight women—and eight alternates to sit in judgment of Massino. The trial was scheduled to open on May 24, 2004.

Criminal cases have their special rhythm. After an arrest and not guilty plea, the defense has to work out a strategy to beat the case or else fold up and plea bargain, hoping for a break. In Massino's case, a plea was out of the question. As the man who was heir to a Mafia tradition of leadership laid down by patriarch Joseph Bonanno, Massino had always sung the praise of the crime family that never had a made member turn informant. Besides, he denied to his family, lawyers, and anyone else who listened that he had anything to do with the murders the government was trying to pin on him.

Before jury selection even began, David Breitbart's strategy was to first chip away at the indictment. He believed history and the law were on his side. Massino had already been charged before with complicity in the May 5, 1981, murders of the three captains—Dominick Trinchera, Philip Giacone, and Alphonse Indelicato. In 1987, a federal jury in Manhattan had found him not guilty of conspiring to kill the three men. To a layman, it sounded like Massino had been cleared of the murders. Well, not exactly.

In the 1987 trial, the charge involving the murder of the three captains was a murder conspiracy charge that was believed to be one of a number of racketeering acts committed by Massino. He was not charged with actually committing the murders but with agreeing and plotting to carry out the crime. Under U.S. Supreme Court rulings dating back to 1932, the government was not prevented from bringing new murder charges against Massino because a substantive crime and a conspiracy to commit the crime weren't the same offense. In other words, there would be no double jeopardy under the Fifth Amendment of the U.S. Constitution. It was Breitbart's job to find a way around that rule of law.

Breitbart was assisted in trial preparation by Flora Edwards, a former official at the City University of New York who gravitated into criminal law. Edwards liked legal research and writing and took pride in the nickname "Princess of Paper" because of the facility she had with the written word. Together, Edwards and Breitbart fashioned an argument that held that Massino's 1987 acquittal prevented the government from now retrying certain issues decided by the jury in the earlier trial.

A key to the defense argument was that in acquitting Massino in 1987, the jury decided that he didn't intend to kill Trinchera, Giaccone, and Indelicato, something the federal government was now attempting to try him for again in 2004. The prosecution's response was that the 1987 jury could have acquitted Massino of the murder conspiracy on the grounds that the government failed to prove that he joined the plot, than that the prosecution failed to prove he had the intent to kill the three men.

It all sounded like a great deal of legal hair splitting. But if the earlier verdict was based on a lack of evidence of a conspiratorial agreement instead of on an intent to kill the three captains, then the government was within its right to bring the latest charges to trial. To decide that issue, Judge Nicholas Garaufis had to read the mind of the earlier jurors and Judge Robert Sweet based on the old trial record. After reading the transcripts, Judge Robert W. Sweet's jury instructions, and the 1987 verdict sheet, Garaufis agreed with the prosecutors, and in a ruling dated March 24, 2004, he told the lawyers why.

"The question for the court to decide, therefore, after examining the 'pleadings, evidence, charge and other relevant matter,' is whether Massino has carried his burden of proving that the 1987 jury 'necessarily' decided that Massino did not intend to cause the deaths of Indelicato, Giaccone, and Trinchera," Garaufis stated. "After conducting such an examination, I conclude that the 1987 jury did not necessarily make such a finding."

Garaufis went on to say that "I conclude that a rational jury in 1987 could have based its acquittal on the government's failing to prove beyond a reasonable doubt that Massino entered into an agreement to murder Indelicato, Giaccone, and Trinchera."

Massino's attempt to whittle down three homicide charges in the indictment had failed. He also faced another problem. Though seven homicides were charged in the indictment, Greg Andres wanted to bring out during the trial other killings and murder conspiracies from the early 1970s through 1999 that the government believed Massino played a role in, as well as acts of loan-sharking, extortion, theft, hijacking, arson, and illegal gambling. Andres even believed that the accusation of Massino shoplifting a bottle of aspirin while on the lam in Pennsylvania was a prior bad act that the current jury should be aware of. The reason for bringing out such evidence, Andres argued, was to give background to the racketeering conspiracy for which Massino was standing trial.

There were seven uncharged murders and murder plots Andres believed he could bring out during Massino's trial. The murders the government wanted to incorporate in the trial, despite the fact that they weren't charged in the trial indictment, included the killing of Vito Borelli, Joseph Pastore, Carmine Galante, Gerlando Sciascia, Robert Capasio, and Joseph Platia. The latter two homicides occurred around July 1984 and were ordered by Massino while he was out on bail after returning from his time as a fugitive, Andres told the court. Andres also said that Massino had a hand in the plot to kill Bruno Indelicato, the son of one of the murdered three captains, Alphonse Indelicato.

Breitbart and Edwards said that the admission of such evidence of uncharged crimes was highly prejudicial to

Massino and in the case of the shoplifted aspirin was irrele-
vant. Garaufis largely disagreed. On May 21, 2004, the Friday before Massino's trial was scheduled to start, Garaufis
said he would allow Andres and the prosecution team to use
evidence of a number of the killings, including the slaying of
Galante, to show not only the level of trust he had in his
turncoat brother-in-law Salvatore Vitale but also to show the
dimensions of the Bonanno racketeering enterprise. But Garaufis ruled that evidence of the killing of Vito Borelli, murdered because he insulted Paul Castellano with the "Frank
Perdue" quip, had no place in the trial. That murder, Garaufis said, just didn't seem connected to the Bonanno enterprise which Massino was accused of running. The aspirin
shoplifting incident also had nothing to do with the racketeering case and was also out, said Garaufis.

Josephine Massino and her daughter, Adeline, happened
to be in court while Garaufis was reading his decision on the
evidence about the uncharged crimes. The meaning was
plain to them, although the legal reasoning that allowed the
government to use so much bad evidence certainly wasn't.
Massino shot a glance over to his wife that said it all. It had
been a bad day.

New York's major tabloid newspapers make it a habit of
running major stories, dubbed "curtain raisers" on the weekend before big trials. On Sunday, May 23, 2004, all the city's
dailies ran big stories about the Massino trial that was opening the next day. The articles varied in length with *Newsday*
doing the longest. Short sidebars were also done about the
defense attorneys and prosecution team. The stories had the
same general tone: Joseph Massino, the last big Mafia boss,
was on trial for being a murderous leader, and some of his
closest friends were going to testify against him. Life in
prison was the only thing in his future.

That Sunday morning at her Howard Beach home,
Josephine Massino opened up a copy of *New York Newsday*.
The front page jolted her. There in the center of the page was

a color picture of her husband, somber-faced, his hair neatly combed, and wearing the black pullover he was arrested in on January 9, 2003. It was his arrest photo and arrayed around it on the page were pictures of four other Mafia bosses of the past: Carlo Gambino, Paul Castellano, John Gotti, and Joseph Bonanno. THE LAST DON: MASSINO TRIAL SAID TO BEGIN THE END OF AN ERA FOR ORGANIZED CRIME BOSSES, the headline said.

None of the other tabloids had placed the Massino story on the front page with such prominence. But each paper had something. Suddenly, seeing the story like that, underscored for Josephine Massino that the trial was starting and that it was indeed show time. She spoke with her daughters and decided to do something she never expected to do. Josephine Massino wanted to talk to the news media. So did Adeline and Joanne. The crush of stories had overwhelmed them. Seeing it all splayed in the papers made them finally want to speak out to show the world that Joseph Massino was not a monster.

The Massino women had been very guarded with the press during jury selection, but would occasionally engage in small talk with me during courtroom breaks. That Sunday, digging out my business card, Joanne Massino called me and said her mother urgently wanted to talk. Detouring from a trip to Shea Stadium where the New York Mets were playing the Atlanta Braves, I wound up in Howard Beach, hoping that none of the women would change their minds.

For over two hours Josephine Massino and her daughters talked about Joseph Massino and what the betrayal of Salvatore Vitale had meant to them personally. They were circumspect to be sure and didn't want to talk about any of the allegations at the center of the trial that was opening the next day. They also didn't want to answer some questions about the merits of the case or things like whether Josephine knew where her husband had been in the years he was on the lam. Though emotionally vulnerable and unsure of what to say,

Josephine Massino and her daughters tried to paint a picture of Joseph Massino that portrayed him as an average Archie Bunker kind of guy with a big heart. They said he was a man who doted on his four grandchildren.

"Forget me and my sister—his grandchildren [mean] everything to him, everything to him, and that is the truth, and anybody will tell you that," said Joanne.

Adeline pulled out a cache of letters Massino had written on average about twice a week to his grandchildren while in jail. Not a literate writer, Massino tried to hold out hope for the grandchildren that he would see them again, ending one note to a granddaughter who shared his liking for food with the closing comment "until we eat again."

The women recounted some of Massino's acts of kindness, such as his donation of juice, coffee, and baked goods for one of his granddaughter's grade school graduations or the way he paid the funeral expenses for the burial of a brother-in-law whose family was cash strapped. The Massino women were true believers in his goodness, something that seemed to blind them to the ugliness of the charges and the mounting evidence against him.

As expected, the women excoriated Vitale, portraying him as a vain, unloving, and selfish man. His actions in turning on Massino were the ultimate in betrayal, actions they believed were motivated by a deep-seated jealousy Vitale had for the close relationship his sister's family had.

"He was a dirt bag," Joanne said.

The morning after the interview was May 24, 2004, and the media hordes had descended on the Brooklyn federal court and set up camp in Cadman Plaza. The park space had a large grass playing field that was fringed by tall trees. The massive gray stone Brooklyn War Memorial, which is big enough to contain rooms, loomed over the plaza. Television news crews and still photographers parked their vehicles along the park's walkway. The park was the best location to photograph attorneys, defendants, and their families because they invariably had to walk straight across the playing field to get to the court house.

Josephine Massino and her two daughters parked in a nearby indoor lot. As they crossed into the park, the photographers began to buzz about their arrival and started photographing them in a flurry of activity. One image captured Josephine Massino peering over her sunglasses as she realized the anonymity she had enjoyed over the years as a Mafia wife was now gone. Her daughters, who had paused in the park while Joanne bent down to tie her shoe, walked by the phalanx of photographers moments later. They walked together, looking a little bewildered and defiant.

Inside, Judge Nicholas Garaufis came into the courtroom at 10:15 A.M. and called the case to order. Massino sat at the defense table with Breitbart—Flora Edwards was delayed because of a traffic problem. At the prosecution table were Assistant U.S. Attorneys Greg Andres and his two cocounsel, Mitra Hormozi and Robert Henoch. Also seated at the prosecution table were the two FBI agents whose number crunching and investigation had started the chain of events that led to this particular day: Jeffrey Sallet and Kimberly McCaffrey. Seated with them was Samantha Ward, a paralegal who worked on the case and helped prepare it for trial.

After some housekeeping matters were discussed, Garaufis took one last look around the courtroom.

"We're ready, everyone?" Garaufis asked.

"Yes," answered Andres.

"Let's bring in the jury," Garaufis ordered.

CHAPTER 20

"They Didn't Die of Old Age"

Robert Henoch was known to some as "Colonel" for a very good reason. He was one.

A slender, bespectacled man, Henoch was a lieutenant colonel in the U.S. Army Reserves while he worked as a prosecuting attorney. Low keyed in court, Henoch honed his skills after graduating from George Washington University School of Law in 1993 in the office of Manhattan District Attorney Robert Morgenthau.

The Manhattan District Attorney's Office is one of the biggest and most visible prosecutorial offices in the country and a lot of the young lawyers who work there wind up doing well. A good attorney can make a career in public service there and many have gone on to major government jobs, including Henoch's top boss, Brooklyn U.S. Attorney Roslynn R. Mauskopf.

Still, as rewarding as a local job in the district attorney's office can be, an attorney who likes criminal law and prosecuting cases can use it as a springboard to the next level up, the job of a federal prosecutor. Henoch, who sharpened his skills doing homicide investigations and trials in Morgenthau's office, took the plunge by joining the Brooklyn U.S. Attorney's Office in 2002.

Among the prosecution team Henoch was the newcomer. Greg Andres had joined the office in 1999, while Mitra Hormozi had signed on in 2001. Even though he was the baby of the team, Henoch knew his way around a courtroom and with his military background—he served in Qatar during the Second Gulf War—he wasn't intimidated by the need to address a jury. It fell to Henoch to deliver the opening statement against Joseph Massino. Even David Breitbart was impressed by what he saw.

Speaking as though he was addressing a general staff at the War College, Henoch didn't have to use notes. Standing straight and looking directly at the jurors, he told them just how bad he thought the defendant was.

"This trial is about the vicious, violent, cunning and murderous rise to power of Joseph Massino," Henoch said in the first seconds of his opening remarks.

Pow. That kind of opening remark summed it all up and if he wanted to just set the scene with one sentence, Henoch could have sat down at that point. But openings are used to tell juries what the evidence will show that supports the government's view of the defendant and in the case of Massino there was a lot to tell.

Some lawyers rely on notes, but as Henoch stood in front of the jury box, his eyes scanning the members of the panel, he spoke with not a piece of paper in sight. He had effectively memorized what he had to say. Pointing to Massino, Henoch said that he was the boss of the Bonanno crime family, an organization that made money through crime: loansharking, gambling, arson, extortion, racketeering, and murder. Massino started off as a lowly associate in the mid-1970s and steadily worked his way up the chain to soldier, captain, and finally the boss of what Henoch said was "a criminal organization that acts outside the laws of the United States and the laws of New York State."

Massino had been boss for over twenty-five years and didn't suffer fools gladly. It was at that point in the early moments of his opening statement that Henoch spoke about the men whose deaths the government believed Joseph Massino had engineered: Philip Giaccone, Alphonse Indelicato, Dominick Trinchera, Dominick Napolitano, Cesare Bonventre, Anthony Mirra, and Gabriel Infanti.

"Indelicato, Infanti, Trinchera, all these men, they didn't die of old age, they didn't die of cancer, they died because they were a threat to the defendant in his struggle for power and control over this family," said Henoch.

Henoch ticked off a host of racketeering acts that Massino had been charged with and for five minutes went over again the various murders, extortions, arsons, gambling rackets, and other crimes the government intended to prove.

How was the government going to prove the case against Massino? Henoch told the jurors that "cooperating witnesses," men who had committed crimes and were arrested, would be trooping into the courtroom to say what it was Joseph Massino had done. There would be other evidence that would corroborate what the witnesses would say, he added.

It is obligatory in Mafia trials that the government attempts to sketch out for the jury the organization structure of an organized crime family. This is done because indictments, such as the one against Massino, allude to a crime family that has a structure that harkens back to the old days of Salvatore Maranzano and his fascination for organization based on the Roman legion.

Cosa Nostra, said Henoch, is an Italian phrase for "Our Thing" or as some say "This thing of Ours." But it is also known as the Mafia, which in New York is comprised of the Lucchese, Colombo, Gambino, Genovese, and Bonanno families, Henoch explained.

Massino may have gotten his hands dirty as a lowly member of the family in the early days, but as he moved up, he became more careful to protect himself. By the 1990s, Henoch said, a cautious Massino didn't want people referring to him by name because of the prevalence of wiretaps and bugs.

"He puts out the word, that if you are going to refer to me, touch your ear," said Henoch.

Massino also expected respect, the prosecutor said. Pulling out a chart of the Bonanno crime family hierarchy, Henoch explained that the lowly soldiers and associates had to show respect by giving Massino a cut of the profits in exchange for the protection his rule afforded them.

"So if you are down here, committing crimes," Henoch said, pointing to a soldier's position on the chart, "you have to pay up the chain. Money sort of defies gravity in the Bonanno family. It flows upward. It doesn't flow downward."

For several minutes, Henoch explained for the jurors the ways of mob life. He alluded to how the Mafia family had a chain of command much like the army that had to be followed. Associates talked to soldiers, who then talked to captains. When disputes arose, Henoch said, there was a "sitdown," a conference or negotiation.

"It is sort of a mechanism used to control the victims of greedy and violent men," said the prosecutor. "That is essentially what a sitdown is."

For most of the morning, Henoch explained the ways of the mob for the jury and then went into his summary of the Bonanno crime family history and the bloodshed that was a part of it. Rastelli was portrayed as a key individual in Henoch's remarks because the late Bonanno boss was the one who elevated Massino to the position of captain after Carmine Galante was killed in the first power struggle of the era. In 1981, factional fighting led to the deaths of Trinchera, Giaccone, and Indelicato, said Henoch, and it was Massino who did Rastelli's bidding and orchestrated the murders.

The embarrassing revelation in 1981 of the Joseph Pistone undercover FBI penetration of the Bonanno family caused trouble for three members of the clan: Dominick Napolitano, Anthony Mirra, and Benjamin "Lefty Guns" Ruggiero. While Ruggiero got lucky and was arrested in August 1981, Mirra and Napolitano weren't and wound up dead.

An important element of Massino's hold over the crime family, according to Henoch, was the fact that Massino inducted his captains and soldiers into the family and sometimes even their sons.

"That is going to minimize the chances, by the defendant's estimation, of those people cooperating against him," said Henoch.

With lunchtime looming, Henoch then revealed how the FBI agents began their financial investigation of the Bonanno family and discovered how Barry Weinberg was getting checks from Salvatore Vitale and Massino. It was in this description of the genesis of the investigation that Henoch spoke to the jurors for the first time the names of the key mob turncoats who would be taking the witness stand. With Weinberg unmasked and found to owe millions in back taxes, he cooperated against Frank Coppa and Richard Cantarella, two captains who had been appointed as part of a committee to run the crime family in the 1990s, said Henoch.

Charged with extortion, both Coppa and Cantarella gave "tons and tons" of information to investigators about organized crime. They turned on everybody and talked about Salvatore Vitale, James Tartaglione, and others. From there, other things happened, explained Henoch, leading in 2002 to "something truly extraordinary." Though he didn't say his name, James Tartaglione, a captain in the crime family, decided to wear a wire.

"This wire, you'll hear some of these recordings, is truly extraordinary," said Henoch. "They show that this enterprise exists, they show that the defendant is associated with it, they show that there's a pattern of racketeering activity that's been going on during the course of this indictment. They are really a window onto the soul and inner workings of the Bonanno family."

Stomachs were grumbling and jurors, along with the press, spectators, and Massino, who was looking forward to lunch brought in by his wife, were shifting in their seats waiting for Henoch to end his opening remarks. He wrapped it up fairly quickly, asking the jurors to use their common sense, reason, and logic to make a decision. Henoch said he was confident that the jury would find Massino guilty on every single count in the indictment.

It had been a good opening statement, delivered by Henoch in a crisp style that echoed his military experience.

But Breitbart had a problem.

The defense attorney objected to Garaufis that Henoch didn't indicate to the jury "one iota" how he intended to prove the charges. Instead, the government attorney spouted a first-person story of what he believed to be the history of Joseph Massino and the Bonanno crime family, said Breitbart. The result was a faulty opening because Henoch didn't indicate what any witness would say, something that was the sin qua non of an opening statement. "For those reasons I move to dismiss," said Breitbart.

The defense attorney's move was an unexpected gambit and seemed to take Greg Andres, the lead prosecutor, momentarily by surprise. But he then rebutted Breitbart by saying that indeed Henoch had said that there would be the testimony of Massino's accomplices, documentary evidence, and other things. The government was under no obligation to spell out what each specific witness was going to say, said Andres.

Garaufis had an easy way out of the situation. He simply reserved his decision and asked Breitbart to come back at some point with case law and court decisions that dealt with the subject. With that, the court adjourned for lunch and the jury left the courtroom. Massino was passed a bag by the marshals that contained his lunch since he was allowed to eat in the courtroom and work with his attorneys. To keep prying eyes away from Massino as he ate, the marshals taped white paper over the windows in the courtroom door.

After lunch, the defense had its turn at an opening statement and that fell to Breitbart. The defense attorney was not a tall man, but he had a nonchalance that gave him an easy manner when addressing a jury. He recognized right from the start that Henoch's opening, with all the talk of murder, arson, and other crimes, had made Massino look like evil personified. But since Massino had pled not guilty to the charges, he had put in issue every fact that was going to come from the mouths of the witnesses.

Breitbart readily acknowledged that while Massino may be the boss of the Bonanno family—the attorney stayed away from the term *crime family*—that in itself wasn't enough to convict him of anything.

"They must prove the underlying acts contained in the indictment, to satisfy their obligation and their burden with regard to proof," said Breitbart about the government's need to prove the case.

Since Breitbart had been one of the defense attorneys in the 1982 federal trial involving the conspiracy to murder the three captains, he had the ability to refer back to that case, and he played it to the hilt by pointing out that the Massino trial was the third time the homicides were being tried. The first time in 1982 involved "Sonny Black . . . Jimmy 'Legs' Episcopia and Nicky Santora and Anthony Rabito and Anthony Ruggiero." But Breitbart then said something that was puzzling. Not only was he wrong about Episcopia being convicted of the murders (he pled out to a different racketeering act) but he also implied that somehow the FBI learned that the case was "all nonsense."

Turning to the 1987 federal trial of Massino, Breitbart told the jurors that he was prosecuted for the conspiracy to commit the murder of the three captains and that a jury found that the charge was not proven.

"And now they come up with a new theory in 2004," said Breitbart to explain why the three murders were still an issue. "He's charged not with the conspiracy to murder, but with the murder, that he was an active player or an aider and abettor, that he was involved in the shooting of those three men."

Breitbart's point was that Nicholas Santora, who had been convicted in the 1982 case, was said by new witnesses not to have been involved in the murders.

"The FBI makes mistakes," said Breitbart. "Often they do it intentionally."

The attorney also took a stab at telling the jurors that information about some of the homicides charged against Massino was all screwed up. Breitbart said Dominick "Sonny Black" Napolitano had size seven shoes but that the body found in Staten Island had size eleven feet, according to postmortem X-rays. Witnesses would testify that Napolitano was shot a total of four times, but the body found had only one bullet that appeared to be a .45 caliber, which was not the caliber mentioned by witnesses. It was these inconsistencies and contradictions that Breitbart hoped would plant reasonable doubt in the minds of jurors.

The FBI believed Cesare Bonventre was killed because of Massino. But Breitbart stated that the dead man was not only a drug dealer but he also had a sideline of kidnapping people for ransom. The old Bonanno boss, Philip Rastelli, had been angered by Bonventre's kidnapping spree and that was why Rastelli ordered the Canadian captain killed, said Breitbart.

So it went with each homicide. Breitbart trotted out information that ran counter to the theory that Massino had the motive to order the murders.

Well aware that the government's main ammunition against Massino was the words of the witnesses, Breitbart suggested strongly to the jury that each of them had a motive to lie.

What was worse, he said, was that they had been manipulated into turning on Massino.

"How do they recruit a witness? Do they bribe them? Do they torture them? You better believe it," the attorney said.

Those remarks brought an instant objection from Andres, but Garaufis let Breitbart soldier on, even to the point where the defense attorney made the grandiose promise that "I am going to prove to you that the same methods being used in Iraq" were being used in the federal jails where the witnesses were kept before they began cooperating against Massino. Sleep deprivation, solitary confinement, constant surveillance, and promises of leniency on sentencing were all the techniques the government used to get the witnesses to cooperate and testify.

Breitbart's remarks about Iraq refered to the Abu Ghraib scandal involving mistreatment of Iraqi prisoners by U.S. military forces, something that had recently been in the news. The reference to Abu Ghraib drew gasps from some spectators and smirks from some in the news media. The Gulf War reference seemed overblown. Breitbart was going to have to really make good on that claim.

The point Breitbart wanted to drive home was that the witnesses had committed numerous murders but that they could get special letters that might help them get light sentences.

"Is that seduction? Is that bribery? Is that torture? I most respectfully suggest it is," he said.

The mobsters who turned on Joseph Massino, Breitbart noted, were each "a master at the lie" as shown by the fact that they had lured various victims to their deaths by lying.

"Do you think they say to Tony Mirra, 'Tony, come with me, we are going to shoot you in the head twice,'" said Breitbart. "No, they have to be so convincing, they have keep a straight face, they have to contort themselves in a way that will convince the individual [victim] that they are going for a joyride, they are going for an important meeting, they are going for a meal, they are going for a drink."

The bottom line for the mob witnesses, said Breitbart, was that all they had to do was say, "Joe [Massino] told me to do it," and they could go home once the judge gave them a light sentence no matter how many murders they did.

Breitbart concluded his opening remarks by saying the seven homicide charges against his client were a sham created to make what was a gambling case into something bigger. He told the jurors they would discover that for themselves and vote to acquit Massino.

The prosecution's first big witness was Anthony Giliberti, the former Teamster official who had been a witness against Massino, Philip Rastelli, and several other Bonanno family members and associates in their 1985 trial in the Brooklyn federal court that led to their conviction. Giliberti was the man who Massino was accused of conspiring to kill through a failed assassination attempt. According to the prosecution, Massino's motive was to prevent Giliberti from ever testifying against him.

When Giliberti took the witness stand this time around against Massino, he was frail and had a lot of physical problems. He was questioned by Mitra Hormozi. A thin woman with a fine-boned face and eyes that bespoke of her Iranian ancestry, Hormozi brought a softer presence to the prosecution table. She had been assigned to the Massino trial team in early 2003 and was responsible for debriefing and preparing Richard Cantarella for trial.

If Andres seemed driven, edgy, and ill tempered, Hormozi was smooth, easy going, and chatty. She would take teasing about her long engagement to her boyfriend because one trial or another, seemed to push her nuptials further into the future. "He is going to leave you," Cantarella once joked with her. Even Massino warmed up to her, telling her to eat and gain weight. When Hormozi told Massino that it was okay to be thin—just look at his svelte wife—the crime boss said Josephine had lost weight because of one thing: "stress."

Under Hormozi's patient questioning, Giliberti revealed in his testimony that he had a fine career as a union thug.

"We stopped a lot of nonunion people from working in the union territory," Giliberti said. "If we couldn't organize them, they wouldn't cooperate, we'd burn their trucks down . . . or cut up their tires or do something to make it miserable for them."

Giliberti talked about union slush funds supplied by shakedowns of moving companies. Some of the money was placed in envelopes and given to "some people I know," said Giliberti, referring to Philip Rastelli. It turned out that Giliberti's ties to Rastelli were more than just money. His sister, Mildred, had married Rastelli's brother, Carmine.

Giliberti said he and Massino once had an altercation at a restaurant in Queens known as Bow Wow in which the defendant punched him and threatened to kill him. He also recounted how he was shot nine times outside his house. But at times Giliberti seemed confused and hesitant, feeling the affects of various medications.

"I feel like an old man," Giliberti said at one point. "When I'm walking down the street and the medicine starts affecting me. I don't know why, but it does."

He sometimes went off on tangents, referring to Hormozi as a "nice young lady, old enough to be my daughter, I wish she was." Queried about his love life, Giliberti said, "Sure, I had a lot of girls."

Asked if he could pick out Massino in court, even when the defendant was asked to stand up, Giliberti said he didn't recognize him.

"If that's Joey Massino, he's really changed a lot. I don't know that guy," Giliberti said.

At one point, Garaufis seemed concerned that Giliberti's ramblings might be an indication that medical reasons might be interfering with his ability to testify and asked Hormozi if that was the case.

"Not that we're aware of," she said. "He has Parkinson's disease. I also believe he's just very nervous right now."

"To this observer, it looks like he's having an Alzheimer's episode," interjected Breitbart.

"Judge, he doesn't have Alzheimer's," said Andres.

"Thank you Doctor Andres," Breitbart said sarcastically.

"Thank you doctors all," said Garaufis, who then indicated that he hoped that Giliberti wouldn't have to testify much longer.

Because of his problems recalling events, his ramblings, and his gratuitous remarks, Giliberti didn't make the greatest of impressions; in fact, he got the government's case off to a rocky and embarrassing start. He did testify about the conflict he had with Massino and the fact that he had been shot, circumstantial evidence that might tie Massino to the assassination attempt. But he admitted he never saw anyone give the orders for the shooting, and he didn't recognize who actually fired at him.

But if Giliberti wasn't an impressive witness for the government, there were plenty more who would be.

CHAPTER 21

"They Thought They Might Get Killed"

Frank Lino was born in the Gravesend section of Brooklyn, went to Lafayette High School, and at the age of fifteen he started doing petty crimes. He moved up from doing stick-ups with the Avenue U Boys to freelancing at the age of eighteen for New York's Mafia families. He became a member of the Bonanno family on October 30, 1977. He was twenty-seven years old.

It was at 2:45 P.M. on May 26, 2004, that a sixty-six-year-old Lino walked into Judge Nicholas Garaufis's courtroom. There had been a number of witnesses who preceded Lino: ex-Teamster thug Anthony Giliberti, former FBI agent Patrick Marshall, FBI supervisor Charles Rooney, and organized crime expert Kenneth McCabe. But Lino was the first of the vaunted Bonanno crime family witnesses to take the stand against Joseph Massino and the moment was clearly historic.

Dressed in a black open-necked polo shirt and tan slacks, Lino seemed to groan as he sat down in the witness chair. He had thin, gray hair and a face rounded by age and weight. He didn't look comfortable on the stand, and he had an air of unpleasantness.

It was lead prosecutor Greg Andres who questioned Lino in his direct testimony. It would be necessary through Lino's testimony to set the tone of the trial and for the government to show that its cooperating witnesses could bury Massino as had been promised to the jury in Robert Henoch's opening remarks. Since Andres was the architect of the prosecution, he knew that Lino had to sound credible and hold up under David Breitbart's reputation as an effective cross-examiner.

Like Henoch, Andres was thin and hungry-looking, his well-tailored suit draping over a slender frame in a way that denoted a comfortable upbringing. Andres was married to the daughter of noted First Amendment litigator Floyd Abrams, and was herself a prosecutor in the U.S. Attorney's Office in Manhattan. Andres was driven in his job. A workaholic, he would return telephone calls as late as 1:00 A.M. He was never far from a cup of coffee or Coke, sometimes walking into a courtroom with a beverage and a nonchalance that angered the wife of one reputed Bonanno captain who happened to be in court. Andres's brusque manner alienated some who worked with him, and he had clearly replaced colleague Ruth Nordenbrook in charge of the case.

But even if Andres was hard to work with, he had an energy and relentlessness that was so necessary to corral the many pieces of the Massino investigation. This trial was his baby and it was only natural that he handle the questioning of Lino, the first really big witness.

The initial questioning of Lino covered the usual stuff. He recounted his criminal history, which included an arrest in 1962 on charges he aided and abetted the murder of two detectives. Despite the fact that Lino said he was beaten in police custody, he refused to cooperate with the investigation of those police murders and was never charged. He admitted being involved in illegal gambling, extortions, and selling marijuana and cocaine. Lino also admitted to committing six murders.

Under Andres's questioning, Lino identified Massino in court as the boss of the Bonanno family. He also said that it was Massino who actually changed the name of the family to that of the Massino family.

"Why was the name changed?" Andres asked.

"Well, because Joe Bonanno, he wrote a book about the Commission, they just wanted to do away with his name," answered Lino.

"What did people think about Joe Bonanno after he the wrote the book?"

"They said he betrayed, you know, the family," replied Lino.

Lino recounted how he learned that Massino was only to be referred to in conversations by a touch of the ear and that the defendant held court at J&S Cake Social Club and Casablanca Restaurant in Queens. He spelled out some key Mafia rules and customs: no disrespect for the wives and daughters of members, no cooperation with law enforcement, no guns were to be brought to meetings, no drug dealing, although that was ignored, and if you got in trouble the family would pay your legal fees. Massino had offered him $75,000 for legal fees once, said Lino.

When he was arrested in January 2003, Lino said the crime family had about 12 key captains, 100 soldiers, and somewhere between 200 to 500 associates. But since the defense had already conceded that Massino was involved in the Bonanno family and scores of photographs had been shown of Massino and others meeting together, the importance of Lino's testimony lay not so much in the structure of the crime family but on whether he would be able to tie Massino into the murders that were at the center of the case. For that, Lino's words were spellbinding.

It was around 1981 that the Bonanno family factional infighting had developed. Three captains, Alphonse "Sonny Red" Indelicato, Philip "Lucky" Giaccone, and Dominick

"Big Trin" Trinchera had been vying for control of the family and the fight had split the Bonanno family, as well as the other New York Mafia clans. Some in the Genovese family supported the three captains, while John Gotti backed Massino and Dominick "Sonny Black" Napolitano, said Lino.

Two meetings had already taken place, one at Ferncliffe Manor in Brooklyn and another at the Embassy Terrace, also in Brooklyn, when yet a third sit down was called to resolve the disputes within the family. The three captains had already been suspicious of such meetings and had hidden some guns at a bar Lino owned near the Embassy just in case.

"They says that if they don't come back we should retaliate," said Lino, referring to the three captains.

Lino explained that he didn't think there would be trouble because a parade had been planned in Brooklyn for the return of American hostages from Iran. In fact, the Embassy meeting was peaceful, even though it didn't resolve anything, said Lino. A third meeting was called, this time at a social club on Thirteenth Avenue and Sixty-seventh Street in Brooklyn run by Salvatore Gravano of the Gambino family. The three captains were still suspicious and wanted Lino to come along but decided that Indelicato's son, Bruno, should stay away.

"They thought they might get killed," explained Lino, "so they says if I would go with them."

"Why didn't they want Bruno to go," asked Andres.

"Because if we got killed he would retaliate," said Lino.

The three captains and Lino met some other Bonanno associates after 7:00 P.M. at the Sage Diner on Queens Boulevard. Though Lino didn't know it, FBI agent Vincent Savadel had by this time already seen Massino and others leave the J&S Cake Social Club in Maspeth in a hurry. After being driven to Brooklyn, the three captains and Lino left their cars at Nathan's Restaurant on Eighty-sixth Street and

Twelfth Avenue and were taken by other cars to the Thirteenth Avenue social club.

Lino said he and the three captains walked into the downstairs area of the club that looked like a storage area. There were several others in the room, including Massino, "George [Sciascia] from Canada, Anthony Giordano, another couple of Italian guys." Giordano left to go upstairs to see if the meeting room was ready. Giaccone was chatting with Joseph "Joe Bayonne" Zicarelli. Lino said he and Trinchera were talking with Sciascia and Zicarelli. He noticed that Indelicato was conversing with Massino, with Indelicato "holding on to Joe's arm."

Lino remembered that Giordano came downstairs with two guys wearing hoods.

"With hoods?" Andres asked.

"They came down with hoods and shotguns," said Lino.

The recollection was now just too painful. Lino choked up. His eyes squinted and for an instant it looked like he would burst into tears.

"Big Trinny went to charge them and"—Lino again choked up but was finally able to say—"he got killed."

Trinchera had charged at the hooded assailants but was immediately shot dead, dropping right where he was hit, said Lino. Giaccone was up against a wall waiting to be shot. Lino testified that Massino hit Indelicato with "an object."

As Lino turned to flee out the door, he said he saw Giaccone get killed. Lino fled so quickly that no one was able to stop him.

The courtroom was quiet enough to hear a heart beat. Lino's dramatic testimony was the first full eyewitness testimony to ever come out about the murders in such detail. Not only did he place Sciascia, Zicarelli, Giordano, and others at the scene but Lino also testified that Joseph Massino was indeed in the room and had actually assaulted Indelicato. It was direct evidence that was damaging to Massino even though the defendant had not been observed firing any shots. What followed next in Lino's testimony was even worse.

Running for his life, Lino ran up the block on Sixty-eighth Street, jumping over fences and finally coming to a home where the occupants let him make a telephone call to his son, Frank Lino Jr., who drove out to Brooklyn to pick up his father. Lino said he then was driven to the home of his sister in Staten Island, where Frank Coppa, who had already been alerted by Lino in another telephone call, arrived to talk things over. Coppa took Lino to his home, where Lino's cousin, Eddie Lino, a member of the Gambino crime family, called to ask for a meeting.

Driving back to his sister's house, Lino said he met with Eddie Lino and several key members of the Gambino crime family: underboss Aniello Dellacroce, soldiers Gene Gotti, Angelo Ruggiero, and Frank DeCicco. The appearance of the Gambino crew showed the range of the alliance that Massino and Napolitano had forged with the other families in carrying out the murder of the three captains. During the meeting, Dellacroce told Lino he was never a target of the murder plot but that he couldn't be told in advance because the plotters thought he might tip off the targets. Dellacroce then told Ruggiero and DeCicco to make sure others disposed of the bodies of the three captains.

On May 6, 1981, Lino said he was called to a meeting at Massino's home on Eighty-fourth Street in Howard Beach. Inside were Napolitano, Sciascia, Zicarelli, Salvatore Ferrugia, as well as Massino. During the meeting, Ferrugia, the nominal street boss of the Bonanno family, said the war was over and that Lino would remain as an acting captain if he "could bring everybody in," meaning convince any members of the three captains' crews to lay down their arms and not cause trouble.

A few days later, Lino recalled, he brought Coppa and Jerry Chilli to Massino's home. It was there, said Lino, that Massino told the men that "everything was over with" and that Coppa's $25,000 loan-sharking debt to the now dead Giaccone was to be paid to Massino. The only two allies of the three captains who didn't come in to meet Massino and the other victorious captains were Bruno Indelicato (Alphonse's son) and Thomas "Karate" Pitera, a Bonanno soldier who specialized in murder. Bruno Indelicato was reputed to be a cocaine abuser and wild with a gun, two qualities that led Napolitano to farm out a hit contract to undercover agent Joseph Pistone to preemptively kill the dead captain's son.

The spate of meetings at Massino's house, as described by Lino, showed that the defendant had benefited from the three captains murder and was active in consolidating the gains for his side. It was another piece of evidence tying Massino to the triple homicide.

When Andres finished leading Lino through the events of the three captains murder, he quickly shifted to August 1981 and the murder of Napolitano. Lino said that he first got wind that something was in the works when his cousin, Eddie Lino, told him that if he wanted to show his faithfulness to the victorious regime in the Bonanno family that he should take part in an upcoming "contract" for a murder.

Lino said he wasn't told of the intended victim, only that Massino and Sciascia said they needed a place for a killing. Lino testified he responded by taking the two men, along with Frank Coppa, to the Staten Island home of Ernest "Kippy" Filocomo, the father of Bonanno associate Ronald Filocomo. It was decided that the killing would take place in the basement.

Three or four days before this murder, said Lino, Massino told him that the victim was to be Napolitano. Massino said that it was going to be Lino's job to drive Napolitano and Bonanno captain Steven "Stevie Beef" Cannone from the Hamilton House, a restaurant once popular in Bay Ridge, to Filocomo's home.

The day of the killing, Lino said he picked up Napolitano and Cannone as planned at the restaurant's parking lot and drove over the Verrazano Narrows Bridge to Staten Island. At the intersection of Victory Boulevard and Richmond Avenue, Lino noticed Massino and Sciascia waiting in a van, which followed at a distance the car that was carrying Napolitano.

"When you got to Kippy's house, what happened?" Andres asked.

"Sonny Black and Stevie Beef got out of the car with me," said Lino. "We went to Kippy's house, Frank Coppa was at the door."

"I asked him where's everybody, he says they are downstairs," continued Lino. "I started to walk with Sonny Black who is behind me. As we start going down the steps, the door, somebody slammed the door, shut it. I threw him down the steps. He got killed."

"Who did you throw down the steps," inquired Andres.

"Sonny Black," said Lino.

Under more questioning, Lino explained that Napolitano sensed something was wrong when he heard the door slam and that Lino had to grab him by the shoulder and toss him down five cellar steps.

"He fell to the floor," remembered Lino. "Then he, Ronnie Filocomo walked over, shot him . . . my cousin Bobbie, he shot him, then the gun jammed. Ronnie came over, shot him two more times."

Lino added that when one of the guns jammed on the second or third shot, Napolitano uttered the final words, "Hit me one more time and make it good."

After the killing, Lino said that Coppa asked him to get Napolitano's car keys so that his car could be commandeered.

"What did you do with the keys to Sonny Black's car?" Andres asked.

"I went outside, gave them to Joe," Lino explained, referring to Massino, who was sitting in the van with Sciascia and a few other men.

At the van, Massino asked if everything was all right and Lino said he responded by saying "yeah." Lino then returned to the house where the others were wrapping Napolitano's body in a body bag Lino said he had received from a friend who worked in a funeral parlor. Napolitano's corpse was to be placed in a grave that had already been dug in a wooded area. But after driving to the site at about 9:00 P.M. Lino said the hole couldn't be found so the body was placed in a wooded area near a stream.

The import of Lino's testimony was readily apparent to the courtroom audience. He had put Massino directly into the planning of the Napolitano murder and placed him at the scene of the killing. By this point in the trial, Lino had implicated Massino in four homicides and did further damage by testifying that Massino had tried to recruit him to serve as part of a special hit team with Anthony Graziano as a way of not having too many people know about family murders.

Lino testified about one other homicide, that of Gabe Infanti in the winter of 1987 when Massino was in prison. Sal Vitale and Anthony Spero planned the Infanti murder, according to Lino's testimony, at his Brooklyn Mother Cabrini Social Club. Infanti was actually killed at a warehouse in Queens where Frank "Cheech" Navarra had some loft space. Lino didn't actually see the murder but testified that Louis Restivo, a family soldier, had brought Infanti to the location. When Lino finally did enter the building, he said he went into the loft and found Infanti face down on the floor bleeding and dead. Vitale was also present, as were Thomas Pitera and Restivo, said Lino.

Infanti's body was ultimately buried in a shallow grave in Staten Island near a pool company, said Lino, adding that lye had been tossed in to disintegrate the corpse. A few years later, after Pitera was arrested and Vitale feared he might cooperate, Lino said an attempt was made to dig up Infante's body but that no remains were found.

After the murders, Lino was questioned by Andres about

a wide variety of Bonanno family businesses including loan-sharking, gambling, and how money was passed up to the family administration. According to Lino, Massino ran a big loan-sharking business and had loaned him about $500,000 over the years with resulting interest payments totaling $1 million. Lino also admitted to running as many as 100 Joker Poker gambling machines and added that Massino and Vitale had their own sports betting operation.

Lino said he made a lot of money in the mob and related how he kicked in $100 month to a Bonanno family kitty used to pay legal expenses. Massino himself, Lino testified, sometimes chipped in; at one point, Massino paid $100,000 in legal fees for Lino's son, Robert.

As the first mob cooperator to take the witness stand, Lino had given a gripping account of the murders and in the process had done a lot of damage to Massino. But he was only one witness. It was up to the defense to probe and find ways to attack his credibility and show why he may have had motive to lie. That would be Breitbart's job.

The aim of the defense was to make Lino out as an odious, untrustworthy man who had been pressured by solitary confinement to cooperate and would thus say anything that would earn him his freedom. Lino admitted under Breitbart's questioning that his time in solitary confinement at the Brooklyn Metropolitan Detention Center was tough. The facility kept lights on twenty-four hours a day, and his cell in the Manhattan Correction Center, where he was transferred, was filthy and a "painful" place to stay, said Lino But the wearing affects of solitary confinement didn't amount to the kind of Abu Ghraib–like torture Breitbart had alluded to in his opening statement.

Lino said he decided to cooperate after learning that Vitale had turned.

"When he cooperated, there was no way I was going to win anymore," said Lino. "He was giving all the orders to do all the killings when he was there."

Breitbart questioned Lino about the trial preparation he was put through and got the witness to say that Andres had asked him questions about three or four times and that he had been questioned a dozen times by the FBI agents. But he denied that Andres had ever told him that he could get a "pass" for the six homicides he had been involved with, much like noted turncoat Salvatore Gravano, who was freed even after admitting to having a role in nineteen gangland murders. Lino was also emphatic that prosecutors and the FBI had never said they "wanted Joe Massino."

Breitbart cross-examined Lino about the three captains and other murders but the witness never really gave any significant contradictions from his earlier direct testimony. In short, Lino's account held up, even under Breitbart's close questioning. But Lino did come off as obnoxious, disagreeable, and amoral under cross-examination. He admitted that he didn't care if some of his associates sold drugs near public schools and recounted his own drug abuse. He also snipped back at Breitbart, conduct that irritated some on the prosecution team.

"Isn't it a fact, sir, that you were considered the cheapest guy on the street, you stole from everyone?" Breitbart asked Lino.

"That's not true," responded Lino, who began to chuckle.

Breitbart asked if he said something funny.

"Yeah, I'm laughing at the 'cheapest guy,' you should have been as cheap as me sport," said Lino.

Once, when Breitbart's questioning implied that Lino was lying, the witness dropped any pretense of decorum and responded with a wisecrack, "Why don't you give us all lie detector tests and we will see who is telling the truth."

Another time Lino forgot the line of Breitbart's questioning and said, "I'm not trying to be funny."

"There is absolutely nothing funny about you," Breitbart shot back in a voice dripping with a contempt that spoke to the witness's inhumanity.

CHAPTER 22

"I Didn't Want to Do No More Time"

It was 1977 when Frank Coppa met Joseph Massino at the Fulton Fish Market in Manhattan. The meeting place was symbolically appropriate on a number of levels. The seafood there was always plentiful in restaurants and both men liked to eat. The wholesale market, which occupied a two-block area south of the Brooklyn Bridge, had also been Mafia territory where enforcers from the Genovese crime family controlled rackets.

Massino was introduced to Coppa by an elderly Bonanno captain named Matteo Valvo, who had once been active in a union representing toy and novelty workers and owned a fish store in Brooklyn. Coppa and Massino became fast friends and over the years the two progressed through the ranks of the crime family. It was in the 1960s and 1970s that Coppa saw the potential for Wall Street as a place to illegally make money and got involved in a number of scams selling unregistered securities and manipulating the price of smaller stocks.

After Massino took over as family boss he placed Coppa in a group of crime captains and other high-ranked members who administered family affairs. It was a position of great trust. It also turned out to be a disaster for Massino when Coppa decided to cooperate with authorities.

Coppa, the first Bonanno family member to turn on Massino in late 2002, took the witness stand on June 7. A rotund, balding man, Coppa seemed to lock eyes with Massino for a few brief, uncomfortable seconds in the courtroom. He quickly told the jury that his stock market misdeeds earned him a three-year prison term in July 2002 for stock fraud. Coppa indicated that the thirty-six-month prison term wasn't a problem until in October 2002 he was indicted for the extortion of parking lot entrepreneur Barry Weinberg. That indictment meant that Coppa could be facing as much as eighty more months of prison time.

"I didn't want to do no more time," Coppa said under Robert Henoch's questioning. "I thought about it and I had my lawyer call the agents."

It was early in his testimony that Coppa showed how much Massino had confided in him. By 2000, Massino began to distrust his brother-in-law, Salvatore Vitale, for a number of reasons.

"He didn't like the way he was carrying himself, like he was a big shot," said Coppa. "He didn't like the way he was with his family. He had problems with his family and that is what he complained about."

There was more for Massino to worry about. Coppa said that Massino distrusted Vitale because he knew about "seven pieces of work" they had done together over the years.

"You said 'seven pieces of work,' what were you referring to when you say that?" Henoch asked.

"Murders," replied Coppa, gesturing with his thumb and index finger as if they were a gun. He explained that it was actually Massino who had used that very same gesture in their conversation.

Had Vitale not been Massino's brother-in-law, he would have killed him, said Coppa.

After flirting with the subject of homicides, Henoch

asked Coppa to explain how he had learned of the death of Gabriel Infanti. While on vacation with Massino, Coppa explained, the crime boss said Infante was killed because Massino was afraid he was going to cooperate with authorities in a civil racketeering case. It was a statement that, unlike Lino's testimony, which dealt only with the actual killing, showed Massino talking about the motive he had for the Infante homicide.

Moments later, Coppa recalled that he also had a conversation with Massino about the murder of Bonanno family member Russell Mauro. According to Coppa, Massino said Mauro was killed because "he was heavy into drugs."

The Mauro homicide wasn't something Massino was on trial for. Instead, it was one of those bad acts that prosecutors won the right to bring up at trial to show the defendant's power and control of the crime family racketeering activity. Coppa didn't have any firsthand knowledge about the Mauro killing. But he knew plenty about the death of Dominick "Sonny Black" Napolitano.

Yes, he had opened the door when Frank Lino, Steven Cannone, and Napolitano rang the doorbell at the Staten Island house, Coppa told the jury.

"I opened the door, walked him to the basement door, opened the basement door, Frank Lino went down the basement with Sonny Black, and at that point he got shot," said Coppa.

While not seeing Napolitano get shot, Coppa said he heard three shots as he was walking Cannone to the front door.

"Sonny Black died like a man, he said make it quick." According to Coppa, Robert Lino was one of the shooters in the basement.

It was Frank Lino who gave Napolitano's car keys to Cannone, said Coppa. Then Lino and Cannone walked to the left up the street to a backup car. Coppa said he walked to the right to go to his car.

Coppa never testified that he saw Massino in the vicinity of the Napolitano murder. But he did say that Lino told him Massino had been waiting at the street corner for Cannone. Taken together, Coppa's testimony buttressed Frank Lino's testimony about Massino's whereabouts and involvement in the homicide. (Oddly, Coppa was unable to recognize a photo taken of Napolitano when he was alive.)

At the same time that Napolitano's body was being driven away in the back of a Cadillac, Coppa said he and Frank Lino went to a church feast in Brooklyn.

To underscore the close relationship between Coppa and Massino—as well as to lay the groundwork for some more damaging testimony—Henoch showed the jury some vacation photos Coppa had given over to the agents. They showed Massino and him mugging it up in France. One comical shot showed both portly men towering over a small Fiat, while another had them side by side, Massino's stomach stretching his polo shirt and Coppa's belt cinching tight across his midsection, making him look like a sausage casing. Some jurors seemed amused.

But the business in Monte Carlo was not all amusing. It was there, Coppa testified, that Massino talked about the death of Philip Giaccone, one of the three captains slain in 1981.

"He wasn't sorry that Philly Lucky got killed because [Massino] didn't like him," said Coppa.

Coppa wasn't present during the murder of the three captains, but his testimony corroborated a key part of Lino's earlier statements to the jury. Coppa said that Lino did call him immediately after the killings and sounded very traumatized, saying that Massino had been present along with others at the time of the shootings. Coppa also said, just as Lino had recalled, that he went with Lino to Massino's house after the shootings and that Lino had a discussion with Massino.

As he had told the FBI in his earlier debriefings, Coppa testified that he had paid millions of dollars over the years to

Massino and the Bonanno crime family in the form of tribute and loan-sharking fees. The payments for the loans to-
taled thousands of dollars a month, often going through
Vitale to Massino, said Coppa. Christmas gifts of up to
$20,000 were also paid to Massino. Testimony about the
money was being used by the prosecution to flesh out their
financial case against Massino, who was also on trial for
loan-sharking and money laundering, in an effort to get at
the millions of dollars he made as a mob boss.

Things got tense in the courtroom for the prosecution
when Coppa's son, Frank Coppa Jr., a reputed member of the
crime family, appeared in court during Breitbart's cross-
examination. Garaufis called for a sidebar, a conference by
the side of his bench out of earshot of jurors.

The presence of his son was "torturing" Coppa, said Andres, and he strongly indicated that he thought Massino
might have passed an order to have Coppa's son come in the
courtroom "upon penalty of death" if disobeyed. The prosecutor wanted any cross- examination of Coppa to steer clear
of references to his son.

Breitbart and Edwards were perplexed by the notion that
Coppa's son had come to a public courtroom simply to intimidate his father. It was a notion that seemed rooted in the
scene in the film *The Godfather,* where the brother of one
mafioso was brought in to shame his sibling into silence before a congressional committee. But in reality, Coppa was
under an obligation to testify truthfully, he had signed a cooperation agreement with the government, and his future
liberty depended on his being a useful witness. It sounded
implausible that Coppa could or would be intimidated by the
presence of his son. In the end, it was a tempest in a teapot
and Breitbart said he hadn't even planned to ask Coppa
about his son.

But Breitbart brought out other things that must have
caused Coppa to squirm in his chair. For instance, Coppa admitted on cross-examination that he had lied to a judge in a

1990s stock fraud case to hide his true financial status. He also admitted to the jury that he still had a net worth of $2 million, an amount he hoped wouldn't be used to repay investors who had lost $5 million in his schemes.

In an attempt to show that Coppa may have killed a gay entertainer, Breitbart asked him about an alleged incident at Sammy's Steakhouse Restaurant in Manhattan, a place that had a showcase theater. Coppa said the theater was a gay scene with transsexual entertainers. Breitbart dropped a titillating question when he asked Coppa if anyone had ever walked in on him having sex with a male entertainer playing the role of the singer Cher.

The question brought an immediate objection from the government and Garaufis called for another sidebar.

"Is there some relevance to the question here?" Garaufis asked.

"Yes, he murdered Cher," said Breitbart. "It wasn't Cher though, it was the boy that he was having sex with."

Breitbart explained that Ronald Filocomo, the man who was identified in testimony as being one of the shooters in the Napolitano murder, had walked in on Coppa, who was mounted on the performer. Breitbart said his source of information was Filocomo, who he spoke with in his jail cell.

Garaufis waivered and thought such testimony would be prejudicial. Breitbart then asked that the court order Filocomo to testify, which Garaufis had no power to do.

Finally, Garaufis allowed Breitbart to ask Coppa if he had a "relationship" with Cher and if he killed him. Coppa said Cher was actually his accountant but denied killing the performer, whose first name was Joseph.

Coppa had a lot of baggage affecting his credibility because he had admitted under Breitbart's questioning to having lied to a federal judge during one of his earlier stock swindles to shelter some assets.

"Would it be fair to say that if you lied to save a few dollars you would lie to save your life," Breitbart asked, referring to Coppa's cooperation agreement.

"No," Coppa responded. "Because if I lied I wouldn't be saving my life."

Coppa said that under the terms of his cooperation agreement with the government prosecutors would write a letter to his sentencing judge in an effort to get him a lower sentence. He admitted that he spoke to prosecutors about the sweet deal Sammy Gravano got in the John Gotti trial. Gravano received a five-year sentence from the court in return for his cooperation on the Gotti racketeering case.

"Hopefully I will get out of jail soon," said Coppa.

Though he was the first Bonanno family member to turn on Massino, the impact of Coppa's testimony was more to buttress the compelling details Lino had spelled out on the Napolitano homicide. He also backed up Lino's account of the crucial meeting with Massino after the murder of the three captains. The offhand remarks Massino had made about the killing of Gabe Infanti was also powerful circumstantial evidence. Unlike Lino, whose sparring with Breitbart made the mafioso sound like a bully boy and thug, Coppa seemed matter-of-fact.

CHAPTER 23

"This Is for Life"

It was never made clear why James Tartaglione had the nick-name "Big Louie." When he took the witness stand in the Joseph Massino trial, the bony sixty-six-year-old Tartaglione had a unique position among the witnesses in the case. While the others decided to cooperate with the government after being arrested, he had decided to help the FBI while he was very much a free man.

Of course, at the time he decided to cooperate Tartaglione might not have remained a free man for very much longer. Because he had so many dealings with Salvatore Vitale, Tartaglione sensed that when Massino's brother-in-law became a cooperator that it was only a matter of time before he would also be named in a federal indictment. It was then that he decided to reach out to prosecutor Ruth Nordenbrook.

On the witness stand Tartaglione, dressed in a sports jacket and open-necked shirt, recounted for hours his involvement with crimes and details of the inner workings of the Bonanno family. He was in a good position to explain these things because Massino had entrusted him with the job of being on committees that oversaw the workings of the family. It was also Massino, said Tartaglione, who told him about contacts the family had maintained with the other Mafia groups in New York dealing with the construction and gasoline businesses.

The more important aspect of Tartaglione's cooperation, however, was that during the time he was able to travel freely he agreed to wear recording devices in 2003 and secretly tape his conversations with various high-ranked Bonanno family members. He also taped some of the lawyers who had been representing them. Some of the tapes would become useful pieces of evidence as the Massino trial unfolded.

However, just before trial in March 2004, the revelation that Tartaglione had been taping his own attorney, Scott Leemon, who also had some contact with Massino, caused a furor. Court records showed that Tartaglione had recorded at least five conversations with Leemon in 2003. David Breitbart was furious because Leemon had been part of joint defense strategy meetings involving several defendants in the case. As a result, Breitbart suspected that the taping of Leemon was done to spy on the defense camp and he made a motion to either have Andres removed from the case or the tapes made by Tartaglione suppressed.

Anticipating problems of this sort, the government had set up a "firewall" that insulated Andres and the other Massino prosecutors from knowing what the Leemon recordings had revealed. That kind of insulation was created by having Assistant U.S. Attorney Bridget Rohde and an FBI agent review the recordings. In a pretrial ruling, Judge Nicholas Garaufis decided that the taping of Leemon was not improper and allowed it to continue.

On the witness stand, Tartaglione told jurors about some of the facts of Mafia life. Like the other witnesses, he said the Bonanno family was known as the Massino family. The boss of a mob family is akin to taking care of the crime family members like a regular father.

"He has to take care of all of his children," said Tartaglione.

Tartaglione was first made a member of the Mafia in 1983 and about a year later he rose to captain. After Massino came out of prison in the early 1990s, Tartaglione said he was placed on the committee that administered the family. Once in the Mafia you did what the family and the boss wanted you to do, he said.

"This is for life," said Tartaglione about the commitment a member of the Mafia makes.

Tartaglione admitted being involved in murders, assaults, car theft, extortion, hijackings, and loan-sharking. He met other crime family members at weddings, wakes, and social clubs like John Gotti's locales on 101 Street in Corona and in Manhattan at the old Ravenite Social Club on Mulberry Street.

Tartaglione implicated Massino in an arson of the office of Doctor Leifer, a dentist who had been friendly with both Massino and his wife, Josephine. Leifer wanted the office burned, Tartaglione testified, so Tartaglione and Sal Vitale took part in what was described as straightforward crime. Leifer gave Vitale the keys to the back door of the building for easy access. Five gallons of gasoline was then poured throughout the premises and lit. But Tartaglione said the building didn't burn down completely and Massino later told him "you did a bad job," nevertheless paying him $1,500 for the night's work.

Like the film *Rashomon*, in which a crime was retold cinematically from the viewpoint of various witnesses, prosecutors had numerous witnesses against Massino relate what happened during the murder the three captains. Each account was different because it was told from separate recollections of the witnesses who were involved in different ways. While differing, the accounts merged to give a complete picture of what happened in and around the Brooklyn social club where the slayings took place. Each account also implicated Massino. In the case of Tartaglione's testimony, he was the first witness to talk about how Massino was intimately involved in the preplanning and direction that led to the murders.

Questioned by Mitra Hormozi, Tartaglione said he showed up at Massino's Queens social club the day of the murders and overheard the crime boss asking Duane Leisenheimer if he had the scanners and walkie-talkies. Satisfied with the answer, Massino then told everyone present—including Vitale, Dominick "Sonny Black" Napolitano, and Leisenheimer—"Let's go."

According to Tartaglione, the van he was transported in also carried Anthony Rabito. The driver was Napolitano. At the "location," said Tartaglione, he and the others sat in the van until a message came over the walkie-talkie telling them to go into the club.

After driving toward the club, Tartaglione recalled, he saw Vitale being hugged and kissed by other Bonanno members on the scene.

"I gave Sal a big hug and a kiss," said Tartaglione. "At that particular point I knew that somebody was killed."

Inside the club, Tartaglione said he saw Rabito, "Boobie" (John Cerasani), and others who he refered to as "Italian guys," meaning Sicilians. He noticed that those inside the club were wrapping up three dead bodies. Vitale then asked him to pick up spent shell casings on the floor.

The bodies were placed in a van and then Tartaglione said he was asked to follow the vehicle with the bodies as it was driven to Woodhaven Boulevard. On May 5, 1981, Tartaglione was not yet a made member of the Mafia and he wasn't told that day of the identity of the three victims. But through gossip he learned they were Philip Giaccone, Dominick Trinchera, and Alphonse Indelicato.

Apart from his recollection of the moments at Massino's club, Tartaglione's testimony didn't mention Massino at the scene of the three captains murder. However, he said that one day at a restaurant Massino walked over to him and said, "Louie, you did a good job."

There were other things that Tartaglione remembered that seemed to link Massino to the three homicides. He said that Massino talked to him about going to Florida to seek out Bruno Indelicato, the son of the dead captain, whom many feared would strike back in retaliation for his father's murder. (Tartaglione never went.) Not long after that, Vitale told him "we might have a problem," referring to the fact that one of the bodies was rising through the ground at its burial place in Queens.

Another part of Tartaglione's testimony was circumstantial evidence that Massino might have had something to do with the killing of Anthony Mirra, although it was hardly compelling since the murder took place before Tartaglione became a made member of the family, so he wasn't privy to a lot of inside information. He testified that at Massino's J&S Cake Social Club he overheard a conversation in which Massino, referring to the Mirra homicide, told James Episcopia that they should have taken the cash Mirra was believed to have in his socks.

But there was one murder that Tartaglione knew a lot about because he was closely involved. Having been told by Vitale that the crime family wanted him "to do work," Tartaglione understood that to mean a homicide. FBI agents had learned that the actual groundwork for the murder of Cesare Bonventre was laid sometime in 1984, when Massino was on the lam and he met with Louis Attanasio in Pennsylvania. Vitale and Tartaglione were present when Attanasio and Massino went for a private walk. Though he wasn't privy to any conversation Attanasio had with Messino, Vitale later told investigators that Attanasio had related that Massino had said Bonventre had to be killed.

Though he didn't recall a precise date, Tartaglione testified that he went to a garage off Grand Avenue and Fifty-seventh Street in Queens one day and waited. When a car arrived inside the garage, one of its doors opened and Bonventre's body was pulled out, he said. It was then that Bonventre was shot by Attanasio as the mortally wounded man lay on the garage floor, said Tartaglione.

Through his testimony, Tartaglione gave evidence on five of the seven homicides the prosecution was trying to pin on Massino. He also testified about several other killings that didn't involve Massino but that Vitale was involved in: Antonio Tomasulo, *New York Post* supervisor Robert Perrino, and Russell Mauro.

Perhaps the most interesting piece of evidence Tartaglione provided to investigators in the case were the recordings he secretly made of his crime family brethren. Never before had such a high-ranked member of the Bonanno family agreed to wear a wire and Tartaglione did so not only during meetings with his own lawyer but also with several members of the crime family administration who were running the family while Massino was in jail awaiting trial.

Tartaglione made tapes for several months and finally ended his covert surveillance in January 2004. Andres and the prosecution team didn't introduce all of Tartaglione's recordings into evidence but did play several tapes for the jury. Of course, Massino was in jail when the recordings were made and his voice wasn't captured. But he is alluded to several times on the tapes and in fact Tartaglione repeated for the jury the old story that the crime boss is only mentioned in conversations indirectly as "that guy" or "the ear."

One of the recordings showed the fear that Vitale's wife, Diana, had that Massino was going to kill her husband. Vitale had been so frightened of his brother-in-law at one point that he stayed away from him. According to Tartaglione, Massino was asked point-blank by Diana, "Are you going to do anything to my husband?"

On another recording, Anthony Urso, who was acting family boss after Massino was arrested, complained about the flood of informants and turncoats infecting the family and said that as a deterrent they should be killed, along with their families.

"You tell them, 'Whomever turns, we'll wipe your family out,'" said Urso.

On another tape, Vincent Basciano, the Bronx hair salon owner who later became the reputed acting boss of the family, was heard expressing undying loyalty to Massino.

"I got 100 percent faith in him," said Basciano. "Listen to me. If I'm your fucking guy, if I'm gonna walk on hot coals, if I gotta fucking jump in the ocean, let me do it for one guy."

Basciano's statement of loyalty reflected an old way of thinking, an unswerving allegiance to the boss of the family. As events would later play out in the Massino saga, such fealty would be terribly misplaced.

Tartaglione taped enough people in the crime family to keep investigators busy for months. Prosecutors used only a handful of the recordings at Massino's trial. But through interviews, court records, and other documents it was learned that Tartaglione got his fellow gangsters to talk about a wide array of things, ranging from their favorite restaurants, dating problems, and the best defense attorneys to use in case of trouble. The evil done by turncoats like Sal Vitale, Frank Coppa, and Frank Lino were also talked about at length.

According to some of the conversations, the Bonanno family was under the delusional perception that because the government wanted to use more than one informant that there must be problems with the case against Massino. Somehow, said reputed Bonanno underboss Joseph Cammarano on one of the recordings, Massino's good memory would be used to trip up Vitale on the witness stand. He was the Mafia elephant who never forgot.

Vitale had earned a special opprobrium from the Bonanno gangsters. Tartaglione believed that Massino's brother-in-law could take everyone down but didn't think he had been an informant as far back as five years, which is what some in the Bonanno crime family believed. If that was the case, Massino would have been arrested a long time ago and

Vitale would have made a run at being boss of the family, a hypothetical scenario that, had it played out, would have made a crime boss a cooperating witness from the moment he took command.

In their meetings with Tartaglione, both Cammarano and Urso, according to records, bemoaned the fact that the FBI was so vigorously pursuing the crime family and even trying to use the death penalty against Massino in the second case. But at least one Bonanno boss didn't think the federal government would really try to use the death penalty against Massino. They had bigger concerns. They had to hunt for Osama bin Laden.

CHAPTER 24

"He Is a Rat"

When he took the witness stand at the trial of Joseph Massino, there was one thing that Richard Cantarella wanted to be sure about: he had to be well dressed for his appearance.

On the streets of Little Italy, Cantarella had always been known as being a man fastidious about his appearance. His coiffed hair was styled so neatly that the moniker "Shellack Head" stuck to him like his styling gel. When it was his time to testify, Cantarella made sure that his wife brought him half a dozen boxes of new shirts from Neiman Marcus. Star witnesses, even if they would scramble your brains with a bullet, have to look good.

Dressed in a dark suit and a white open-necked shirt that was right out of its package, Cantarella walked into court on June 10, 2004, as the fourth major mob turncoat in the Massino trial. He also had on a pair of tinted sunglasses.

Though he was an admitted killer, Cantarella was, like Frank Coppa, a man with a head for business. He had been involved in parking lots when Salvatore Vitale approached to say that he and Massino wanted to become involved in the same business. Three parking lots became the object of partnerships with Massino's portion being held in the name of his wife, Cantarella told the jury.

But Massino just didn't approach Cantarella for business out of the blue. The well-dressed gangster had made a quick and steady rise through the ranks of organized crime until he had become one of Massino's captains. Eventually, Cantarella was appointed by Massino to be part of a committee to run the family affairs, taking over a spot that had been vacated by James Tartaglione.

Cantarella had come from a personal family line that had substantial ties to the Bonanno crime clan. His uncle, Al Embarrato, had been a longtime Bonanno captain and his cousin, Joseph "Mouk" D'Amico, had been a soldier. After Cantarella was inducted in 1990 with Massino as his main backer, he began to dine with the crime boss at J&S Cake Social Club, as well as at CasaBlanca Restaurant in Maspeth, a place Massino owned with soldier Louis Restivo.

Since he had developed a good rapport with prosecutor Mitra Hormozi, she handled Cantarella's direct examination on the witness stand. Cantarella's real value to the prosecution was not just in his explanation of the structure of the Bonanno family and Massino's eating schedule but in the ability to tie the defendant into the Anthony Mirra homicide. Questioned by Hormozi, Cantarella told the jury that on a trip to the northern end of Little Italy with Embarrato, Cantarella stayed outside while Embarrato entered a building. Coming back to the car, Embarrato turned to Cantarella and gave him some sober news.

According to Cantarella, his uncle stated, "'I just got an assignment from Joe Massino to kill your cousin Tony, he is a rat.'"

Mob insiders and investigators knew that Mirra was on thin ice ever since the revelations surfaced that FBI agent Joseph Pistone had infiltrated the crime family. It had been Mirra who first met Pistone and used him as a driver. Eventually, Pistone used his entrée with Mirra to become close to others like Dominick "Sonny Black" Napolitano and Benjamin "Lefty Guns" Ruggiero. The results were disastrous for the Bonanno family.

The actual killing, Cantarella testified, was done by D'Amico, who fired into the right side of Mirra's head in a parking lot in lower Manhattan's West Side. A shaken D'Amico then got into a getaway car that Cantarella said he drove.

Cantarella also told of his involvement with a number of other homicides. Those killings, he said, didn't involve Massino. But the events surrounding one murder, that of *New York Post* distribution supervisor Robert Perrino, revealed the depth of the penetration the mob once had at the tabloid.

The mob never had anything to do with the editorial functions of the *Post* or its executive offices. Instead, the Mafia was able to exploit the central weak point in any newspaper's operation: the distribution system. If a newspaper can't get its newspapers out to the newsstand, its circulation is dealt a fatal blow, particularly for a publication like the *Post*, which depended for its survival on single-copy sales on the street.

The distribution system at the *Post* was like a Christmas tree for the Bonanno family. On cross-examination by David Breitbart, Cantarella said he was getting paid by the *Post* for a no-show job for about $800 a week from 1985 to 1992. He wasn't the only one reaping benefits. Vitale was pulling in some weekly cash and one of his sons also had a no-show job, said Cantarella. In addition, Cantarella said his cousin, Joe D'Amico, had a job at the newspaper and had clout with the union, which covered the distribution operation. A reputed Bonanno soldier named Joe Torre also had a job as a driver and loader, according to Cantarella.

But in 1992 the investigation by the Manhattan District Attorney's Office was heating up. The prosecutors' targets were Perrino, Al Embarrato, and officials from the union that covered the distribution system workers, said Cantarella. Vitale became concerned about Perrino and asked Cantarella if the *Post* supervisor was showing any signs of weakness that might lead him to cooperate. Cantarella said he told Vitale he didn't see any indication Perrino might become a turncoat. But even that wasn't enough to allay Vitale's fears about Perrino, whom Cantarella said knew about the mob's no-show jobs and that circulation was being inflated by newspapers, which were sometimes dumped in the river rather than returned as unsold.

Perrino, who was complicit in a lot of the Bonanno shenanigans at the *Post*, left his Long Island home on May 6, 1992, and was immediately listed as a missing person. Nothing was heard of Perrino's whereabouts until in December 2003 FBI unearthed his remains from the floor of a warehouse in Staten Island. Frank Lino had provided information to the FBI about the murder and said Perrino's body was taken from a bar in Brooklyn where he was killed to the construction warehouse of a Bonanno family associate. It was at the warehouse that Perrino's corpse was put in a steel drum and covered with concrete. As Cantarella testified, Frank Lino told investigators that it had been Vitale who orchestrated Perrino's murder.

Massino did not know of and hadn't approved of the Perrino murder, said Cantarella. Talking after the homicide, Massino told Cantarella that he was upset with Vitale for ordering the Perrino killing. Had Massino known in advance of the murder, he would not have let it happen, said Cantarella.

Cantarella's testimony showed that Massino was neither involved in the Perrino homicide nor that of Richard Mazzio, which also took place in 1992. But Cantarella had done his damage to Massino with the testimony about the Mirra homicide and his ascendancy to the leadership position in the Bonanno family. He also told the jury that

Massino was involved in plenty of other Bonanno crime family operations including loan-sharking and gambling that involved games of baccarat and Joker Poker machines.

After Cantarella finished testifying, the prosecution called his cousin, Joseph D'Amico, to the stand. D'Amico was the fifth Bonanno family member to turn against Massino. Like his cousin, D'Amico dressed well, wearing a gray suit, a white shirt, and a rose-colored tie. While the other turncoats were uncomfortable as witnesses, it was D'Amico who expressed how distasteful his life as an informant had become.

D'Amico told the jury that his own mother had been a loan shark. But he denied a fanciful story that had been circulating among Mafia cognoscenti for years that she had paid the late Carmine Galante up to $50,000 so that her son could be inducted into the crime family.

"If that was true I would like my money back," D'Amico quipped.

D'Amico said he liked the mob life and told the jury that his induction in 1977 into the Mafia took place in the kitchen of an apartment in Little Italy. It was during the ceremony, D'Amico recalled, that one of the participants asked him, "Would you leave your own family and protect someone in this family first?" His response was a simple "yes."

Asked about the Mirra homicide, D'Amico confirmed what Cantarella had said earlier. Mirra had embarrassed the family and had committed an unforgivable sin when he brought undercover agent Joseph Pistone within the orbit of the Bonanno family. D'Amico admitted that he shot his cousin in the head.

Mob life was clearly what D'Amico had lived for. He seemed to revel in the excitement and danger. He told the jurors that he even had John Gotti as a wedding guest, and he submitted a picture into evidence that showed a smiling Gotti shaking the hand of a beaming D'Amico, all dressed up in a black tuxedo and sporting a white bow tie.

Cross-examined by David Breitbart about leaving Mafia life, D'Amico said he had done so reluctantly.

"I rather not be here," D'Amico said. "I rather be where I was, living downtown."

Any other place would suit D'Amico fine. He just would rather not be in the Brooklyn courtroom facing the stares of Joseph Massino.

CHAPTER 25

"I Had Killed for Him"

The first month of the trial seemed a surreal spectacle for the family of Joseph Massino. It followed a routine in which Josephine Massino would drive in from Howard Beach, sometimes accompanied by both of her daughters, and then run the gauntlet of news photographers outside the courthouse in Brooklyn. Once inside, she would take her seat in the front row of the public seating in an area the U.S. Marshals had reserved for the defendant's family.

If Josephine got to court early enough before the session started, she would be able to converse with her husband about family finances, which because of restraints put on their bank accounts by the government, could not be easily accessed. Massino always thought a lot about food and he often asked his wife a central question: "What did you eat?" He knew that the stress of the trial was causing her to lose weight and that was bothering him. There had also been an unexpected complication. Josephine's older sister, Anna, had suffered what appeared to be a stroke a few days after opening statements and this meant hospital visits at the end of the day.

It was always something. Massino learned of his sister-in-law's medical trauma during a visit by his wife and daughters to the Brooklyn jail where he was being held. He immediately sensed a problem from the depressed look on the faces of his wife and daughters.

"Let Mommy tell you," Joanne told her father as he pressed for details.

"What?" Massino asked again.

"Let Mommy tell you," she insisted.

Finally, as Josephine Massino began to relate the story of her sister's travails, the weeks of tension and stress became unbearable. She broke down as she told Massino the details. Her sister had been the center of gravity for the family. One of Josephine Massino's problems, and she had many at this point, was that she kept her emotions pent up as the problems began to mount. With Anna out of action, Josephine had no one to seek solace from. She had no outlet. She told friends she didn't want to go for walks, talk to a priest, or do things that might release the tension.

Even if the Massino women wanted to escape the reality of their lives, it would have been difficult to get away entirely. The newspapers and television stations were running daily coverage of the trial, with gory details of the three captains and other murders played out in bold headlines. Pictures of Josephine Massino and her two sisters were shown to the jury because they also captured Massino himself in the presence of other mobsters. Even a surveillance photo taken at the Sands beach club in Atlantic Beach when Adeline had her wedding was shown. When Frank Coppa testified, the jury saw his holiday snaps, which showed him and his wife with Massino and Josephine in Paris and Monte Carlo. Nothing seemed private anymore.

For the Massino women, the trial seemed unreal. Of course, they understood that events involving their very own family were being portrayed. But it all sounded like some movie.

On June 28, 2004, things got even more personal. Josephine Massino had been waiting for weeks for her brother to take the witness stand. There had been rumors that Salvatore Vitale would have been called early. Instead, the prosecution intended to use him as the capstone to a case that was getting increasingly stronger with each witness appearing to buttress what the preceding ones had told the jury.

It was 4:20 in the afternoon when Salvatore Vitale finally walked through the rear door of the courtroom, the one that confidential witnesses who were under federal protection always made their entrance. Vitale had reveled in the street name "Good Looking Sal." But while he still had the fading features of an old nightclub lounge lizard, Vitale had not aged well. His face seemed puffy and his hair was no longer dark but mostly gray. It was little known, but Vitale had suffered a heart attack some years earlier. On this day, when he raised his right hand to swear to tell the truth on the Bible held by court clerk Joseph Reccoppa, Vitale was fifty-six years old. He looked ill at ease.

The courtroom was dead silent as Vitale shifted into his seat. His sister, Josephine, sat sphinx-like, her mouth pressed shut and her lips in a straight line that contained her deep-seated rage. Her daughter, Joanne, sat next to her, arms folded in defiance. Adeline clutched a notebook into which she had been writing notes about the testimony of each witness.

With prosecutor Greg Andres as his interlocutor, Vitale began what would be a momentous week of testimony. Things started slowly with Vitale recounting how he had met Massino at the age of eleven or twelve while growing up in Maspeth. Their relationship was what he described a "good relationship" that led to a close friendship. When Vitale returned from a stint in the military, he took a job on one of Massino's catering trucks, using it as a base for numbers running until the early 1990s.

Through the other witnesses, the prosecution had already established some of the practices and procedures of the Mafia—the passing of money from rackets up the chain of command and how the orders of the boss had to be obeyed at all costs—but Vitale had to flesh them out a bit. Moving in broad strokes, Andres had Vitale explain that once Massino went to prison in the late 1980s Massino used him to communicate with Bonanno family members. Vitale said that both he and Anthony Spero were used by Massino as a committee to run the family on a day-to-day basis. About once a month, said Vitale, he visited Massino during this period in prison.

Vitale eventually stopped seeing Massino in prison because the crime boss feared that officials might become suspicious of them and not let him out of prison. He would let his surrogates run things on their own.

"Whatever you and Anthony Spero want to do is fine with me," Massino said, according to Vitale.

Before the prison visits stopped, Massino told Vitale that while Philip Rastelli was the boss, the old mobster was sick and would die soon. Massino liked Rastelli but didn't respect his leadership ability. How smart could Rastelli be—he spent half of his life in jail, Vitale remembered Massino saying. When Rastelli died, Massino wanted Spero to call a meeting. At the meeting of the captains, Massino said someone, either his brother-in-law or James Tartaglione, should second the motion to make Massino boss. Vitale said that Massino had another directive: protect the family at all costs, even if it meant killing someone.

Rastelli died in 1991 and it was during a meeting at a house in Staten Island that Spero held the rigged election and the imprisoned Massino was officially anointed as boss, a job he really already held de facto for years.

He may have loved his sister, but it didn't take long for Vitale to link Josephine to her husband's dealings. He stated that while he was barred from visiting Massino, he communicated with him through his sister. He also testified that Massino continued to make money from criminal activity while in prison and that he passed along the boss's share to Josephine. On the subject of money, Vitale said that it was the key goal of the Bonanno family and that he personally made two or three million dollars from the rackets, cash he split with Massino.

"I didn't have any obligation to do that, he gave me the position I had, he made me what I am," said Vitale. "He made me a Goodfellow, he made me the captain, he made me underboss, I felt any score came to me through the men, it only would be right to give him 50 percent."

It was in the mid-1990s that Vitale said his relationship with Massino changed radically. Though Massino had made him underboss, Vitale said the position was an empty shell. Massino kept captains away from Vitale, forbidding them from even calling his brother-in-law. Christmas gifts were also banned. In Mafia-speak, Vitale was "on the shelf." He had a title but it was just a job as a figurehead. The loss of status had gnawed at Vitale and he felt vulnerable, believing his wife and children would be left in the street if anything ever happened.

Even though he was shelved from 1995 to 2003 and felt degraded, Vitale said he continued to kick up money to Massino and commit crimes for him.

"I had killed for him," said Vitale.

Before the bad blood developed between the two men, Vitale said that he took a strong personal interest in Massino's family, particularly when the crime boss was in prison.

"I was taking care of my sister and her children . . . support her, take her out to dinner, keep her strong," explained Vitale.

Josephine showed no reaction to that comment, but her daughter, Joanne, bolted from her seat in a huff, muttering, and walked out the courtroom door. The brief flurry caught Greg Andres's attention and although he didn't stop his questioning, the prosecutor brought it up to Garaufis outside the presence of the jury.

"There were a variety of people in the audience that told me they heard one of his [Massino] daughters saying that Mister Vitale was lying, it was audible and the jury reacted to that," Andres said. He asked Garaufis to either move the family from its coveted front-row seats or bar Massino's kin from the courtroom.

David Breitbart, who had been having numerous skirmishes with Andres over issues large and small, questioned whether what Andres said was true.

"I didn't hear a word and I was sitting in the well of the court," the lawyer said.

Massino's family kept their seats in the front row, just in time for them to hear the beginning of the worst of what Vitale had to offer. Vitale admitted he committed eleven murders and that eight of them also involved Massino. He ticked off what was now a familiar list of victims for the jury: Joseph "Doo Doo" Pastore, Philip "Lucky" Giaccone, Dominick Trinchera, Alphonse "Sonny Red" Indelicato, Dominick "Sonny Black" Napolitano, Cesare Bonventre, Gabriel Infante, Anthony Tomasulo, Robert Perrino, Russell Mauro, and Gerlando Sciascia.

Three of the murders, Vitale said, were ordered by both himself and Anthony Spero. Those victims were Perrino, the *New York Post* supervisor, Tomasulo, who was threatening Bonanno members and cheating on gambling earnings, and Mauro, a Bonanno member who was abusing drugs and suspected of talking to law enforcement.

The significance of Vitale's grim list of victims was not lost on anyone in the courtroom. While other witnesses like Frank Coppa, Frank Lino, and Joseph D'Amico talked knowledgeably about one, two, three, or four of the murders, Vitale had a wider field of vision. He could implicate Massino in all six charged murders, plus a few more as a bonus for the prosecution. The list of victims set up hours of testimony from Vitale about the murders he and Massino took part in during their decades in the Bonanno family. It was "This Is Your Life Joseph Massino" through the story of gangland hits.

Vitale didn't play a role in actually killing Pastore, Massino's old cigarette smuggling partner. But he agreed to clean up the small apartment on Fifty-eighth Avenue in Maspeth after the murder when Massino asked him to do so. Vitale also related how Massino, just before Pastore was killed, asked his brother-in-law to borrow nearly ten thousand dollars from the victim, money that would never be repaid.

"I went upstairs with a bucket and brush and cleaned up the area," said Vitale. He didn't find a body but he did see a mess. "All blood, all over the place, even inside the refrigerator."

The murder of the three captains occurred at a time when Vitale was not yet a member of the crime family. But he played a key role nonetheless. What he had to tell the jury put Massino squarely in the planning and execution of the slaughter. As he had told the FBI in his many hours of debriefings, Vitale said that Massino had solicited the advice of Gambino boss Paul Castellano and Junior Persico of the Colombo family when he learned that the three captains were supposedly arming themselves.

"Joe Massino said they said you have to defend youself, do what you have to do," Vitale stated.

Pressed by Andres for what that statement meant, Vitale answered, "Kill the three captains."

Dominick Napolitano, who was aligned with Massino in the power struggle, wanted his new friend Donnie Brasco, who was actually undercover FBI agent Joseph Pistone, to play a significant role in the slaughter of the three captains, Vitale remembered. But he said that a wary Massino said no.

Vitale, who had earlier obtained drop cloths and rope with which to tie up the bodies, said he was hiding in a closet with Vito Rizzuto of Canada, another Canadian named "Emmanuel," and another man who carried a shotgun. Rizzuto and Emmanuel had pistols and Vitale said he had a tommy gun, which he accidentally discharged before the real shooting started. Everyone wore ski masks.

On the prearranged signal, Gerlando Sciascia running his hand through his hair, everyone in the closet ran out and Rizzuto declared it was a stick up, said Vitale. While Vitale and the shotgun-toting gangster were told to guard the exit door so no one escaped, Lino made his escape before anyone could stop him, Vitale remembered.

Vitale saw all the men in the room when the shooting started and he remembered seeing Massino hit Giaccone, although he didn't tell the FBI that in his debriefings.

"It was all hell broke lose," Vitale said when cross-examined by Breitbart. "It was a matter of seconds, five seconds, ten seconds."

In the eerie moments after the killing, Vitale remembered coming back into the room where the shootings occurred and noticing that almost everyone had left.

"The only one standing in the room with the three dead bodies was Joe Massino," said Vitale. "We just looked at each other to say 'where did everybody go?'"

Vitale stayed around with the others to pack up the bodies in the drop cloths and lift them into a van that was driven to Howard Beach by James Tartaglione. At the intersection of 161st Avenue and Flushing Boulevard, two Gambino crime family members, Gene Gotti and John Carneglia, were waiting to take the corpses away for disposal, said Vitale.

The bloodshed of 1981 continued, Vitale said, with the murder of Napolitano, whose death was arranged by Massino. Vitale said he learned of the plot after Massino summoned him to Howard Beach and took him on a walk-and-talk stroll. Massino was angry, said Vitale, over the Donnie Brasco penetration of the crime family by the FBI and was going to give Napolitano "a receipt" for the fiasco. That term meant that Massino wanted Napolitano dead, Vitale told the jury. He added that his brother-in-law believed that even if he was convicted of the murder of the three captains, he would have the satisfaction of killing Napolitano.

Vitale admitted driving Massino to Staten Island in a van the day Napolitano was killed, and he remembered Frank Lino coming over to the vehicle and saying, "It is over, it's done, he is dead." There was some joking, Vitale remembered, with Massino telling Lino to hurry up in wrapping things up.

Concerning the Anthony Mirra homicide, Vitale wasn't present, but he recalled for the jury two incriminating conversations Massino had about the killing. Once, Vitale overheard Massino tell Al Embarrato that "it's unfortunate but Tony Mirra has got to go." Another time Vitale said Massino told him that "Richie Cantarella and Joe D'Amico killed Tony Mirra in the car."

Vitale also confirmed Tartaglione's account of events leading up to the murder of Cesare Bonventre in 1984, including the private conversation Massino had with Louis Attannasio that seemed to precipitate the planning. It was after that private talk, which took place at Massino's secret refuge while he was on the lam in Pennsylvania, that Attanasio told Vitale of the plan.

"We are going to kill Cesare and I need your help to set it up," Attanasio told him, according to Vitale.

Vitale then told the jurors how Bonventre was driven after he left his car near Flushing Avenue and Metropolitan Avenue in Maspeth to a nearby garage. As the car he was driving approached the garage, Vitale said he blurted out the prearranged signal "It looks good to me" at which point Attanasio, who was in the backseat, shot Bonventre. A struggling Bonventre tried to crash the vehicle, and after he tumbled out of the car in the garage Attanasio shot him again for the coup de grâce, said Vitale.

According to Vitale, Massino passed instructions to Gabe Infanti to dispose of Bonventre's body by dismembering it.

It was a job that failed utterly since the body was found a few weeks later in two steel drums in New Jersey.

The parade of hits kept coming from Vitale as he related to the jury how it was Massino who wanted the hapless Infanti, who had screwed up disposing of Bonventre's corpse and bungled the shooting of Teamster official Anthony Giliberti, killed for his incompetence.

"I want it done and I want it done now," was how Vitale characterized Massino's order to execute Infante.

Louis Restivo, Frank Lino, and Tommy Pitera were involved in the killing of Infanti at a warehouse, said Vitale.

Some murders, such as those of *New York Post* supervisor Robert Perrino and gangsters Russell Mauro and Anthony Tomasullo, didn't involve Massino, who was in jail at the time, said Vitale. But the 1999 murder of Gerlando Sciascia (whose death had come to the notice of Louis Freeh and Charles Rooney at the FBI) was ordered by Massino with the command, "George has got to go . . . call Tony Green [Anthony Urso] and take care of it." According to Vitale, Massino then said he was leaving the following day for a trip to Cancun, Mexico, and asked that the murder be done by the time he got back.

To make it look like Sciascia was killed as part of a drug deal gone bad, his body was dumped on the street in the Bronx. To bolster the impression that the mob had nothing to do with Sciascia's death, Massino ordered his captains to not only attend the wake but also to ask around about who would want to kill the Canadian gangster, said Vitale. But all of that mock concern, he added, was simply a smoke screen to divert suspicion from the Bonanno family. Even so, Vitale said that Vito Rizzuto, the crime family's key member in Canada, never did believe Sciascia died over drugs.

Evidence about the murders was bad enough. However, Vitale had plenty of insight into the financial dealings of his brother-in-law, matters that were at the core of the government's allegation that Massino had amassed a fortune through a life of crime. According to Vitale, he and and Massino ran a loan-sharking operation from about 1975 to 1999. Vitale's role, at least in the beginning, was to make collections on the loans while Massino served as the business builder by finding new customers. Over time, Vitale said that he and Massino each earned a million dollars from the lending. Other Bonanno family members took part in the loan-sharking, including Anthony Urso, he said.

Prosecutors also had charged Massino with extorting hundreds of thousands of dollars from a business known as King Caterers and Vitale was well aware of what had happened. The company was located in Farmingdale, New York, which is on Long Island. One of the company principles, said Vitale, needed protection from an encroachment by Carmine Avellino of the Lucchese family. Sometime between 1984 and 1985, the official at King Caterers approached Vitale through an old friend of Massino's in Maspeth and asked for help.

As is common in organized crime when there is a dispute about a business, mobsters will hold a meeting, a sitdown, and hash things out. The negotiations over King Caterers took place on Prince Street in Manhattan and Vitale testified that he, Massino, Avellino, and Bonanno captain Steven Cannone attended. Massino used a bluff to increase his negotiating position by falsely saying that one of the principles of the catering firm was a distant cousin of his. In the end, King Caterers was given to Massino and the Bonanno family, said Vitale.

In return for the protection of the Bonanno crime family, King Caterers worked out employment agreements for Massino and Vitale to act as food consultants over a three-year period, Vitale said. He and Massino were to each be paid a fee of $25,000 with the expectation that both men would become partners in the business after three years.

Eventually, because the principles of King Caterers were

not paying all their taxes, Vitale said that he and Massino decided to set up their own company—Queen Caterers—as a buffer through which they would receive payment for any bogus services they rendered to the King firm. The arrangement was to insulate them from any tax problems King Caterers might have. Vitale figured that at some point the King firm might get subpoenaed and told the company owners to say if the government asked that Massino made the sauce, which he did maybe one time. Vitale further explained that at some point he and Massino sold their share in King Caterers back to its principles for $650,000 in cash, split equally.

As Vitale testified, he dragged his sister, Josephine, into things. Vitale had already told the FBI agents that when Massino was in prison he allegedly paid his brother-in-law's share of money from various illegal ventures to Josephine. On the witness stand, Vitale repeated that and aside from embarrassing his sister he was potentially implicating her in wrongdoing through her acceptance of the funds. He also had said that he kept in contact with Massino while he was in jail through his wife, though he didn't indicate what the substance of those conversations where.

At the same time, Vitale also showed that he was trying to buffer Josephine from the possibility that she could be charged for handling alleged proceeds of crimes. He stated that as part of his agreement to cooperate with the government it was expressly stated that nothing he said could be used against his sister. Vitale also said he had agreed not to testify against his sister. It seems family still counted for something to him.

With her family affairs laid out for the world to see, including some pictures that were meant to be happy family snaps, Josephine Massino became more exasperated. Despite the fact that Vitale wouldn't ever testify against her, Josephine made clear her feelings about her sibling. "I hate that man," she was overheard saying under her breath.

It was on David Breitbart's cross-examination that Vitale revealed the depth of his anger and loathing for Massino. Asked when he decided to become a turncoat, Vitale said it was actually on January 9, 2003, the day both he and Massino were arrested together. Resentment had been festering for a long time.

"He separated me from the [crime] family, he tried to separate me from my personal family," said Vitale. "When I got indicted no one called my wife and children to see if I needed anything."

The latter was an increasingly common complaint among other mafiosi, who resented the lack of attention and concern shown for them once they got arrested. Such cavalier inattention would have been unheard of in Joseph Bonanno's time among the Castellammarese who made up the Mafia. But this was a changed Cosa Nostra, one with a flawed sense of loyalty among thieves. It was a major reason why Vitale decided to flip sides.

"That is when I thought my thoughts and said he don't deserve the respect and honor with me sitting next to him," said Vitale contemptuously, shooting a glance at his brother-in-law. Massino stared back at him.

Aside from some inconsistencies between what he said earlier to the FBI agents and what he said in court about events surrounding some of the homicides, Vitale seemed to hold up well on cross-examination. Andres had some questions on redirect that gave Vitale a chance to reiterate how Massino had taught him everything he knew about organized crime. In a stroke of irony, Vitale recalled that during his induction ceremony in 1984 it had been Massino who had lorded over the proceedings and had made the boastful remark, "We never had a rat in the family."

Vitale's testimony was completed at 4:05 P.M. on July 6. Excused by Judge Nicholas Garaufis, Vitale got up from his chair on the witness stand. He turned without looking at either Josephine, her husband, and her two daughters, and walked out the rear courtroom door. An expressionless Josephine followed him out the door with her eyes. The back of his head, the one she used to stroke when he was a little boy, would be the last thing she would ever again see of the brother.

CHAPTER 26

"Not One We Won"

Salvatore Vitale's testimony about Joseph Massino was like the Rosetta Stone of archaeology when it came to the Bonanno crime family. He had been so close to Massino over the years and had taken part in so many crimes with him that Vitale provided prosecutors with an overview of just about everything the crime boss had done. Vitale also gave meaning and context to a lot of the power struggles and politics of the crime family. It was the kind of stuff a jury could eat up.

But while the prosecution could have finished up with Vitale, there was still about three weeks of testimony that followed him. Next to the Mafia cooperators, much of the remaining testimony was dull and uneventful. Some dealt with crime scene investigations of the arson at the office of Doctor Leifer. An FBI agent told the jury about certain wiretaps that were placed on the telephones of the late Gambino captain Angelo Ruggiero in the 1980s. A low-level Bonanno operative testified about the crime family gambling operations in the cafés and coffee shops of Queens.

About a week after Vitale had finishing testifying, another old friend of Massino's took the witness stand. He was now forty-seven years old and looked more mature than the fuzzy surveillance photograph had depicted. Clean cut and well dressed, Duane Leisenheimer was a changed man. Once a stand-up guy who went to prison rather then testify to a grand jury about Massino, Leisenheimer was now helping the government.

As Leisenheimer settled into the witness chair, his eyes and facial expression showed both recognition and resignation as he glanced at Massino. Under questioning by prosecutor Robert Henoch, Leisenheimer said he had already distanced himself from Massino when in June 2003 he was visited by FBI agents Kimberly McCaffrey and Jeffery Sallet at his home.

The two agents were very direct in what they had to say and handed Leisenheimer a subpoena.

"You went to jail once for this guy, you don't need to go to jail again," McCaffrey said to him.

After retaining a lawyer, Leisenheimer said he met with prosecutor Greg Andres, who took a hard line with him, telling Massino's old friend that he had a lot more to worry about than the contempt charge he had faced in 1984. By this time other witnesses like Salvatore Vitale and Richard Cantarella had been cooperating for months. Particularly in the case of Vitale's cooperation, Leisenheimer was implicated in a lot of crimes.

"It doesn't look good," Leisenheimer said his lawyer told him. He decided to cooperate.

"I had a big decision to make," said Leisenheimer. "I had a family to think about."

Leisenheimer related to the jury his long relationship with Massino, which began in his teens and went on for decades. Massino had been his mentor in crime, involving him as a kind of office assistant in the three captains and Cesare Bonventre murders. It was during the killing of the three captains that Leisenheimer was given the job of sitting in a vehicle a few blooks away from the scene of the murders to monitor a walkie-talkie. Leisenheimer didn't see the shootings but was involved in the cleaning up of the crime scene, describing for the jury Vitale's annoyance when rigor mortis had set in with the corpses.

In the case of Bonventre's killing, Leisenheimer described how Massino had told him while they were on the lam in Pennsylvania that Philip Rastelli was the one who put the murder plot in motion.

"'Cesare Bonventre's gotta go, the old man wants Cesare to go, this is at Marty's instigating,'" Massino said, according to Leisenheimer. He explained that the "old man" was Philip Rastelli and that "Marty" referred to Rastelli's brother, who apparently had passed along the murder message.

Leisenheimer said his job was to find a garage where Bonventre's murder could be facilitated. He found a place that he sometimes used as an auto chop shop off Metropolitan Avenue. After Bonventre's body was driven away in the trunk of an Oldsmobile, the dead man's own car, a 1980s Cadillac, was cut up in the garage, said Leisenheimer. He then drove back to the Poconos.

The only other key witness to testify was FBI agent Kimberly McCaffrey. Because of her involvement in the early stages of the investigation, McCaffrey was able to detail how things got started in the forensic accounting work. Questioned by Andres, she described the discovery of extortion victim Barry Weinberg and the development of his friend, Agostino Scozzari, as witnesses who had a field day making secret tapes.

McCaffrey also gave a window into the finances of Massino and his wife. There were three parking lot businesses in lower Manhattan that she found Josephine had an interest in, along with her brother, Salvatore, and Richard Cantarella's wife, Loretta. McCaffrey also described the compensation each received, ranging in amounts from around $18,000 in some years to as low as $7,500. McCaffrey also described for the jury the discovery of checks Josephine had written to Weinberg for amounts ranging from

$16,666 to $10,000, checks that led investigators to Weinberg as a target for tax crimes. Massino's finances weren't the only ones detailed by McCaffrey. She told the jury how, after Vitale began to cooperate, that agents found hundreds of thousands of dollars he had stashed in safe deposit boxes, in a safe in his home, and in a secret compartment in his attic.

There was one more FBI agent who testified about Massino's finances. Agent Dan Gill had examined the books of King and Queen Caterers. Over an eleven-year-period, said Gill, he found that Queen Caterers, the firm Vitale said was used to hold the extortion money from King Caterers, received $1,048,500 as compensation for distribution to Vitale and Massino.

Massino's tax returns were also submitted to the jury and showed a steady growth in income. From 1992 when Massino and Josephine had shown a gross income of $121,667, the amount grew to $411,672 in 2001, with a high of $590,789 in 1998. Some of the income, McCaffrey said, came from real estate investments and occasional lottery winnings. Neither McCaffrey nor Gill said that the tax returns they examined found any criminal tax violations.

Summations began on July 21 and the government's side was presented by Mitra Hormozi. Dressed in a black pants suit, she seemed none the worse for wear after a trial that had lasted nine weeks. She had to digest over 8,000 pages of transcript for the jury.

"All the evidence you have seen is a testament to Joseph Massino, to his ambition. To his ruthlessness and ultimately to his power," said Hormozi. "Ironically, perhaps Mister Massino summarized it best when he told his friend Richard Cantarella in describing himself before he became boss that he was a one-man army, a one-man army for Philip Rastelli. Think about that statement, it is a powerful statement."

Hormozi said that the trial showed that Massino orchestrated the murders of Alphonse Indelicato, Philip Giaccone,

Dominick Trinchera, Dominick Napolitano, Anthony Mirra, Cesare Bonventre, and Gabriel Infante. He also tried to get Anthony Giliberti killed. On top of that, Massino amassed millions of dollars through gambling, extortion, arson, and loan-sharking.

"Every piece of evidence in this case, whether it came from the witnesses, the ballistics, the medical evidence, the crime scene evidence, photographs, every single piece points to the defendant's guilt," she said. "Not a single piece of credible evidence points to any other logical conclusion."

When his turn came to speak to the jury, defense attorney David Breitbart essentially conceded again that Massino was the Bonanno boss. But he hit back with the theme he had pushed all along: that Massino didn't have the authority to have the murders committed.

"There were no murders in the nineties," he said about the period after Massino became crime boss. "He showed a love of life, not a love of death, because murders ceased."

Breitbart returned to his theme from his opening statement that the cooperating witnesses were experts in the "big lie" and could deceive people to walk unwittingly to their deaths. He spewed venom at Vitale, calling him a "degenerate liar" and a jealous, vicious killer.

"If you find witnesses lied about an element in the case," Breitbart told the jury, "you have the absolute capacity to say 'out.'"

Since the government has the burden of proof in criminal cases, it gets a chance to rebut the defense summation and in this case the job fell to Andres. He ridiculed Breitbart's claim that Massino was a peaceful mob boss. No handshakes cemented Massino's rise to power, Andres said; rather, it was bullets and guns. He also noted that far from an interregnum of peace, Massino's reign had been punctured by the murder of Gerlando Sciascia in 1999, a crime not part of the indictment but still shown by the evidence to have occurred.

After a two-hour explanation of the law by Judge Nicholas Garaufis, the jury finally began deliberations on July 26. Four days later, on July 30, the jury signaled it had reached a verdict just before lunchtime. FBI agents, courthouse personnel, news media, and Massino's family all filled up the courtroom. The jury foreperson, a woman, handed up the long verdict sheet to court clerk Joseph Reccoppa, who in turn handed it to Garaufis. The judge glanced at the sheet and then handed it back to his clerk, who gave it back to the foreperson. Reccoppa then asked the jury to announce its verdict.

The words *guilty* and *proven* were spoken twenty-two times, once for every single count in the indictment and also for each of the racketeering acts—the murders, gambling, loan-sharking, arson, and money laundering—that Massino had been accused of.

With the first guilty finding, Josephine Massino clamped her lips ever tighter and began to shake her head. As each "guilty" was announced, Massino's daughter, Adeline, became crestfallen, her shoulders slumping each time the word was spoken. She cradled her chin in her hands, elbows on her knees, as she stared at the floor. When the verdict was finished, Massino shot a glance at his wife and shrugged as if to say, "What can you do?" Finally turning in her seat, Adeline said to no one in particular, "Not one we won, not one," referring to the myriad charges.

Outside the courtroom, prosecutors and FBI agents embraced and kissed. It had been a resounding victory. Breitbart and Flora Edwards were silent, preferring not to say anything. Josephine Massino and her daughter left the courthouse in silence, refusing to speak to reporters, some of whom told them how sorry they felt for them.

The news media had assembled early that morning and by the time the Massino family left the courthouse they were surrounded by photographers. Walking in silence to the Park Plaza Diner, a favorite eatery for the courthouse crowd,

Josephine Massino went into a back dining room. She was accompanied by Michelle Spirito, the wife of reputed Bonanno soldier John Spirito. A cancer survivor who had lost her larynx through surgery, Michelle Spirito couldn't speak but had tears in her eyes.

"I have nothing to say," a distressed Josephine Massino finally said.

As if the verdict hadn't been enough, the jury still had to decide on how much money Massino had to forfeit to the government as fruits of his crimes. Prosecutors were asking for over $10 million and wanted to take the shuttered CasaBlanca Restaurant and a rental property located on Fresh Pond Road in Queens. The government was also going after the home of Massino and his wife in Howard Beach, the home Massino's mother, Adeline, was living in on Caldwell Avenue in Maspeth, as well as the family home Josephine had been raised in, also in Maspeth. Other properties were also in the government's sights, including real estate Josephine received rental income from.

The forfeiture case was actually a small trial that took place immediately after the lunch break following Massino's conviction. FBI agent Dan Gill testified again about Massino's estimated worth and the estimated criminal proceeds he received over the years. It was no surprise that Gill's estimate came to over $10 million. Breitbart put up a meager defense case, essentially asking the jury to have a heart and not put Josephine out on to the street. It didn't matter. The jury ruled that Massino had to forfeit the $10 million.

It is possible that Massino could have written a check for the $10 million, turned over the restaurant property, and thus satisfied the forfeiture. But usually the government will seize what it can find. While many believed that Josephine Massino could be tossed out of her house, that wasn't the case. Because she had the property jointly with her spouse, even if the government took over Massino's half, it was highly unlikely that she could be evicted. She could live there until she died.

Back in Howard Beach at Josephine's home on Eighty-fourth Street, her family gathered for what was sort of a mob family *shiva*. One relative railed about Vitale, saying none of this would have happened if he hadn't cooperated, a statement that was true to some extent, because he proved to be such a pivotal witness. Yet another relative said that while Vitale was a turncoat he was still family.

Joanne Massino had not been in court when the verdict against her father was announced. She learned of it instead in a telephone call. Her own children knew in a vague way that their grandfather had been on trial since their only contact with him in recent months had been either through jail visits or letters. A few days after the verdict her daughter, obviously sensing the distress in the adults around her, asked how things were going with the trial.

"The jury didn't believe Poppy," answered Joanne.

"That's what I thought," the child said.

CHAPTER 27

Endgame

When they want to hide things from prying eyes on the sixth floor of the courthouse in Brooklyn, the metal fire doors get closed. When the black doors are shut, there is simply no way to see who enters and leaves the courtroom where Judge Nicholas Garaufis presided.

It was sometime late in the afternoon of July 30, after the jury had come down with its second verdict giving the federal government over $10 million of Joseph Massino's assets, that court officials closed the fire doors. The hallway was sealed for privacy.

Just before the doors were shut, a federal marshal had walked into Garaufis's chambers and had a word with one of the judge's staff. Federal judges have a number of support staff working for them. Schedules need to be arranged, problems solved, and paper work handled and for that the jurists have a bevy of clerks, assistants, and other aides. Practically speaking, judges are helpless without them, particularly when the unexpected happens.

On the afternoon of July 30, the unexpected happened. One of Garaufis's staffers came into his chambers to say that Joseph Massino wanted a word with him.

The judge's private office faced Adams Street, the main venue for the Brooklyn Bridge and in the late afternoon of July 30, Joseph Massino stood before Garaufis as the traffic went by and the sun was reflecting off the apartment buildings across the boulevard. A court stenographer was the only other person in the room.

Massino had a straightforward but monumental request of Garaufis: the convicted mobster wanted a new lawyer appointed for him so that he could explore possible cooperation with the government. The meeting was short and after Massino was taken back to the holding cell, Garaufis told Greg Andres about what had happened. The judge needed a list of lawyers the government was comfortable with in the role of "shadow counsel" for Massino. Of course, David Breitbart and Flora Edwards were not to be told of this backroom maneuver.

So it was that one of the most seismic events in law enforcement's long struggle against organized crime got underway. Massino was a beaten man. He faced not only the certainty of life in prison and the loss of every tainted penny he had ever made but also the prospect that he could be executed if convicted—a strong likelihood—in the next year's trial for the murder of Gerlando Sciascia. It seemed clear to Massino that he had one card left to play and that was go to with Team America. In all likelihood, this was not a spur of the moment panicked decision by Massino. He had seen the progress of the trial and that the various witnesses were unshakeable in their testimony. The verdict shouldn't have surprised him.

Everybody else had become a rat, so with his own life at stake Massino must have figured an endgame strategy for himself long before the verdict. As a mobster, Massino had a tendency to figure ways of running from trouble. He went on the lam in 1982. When FBI agents paid him a visit in 1984, Massino seemed so spooked that he ran out the back door of his social club. He was a man who had always tried to have an escape plan. He had played the mob game like the good old man he was. But reality now was not in some emotional notion of blood loyalty spawned in Sicilian culture. No, reality was now the fact that in a coffin was the only way Massino would get out of prison. There had to be another way.

From the government's list of lawyers Garaufis appointed Edward C. McDonald as Massino's shadow counsel. The use of attorneys as "cooperating" lawyers has been criticized by some in the legal community as an anathema to the traditional role and function of a defense attorney. For some, it left a bad taste in that an attorney became involved in a legally approved subterfuge on the trial attorney who had zealously defended someone like Massino but yet didn't know the client had changed sides. However, the use of shadow counsel is legal and used regularly.

McDonald had been head of the old Brooklyn Organized Crime Strike Force in the 1980s, ironically the unit that had prosecuted Massino in the 1985 Teamsters case. Leaving government service, McDonald became a partner in a Manhattan law firm, specializing in criminal defense work.

Massino didn't start cooperating with the government right away. There were initial proffer sessions to go through before any agreement could be signed. The government was in the driver's seat and had to be convinced he could help law enforcement. Massino's initial approaches to the FBI were met with skepticism and he was rebuffed, said one law enforcement official.

The first glimmer the FBI had a new mob mole came in early October 2004. At an overgrown lot in the Lindenwood section of Queens, abutting the border with Brooklyn, federal agents and city police began digging. The place had seen excavation nearly twenty-three years earlier after Alphonse Indelicato's body began rising through the soil. Immediately, word leaked out that the FBI Bonanno squad was involved in the dig in a search for the remains of the still missing three captains murder victims. Agents Jeffrey Sallet and Kimberly

McCaffrey, dressed in their FBI raid jackets and accompanied by agency evidence collection agents, watched as the excavators brought in heavy equipment to tear up the ground and concrete at the site.

It wasn't a total surprise that the FBI would start digging again at the Ruby Street lot. One body had already been found there and immediate speculation centered on a new confidential informant having identified the location as a burial ground where other victims could be found. Some thought Salvatore Vitale, who had already told the FBI that Massino had said the three captains had been disposed of together, might have been the source. But according to one law enforcement official, Massino, in an informal effort at cooperation that didn't cost him much, had told the FBI that police had not looked hard enough when they first found Indelicato's body.

The digging went on for about three weeks and after some false alarms the forensic team recovered human bones. It took over two months for the medical examiner to make DNA comparisons, but it seemed like the dig had been productive. A credit card belonging to Dominick Trinchera and a watch traced to Philip Giaccone had been unearthed. On December 20, 2004, the FBI announced that the human remains found at Ruby Street were those of Trinchera and Giaccone.

Massino's secret dealings with the government, though still tentative and with no cooperation agreement signed, continued through the fall. He had not told his family what he was doing but there were hints Massino dropped that he was feeling abandoned by his crime family brethren. When it was announced in court that prosecutors would not be seeking the death penalty against his two codefendants in the Sciascia murder case, John Spirito and Patrick DeFilippo, Massino became depressed over the exultation shown, said a source familiar with the events. Massino was still on the hook for death and after the way his top lieutenants had turned on him he had become very bitter and felt abandoned, the source said.

With McDonald as his advisor, Massino continued his secret talks with the government. This was all done with his regular lawyer, Flora Edwards, kept in the dark while she gamely went on representing Massino in the upcoming death penalty case. In fact, Massino had asked Edwards to stay on the case after it became clear that David Breitbart would not be able to continue.

Just before Thanksgiving word leaked out that U.S. Attorney General John Ashcroft intended to seek the death penalty against Massino for the Sciascia murder. The ruling was formally announced in court by prosecutors Greg Andres and Nicolas Bourtin on November 12. The Ashcroft decision was another part of the government squeeze play on Massino.

Another move by the feds came on November 23, when Massino appeared in court to answer charges to a superseding indictment in the Sciascia murder case. This time the government added two more defendants, acting street boss Vincent Basciano and reputed Bonanno soldier Anthony Donato, accusing them of racketeering acts unrelated to Sciascia. Both in court and in the holding cells, Massino had a chance to chat with Basciano as they all entered not guilty pleas. Massino's machinations with the government remained a closely guarded secret.

On November 29, things took a curious turn. According to a letter filed in court by attorney Flora Edwards, Massino received a copy in the mail of a *Newsday* story about the fact that Garaufis had required closer monitoring of his health status. The article was confiscated and Massino was moved into a segregated housing unit (SHU) and no longer in the general population of the Brooklyn federal jail, said Edwards. Massino told his family of the move into solitary and the fact that the newspaper article had been confiscated.

Edwards said Massino's movement into the SHU made it difficult for him to prepare for trial, all because of a critical newspaper story. On December 22, said Edwards, prosecutor Andres told her that he had recommended that Massino be prohibited from attending codefendant meetings but wouldn't explain why, saying Garaufis was "fully aware of the facts and circumstances." Edwards said she pressed Andres for an explanation but that he stated the movement of Massino into solitary confinement had to do with Bureau of Prison policy regarding inmates on "death penalty" cases. Edwards continued to ask Garaufis to intervene. Little did she know the real story and the fact that the system was playing with her.

With hindsight, the movement of Massino into the SHU and the government recommendation that he be kept from meeting with codefendants Basciano, Donato, DeFillipo, and Spirito should have been a red flag. But a red flag about what? Never before had a crime family boss become a cooperating witness. Government explanations, which can now be viewed as cover stories, seemed plausible. Perhaps Massino had been plotting more crimes or was using codefendant meetings to pass messages to his underlings?

Massino's wife and daughters were also getting strange vibes. Before his move into solitary, he seemed more embittered to them, family sources said. He had lost about twenty-five pounds and in visits after he was placed in solitary he seemed distracted. Massino had said he was angry with the fact that there had been talk about a plot to kill Andres and said it all indicated that the Mafia had degenerated into a pack of animals, said one family source. From his rhetoric, Massino seemed to signal to his wife and daughters that he was considering becoming a cooperating witness. If you do, his family told him, you are on your own.

It was on the night of January 26 that Massino's immediate family learned that they shouldn't try to see him at the Brooklyn federal jail. He had been moved to the Manhattan federal jail, a sign that he was cooperating they were told.

The next day in the Brooklyn federal court another indictment was filed against acting street boss Vincent Basciano for the December 2004 murder of Bonanno associate Randolph Pizzolo. The court papers indicated that a cooperating witness relayed comments Basciano had made in a courthouse holding cell in November about the homicide. The indictment alleged that the cooperating witness also stated that Basciano had proposed the murder of prosecutor Andres, something Massino had alluded to in talking to his immediate family. Astonishingly, the incriminating comments had actually been tape recorded by the witness. Who was this "cooperating witness"? The indictment didn't say, but in a matter of minutes after the court papers were filed word leaked out: the new witness was none other than Joseph Massino. At the jail Massino met one final time with Edwards. He avoided eye contact with her. She left in a few minutes.

On Eighty-fourth Street in Howard Beach, the news that Massino had become a government informant and had taped his loyal surrogate Vincent Basciano was first disseminated over the all-news radio stations and was another in a long series of enormous emotional jolts. Josephine Massino stayed in seclusion, attended to by a close female friend who had sat with her throughout most of the trial. Quick-tempered daughter Joanne railed against her father and in a blast of anger said, "I am done with him, I am ashamed that he's my father."

In an e-mail interview with *Newsday*, Massino's daughter, Adeline, portrayed her father as embittered and having lost the support of his family with his decision to become an informant.

"My mother, my sister and I [have] no reason why he is doing this and probably never will," Adeline said. "Maybe he himself doesn't know that answer."

At least to his daughters, Massino's decision was a betrayal of the code of loyalty to friends he had always preached to them. They also felt betrayed because they supported him throughout his trial, even in the face of embarrassing disclosures about his infidelity. They also feared that their father's actions could endanger themselves and their own families, a not unreasonable sentiment in the dog-eat-dog life that now characterized the Mafia. Adeline said that her mother in particular had been hurt by Massino's actions during his married life and that she could no longer support him. There were hints that a divorce might even be in the cards.

Massino's turning was not officially acknowledged for some months. But the indications he had become a star government witness were plentiful. The clearest signal was the disclosure in May 2005 that the Department of Justice, led by Ashcroft's successor Alberto Gonzales, had decided to reverse itself and not seek the death penalty against Massino. It was an indication that Massino had done some significant cooperating and was catching a break.

Speculation abounded about what damage Massino could do to his Mafia brethren. By any measure, it was believed that he could hurt a lot of people. Basciano aside, Massino could also be expected to testify against other Bonanno defendants, including reputed Canadian crime boss Vito Rizzuto, who also faced charges stemming from the murder of the three captains and other allegations of racketeering. Rizzuto was fighting extradition from Canada after U.S. officials had disclosed in a letter filed with the Canadian courts the evidence against him in the three captains case.

Massino also had information about the Gambino crime family and he could prove troublesome for some of its members, including John "Junior" Gotti, the son of the late boss. Massino's information about the killing of the three captains could also be used to bring additional charges, if prosecutors wanted to go that route, against the late John Gotti's brother, Eugene, who was already in prison.

Massino's cooperating with the government delayed his sentencing in his racketeering case until June 23, 2005. Garaufis's courtroom again filled and in the crowd of spectators were Donna Trinchera, the wife of slain capo Dominick Trinchera, her daughter, Laura, as well as Donna Sciascia, the daughter of murdered Canadian mobster Gerlando Sciascia. The appearance of Sciascia's family members was a clear sign that Massino would also be wrapping up that murder case with a guilty plea.

At 12:48 P.M., a grim-looking Massino entered the courtroom from the holding cell. He was wearing a gray suit and had an open-necked white shirt. He sat at the defense table next to attorney Edward McDonald. Unlike his demeanor during trial, Massino appeared nervous. He kept scratching his face and putting his hand up to his mouth. In the back of the courtroom were FBI agents Jeffrey Sallet and Kimberly McCaffrey. Sallet had been transferred to Washington, D.C., with a promotion while McCaffrey continued the delicate task of handling Massino.

Neither Josephine Massino nor her daughters were in court. Minutes earlier, Josephine had entered Garaufis's chambers with her attorney and acknowledged to the judge that she had signed a forfeiture agreement. She was owner of record for some of the properties listed and Garaufis had to be satisfied that Massino's wife had signed off on what was to be a massive surrender of most—but not all—of the property she and her husband had acquired. Her spouse was not present in the room. After the formality with the judge was over, Josephine Massino left the courthouse, although she was unable to avoid being spotted by *Daily News* reporter John Marzulli.

At 12:51 P.M. in the hushed courtroom, Garaufis asked Massino to stand up. The judge had a few preliminary questions, asking the mob boss how far he had gone in school. Massino answered by saying the eighth grade at PS 73. Prosecutor Greg Andres, who had entered the courtroom with a large cup of coffee from a local gourmet shop, handed up to Garaufis the cooperation agreement Massino had signed earlier that day. So it was official, Joseph Massino the mob boss had signed on as a government witness.

It was well known that upon his conviction for racketeering in July 2004 Massino was going to get life in prison without parole, as well as a stiff fine. Massino acknowledged to Garaufis that he was indeed guilty of the crimes for which he had been convicted by a jury. By doing that, he squelched any chance of appeal and dropped the pretense that he was innocent. The Sciascia murder case was still open—but not much longer.

At 1:06 P.M., Massino said "yes your honor, guilty" when asked if he had orchestrated the Sciascia murder. Garaufis asked Massino to explain.

"As boss of the Bonanno family, I gave the order to kill George from Canada," said Massino.

That simple sentence in itself was amazing not just because Massino admitted his guilt but also because he had dropped the pretension that the crime family was his patrimony. He didn't say "Massino" crime family as he wanted the enterprise to be known. No, Massino instead acknowledged the supremacy of Joseph Bonanno's legacy. It was the "Bonanno family." Massino had just been renting the hall.

Pressed by Garaufis, Massino said that the killing was carried out by "Johnny Joe," who he said was a "goodfella," Patty DeFilippo, and "Mikey Nose." By his words, Massino implicated John Spirito, whose full name he didn't know, DeFilippo, and reputed Bonanno member Michael Mancuso in the Sciascia murder.

Part of Massino's bargain with the prosecutors was that he had to turn over a great deal of his wealth to the government. He didn't write a check for the $10 million, but he could have come darn close. Massino agreed to give the federal government $10,393,350 in assets. An astonishing $9 million of that was in cash ($7.3 million) and other assets like gold bars. He also turned over the property housing the

CasaBlanca Restaurant in Queens as well as two other buildings on Fresh Pond Road. Those properties had been held in Josephine's name. The staggering amount of cash showed that Massino had done very well for a neighborhood tough who never made it out of grade school.

Although the forfeiture agreement didn't spell it out, Massino was able to work out a deal that allowed his wife to keep title to the marital home in Howard Beach, his family's home in Maspeth where his elderly mother lived with her other son, John, and the old house off Grand Avenue where Josephine Massino had been raised. Josephine was also able to keep title to some real estate in Queens and Florida, the agreement indicated, something that allowed her to garner rental income.

Donna Sciascia had filed a letter with the court but asked that it not be disclosed. However, Laura Trinchera, the daughter of one of the slain three captains, allowed her letter to be read in open court and Garaufis did so for the benefit of the public and the news media. Trinchera's letter was the heartfelt statement of a daughter who never got to grow up with her father and lived for years not knowing where he had gone.

"I am grateful that our family now has closure and now my father is resting in his proper place," said Trinchera. "We now have a place to go and say our prayers.

"As far as Mister Massino, he took the opportunity to live out his life, to see his family grow. He took that away from us," she said. "I am here today to support Mister Massino's facing mandatory life in prison. I feel that better late than never."

Garaufis had been presiding over the Bonanno crime family cases for over two years and wanted to have his own say. There had been sixty-seven members and associates of the crime family named in various indictments and fifty-one, including Massino, had been convicted. The overwhelming majority had pled guilty.

"The evidence produced at Joseph Massino's trial last year told a sobering story of an organization devoted to the pursuit of crime and corruption. That evidence detailed the system utilized by organized criminals—and in particular, the Bonanno/Massino crime family—to conduct business, extract revenue from both legitimate and illegal activities, and enforce its rules against members and non-members alike," said Garaufis.

The judge said that the rituals and personalities of the mob "have been deeply romanticized in the popular media of the past thirty years, seemingly with ever-increasing frequency." But the true nature of that life made it prey on human frailty, greed, weakness, and fear, he said.

For the Sciascia murder, Massino was given a life sentence that was to run consecutive to the life term he received for his conviction in July 2004. He was saddled with a $250,000 fine as well.

Since he was cooperating, Massino would be able to seek a reduction in his sentence, assuming the government was happy with his cooperation and filed on his behalf a letter with the court saying so. These so-called 5K letters, named after a section of the federal sentencing guidelines, had become like gold to Mafia cooperators because they could lead to freedom from a long prison sentence.

The sentencing of Joseph Massino took about forty minutes. When it was over, a dour Massino quickly shuffled his way out of the courtroom in the company of federal marshals. He didn't look at any of the spectators. But those who did see his eyes peered into his soul and found nothing. His gaze was as cold, gray, and dead as gunmetal.

Epilogue

Over the years, the death of the American Mafia has been solemnly pronounced many times. In the 1970s, one local New York prosecutor predicted the mob would be dead in a couple of years. When the ruling Cosa Nostra Commission members were convicted in 1986, federal prosecutor Rudolph Giuliani announced that the governing body had been dismantled.

History turned out to be different. The Mafia gained strength through the 1990s. The Commission simply gained replacement members and continued meeting well into the time when Giuliani became mayor of New York City. The simple fact that law enforcement agencies continue to spend time, energy, and money on Cosa Nostra investigations is an indication that the mob is still with us.

But the world of the Mafia in the United States is much different from what it was in the 1930s, when Joseph Bonanno took over the clan that bears his name. No longer is the family composed of leaders who hailed from the same ancestral land around Castellammare del Golfo in Sicily. Those leaders had died off and took with them the ideals of loyalty and solidarity that had been a part of Sicilian culture that allowed the Mafia to flourish. That is not to say that loyalty and solidarity were gone from the mob. Joseph Massino took pride in those ideals when he was rising up in the mob. He remained fiercely loyal to Philip Rastelli and the old notion that the boss was to be followed no matter what.

But for every mafioso like Massino there was another who didn't value loyalty. The modern Mafia had become, as organized crime expert Ronald Goldstock observed, a group of individual criminals with individual goals of making money. With money as the quest of mob life, group loyalty is actually a very tenuous thing. With the right pressure from law enforcement, individual mafioso can be made to turn on each other, says Goldstock.

Some prosecutors are repelled by the amoral nature of men like Massino and those who were in the Bonanno family. The mafiosi are just plan scary to them. Sure, they play by rules. They are just not playing by the rules the rest of society plays by. Motivated by the goal of making money, the Mafia is just another nakedly capitalist venture impelled by greed, policing itself with murder when necessary. Joseph Massino then did what many in La Cosa Nostra have always done. He was ruthless when he had to be.

Not an educated man, Massino had an innate intelligence and realized that being a terrorizing, headstrong thug was not the way to survive in the criminal life. He liked being low key and treated law enforcement with respect. Still, if Massino honored old values like loyalty and group cohesion, he was painfully aware that such things weren't enough to guarantee the crime family could weather heat from investigators. Omerta might have worked to guarantee that mobsters in Sicily wouldn't betray each other. But in the United States, where law enforcement techniques and laws had evolved to a degree never seen in Sicily, omerta became ineffective in ensuring that there would be no betrayal to police. Draconian prison sentences weakened many mafioso, particularly the elderly who hoped they could still live long enough to enjoy something of a life outside of a cell with their sons and grandchildren.

Massino recognized the old adage that you keep your friends close and your enemies closer. He allowed the sons and relatives of older mafiosi to become made members and by doing so gained another form of control over members. Relatives who were Bonanno members could act as a form of checks and balances on each other since they each had something to gain and lose through the crime family. Relatives could also become informants on each other since it was Massino who ultimately controlled punishments and rewards.

But it was family that actually caused the biggest problem for Massino. He elevated his wife's brother to a high position of underboss in the Bonanno group. Salvatore Vitale had been a loyal underling to Massino as the latter rose through the mob. But while he was loyal, Vitale had problems as an administrator. Court testimony showed that a lot of the other mobsters didn't like him. He didn't garner the respect that an underboss should have been accorded. Some believed Vitale was an informant for about five years—although government records indicate that he wasn't—and thought he should be killed. Witnesses testified that Massino even considered doing away with Vitale. Yet, some in the Bonanno family remembered that when questions were raised about Vitale's loyalty and the suspicion that he might be an informant, it had been Massino who went around chastising people and telling them to stop spreading rumors.

Massino allowed Vitale to live. Massino would later be tape recorded in jail saying to Vincent Basciano that "to me, life is precious" and that he wouldn't kill someone unless transgressions were proved "in black and white." However, Massino didn't really work that way. Massino didn't hold courts of inquiry before a murder was allowed. He didn't give the accused the right to file an appeal. His reasons for ordering murders seem to have been as much motivated by fear of informants than any real malfeasance. That being the case, he could have had Vitale done away with as well. It seems Vitale lived and brought about Massino's demise because the crime boss was unable to take the step of murdering the man who had been so close to his own wife, Josephine. Family counted for something. It also cost him.

Though Massino had provided for Josephine and their daughters, he was not above using his own family to advance his stature with law enforcement. Court records show that when Massino was secretly tape recording Basciano in a federal jail, he claimed that Josephine had sent him messages about Bonanno family business and members. Massino obviously said that because he wanted to trick Basciano into revealing how he might be passing messages. What kinds of messages the crime boss actually received from his wife was something only he and she know for sure. But when Massino's remarks about his wife became public, there were tough headlines about it. MOBSTER TAPE TIES WIFE TO BONANNO BIZ, said one headline in the *Daily News*. Those kinds of stories made it seem like Josephine had been running the crime family.

As much as Massino tried to be an astute judge of human nature and frailty, he was brought down by those qualities in others. Elderly mafioso Frank Coppa didn't want to die in prison away from his grandchildren and decided to make a deal. Practical mafioso Frank Lino saw that when other Bonanno members decided to cooperate he had no way of beating the rap and also turned. Embittered mafioso Salvatore Vitale, marginalized by Massino, decided to lash out by cooperating. Even old cronies who were not in the mob like Duane Leisenheimer wanted to get on with their lives, raise their families while they were still young enough, and enjoy life.

Massino could instill fear and a grudging respect in his followers, but in the end that would never be enough to engender undying loyalty. Joseph Bonanno was right when he said that the old notion of the Mafia was gone. Cosa Nostra, "This Thing of Ours," had become for each mafioso "My Thing."

In the end, even Joseph Massino had to agree.

Where Are They Now?

(as of February 27, 2007)

Baldassare Amato (Bonanno soldier): Indicted in January 2004 on various racketeering charges in federal court in Brooklyn. Among the charges were allegations that Amato took part in the murder of Bonanno family associate Sebastian DiFalco in 1992. He was convicted in July 2006.

Greg Andres (prosecutor): After successfully prosecuting Joseph Massino in July 2004, Andres received an award from the Department of Justice for "superior performance by a litigation team" in convicting 35 members and associates of the Bonanno crime family. Massino was included in that total. He was also promoted in January 2006 to the position of deputy chief of the criminal division in the Brooklyn U.S. Attorney's Office. Andres continued to handle trials and in March 2006 was the lead trial counsel in the case of reputed acting Bonanno boss Vincent "Vinny Gorgeous" Basciano.

Vincent Basciano (acting Bonanno boss): The FBI and others in law enforcement considered Basciano to have been the acting boss of the Bonanno family from early 2004 until December of that year. Basciano was arrested in November 2004 on racketeering charges, including the murder of mob associate Randolph Pizzolo. In March 2006, Basciano went on trial for another federal racketeering case that included the 2001 killing of Frank Santoro in the Bronx. He was convicted of racketeering, but the jury came to a mistrial on the Santoro murder. Basciano was also scheduled to go on trial later in 2007 for the Pizzolo murder, a charge that is eligible for the federal death penalty.

David Breitbart (defense counsel): Continued to live and work in New York City and do criminal defense work. He represented model Naomi Campbell when she was arrested for assault in March 2006.

Richard Cantarella (Bonanno captain): Remained a cooperating witness for the federal government. He testified in the March 2006 trial of Basciano and was awaiting sentencing for racketeering.

Patrick Colgan (FBI agent): Was retired from the FBI and working as a private investigator in New Jersey. In March 2006 he testified as a prosecution witness in Brooklyn federal court in the "Mafia cops" trial.

Frank Coppa (Bonanno captain): Remained a cooperating witness for the federal government and was awaiting sentencing for racketeering.

Joseph D'Amico (Bonanno soldier): Remained a cooperating witness for the federal government and was awaiting sentencing for racketeering.

Flora Edwards (defense counsel): Like David Breitbart she continued to work as a criminal defense attorney in New York City. In late 2005 she handled the affairs of Genovese crime boss Vincent "The Chin" Gigante as he became terminally ill and died.

Nicholas Garaufis (judge): As a sitting judge in the U.S. District Court for the Eastern District of New York, Garaufis handled most of the criminal cases related to the federal prosecutors' offensive against the Bonanno crime family. In March 2006 he presided over Basciano's trial. He was expected to preside over Bonanno crime family cases well into 2007.

Robert Henoch (prosecutor): Also received an award for his service as government trial counsel in the Massino case. In 2006, Henoch was lead government attorney in the prosecution of the so-called "Mafia Cops," a trial which led to the conviction of two ex-NYPD detectives accused of being hit men for the Luchese crime family.

Mitra Hormozi (prosecutor): Along with Andres and Henoch, she received an award from the Department of Justice for her work on the Massino case. In 2006 she was co-counsel with Henoch in the trial of the "Mafia Cops." She married in August 2005 and had a baby boy in 2007.

Duane Leisenheimer (Massino associate): He was a federal cooperating witness.

Frank Lino (Bonanno captain): He remained a cooperating witness and was awaiting sentencing for racketeering.

Kimberly McCaffrey (FBI agent): Continued to work for the Federal Bureau of Investigation in New York City. Along with the rest of the prosecution team, she received a Department of Justice award for her work on the Massino case. Her main responsibility in 2006 was the handling of Joseph

Massino after he became a cooperating witness for the government. She had her second child, a girl, in mid-2006.

Patrick Marshall (FBI agent): Was retired from the FBI and living on the West Coast.

Adeline Massino (daughter): Continued to live in Howard Beach with her husband and two daughters. She took a job in the accounting field. In her spare time she busied herself with her children's school, as well as their dance and sports activities.

Joanne Massino (daughter): Like her sister Adeline, she continued to live in Howard Beach in a home near her mother. As a single divorced mother, she raised a daughter and son. A few days a week she worked at her children's parochial school.

Joseph Massino (former crime boss): After the former Attorney General John Ashcroft ruled that Massino was eligible for the death penalty, he moved in earnest to become a cooperating witness for the federal government. He finally signed a cooperation agreement in June 2005 and was placed in the federal witness security program. Massino was expected by many to be called as a witness in 2006 for the trial of his former confederate Vincent Basciano but has never made an appearance in the case. He is said by friends and associates to be exercising and trying to control his diabetes.

Josephine Massino (wife): She continued to live in her Howard Beach home, which she bought with her husband many years earlier. Much of her time was spent in the company of her daughters and grandchildren. Josephine also had been dealing with the recuperation of her sister Anna from the effects of a stroke. Since her husband was convicted in

July 2005, Josephine has not made any public statements about his case.

Ruth Nordenbrook (prosecutor): She was retired from federal government service. Nordenbrook suffered the untimely death of her husband in November 2004 just prior to her retirement. She continued to live in New York, tending a Brooklyn Heights neighborhood rose garden and doing volunteer work.

Joseph Pistone (FBI agent): After retiring from the FBI, he started a second career as an author. Pistone's books included, as co-author, "Donnie Brasco: My Undercover Life in the Mafia," (1987) and, on his own, "The Way of the Wiseguy" (2004). He also co-authored a novel with Bill Bonanno, son of the late crime boss Joseph Bonanno, entitled "The Good Guys" (2005).

Vito Rizzuto (Bonanno soldier in Canada): Referred by law enforcement officials as the "Godather of the Italian Mafia in Montreal," he was indicted in January 2004 on racketeering charges, including the murder of the three captains in 1981. He was ordered extradicted by Canadian courts in 2006 but continued to fight that move with additional legal challenges. Trial was pending.

Charles Rooney (FBI supervisor): Retired from the FBI in fall 2005 and began working as a consultant to the agency.

Benjamin Ruggiero (soldier): Released from federal prison in April 1993 at the age of 79. He died of natural causes in 1995.

Jeffrey Sallet (FBI agent): He moved to FBI headquarters in Washington where he took a job as a supervisory special agent in the organized crime section. He received an award from the Department of Justice, along with the others on the prosecution team, for his work on the Massino case. Sallet occasionally traveled to New York City to help in the prosecution of other Bonanno crime family members.

James Tartaglione (Bonanno captain): Remained a cooperating witness for the federal government. He testified in the 2006 trial of Basciano and was awaiting sentencing for racketeering.

Anthony Urso (Bonanno acting underboss): Pleaded guilty in 2005 to racketeering charges in federal court in Brooklyn. Was awaiting sentencing.

Salvatore Vitale (former Bonanno underboss): Remained a cooperating witness for the federal government and testified in the March 2006 trial of Basciano. During his testimony, Vitale said that his sister Josephine wasn't aware of the details of the crimes he and Joseph Massino carried out. Vitale said he never discussed "street" business with his sister or in her presence. He was awaiting sentencing.

Notes

1. "No Sleep Till Brooklyn" Details of the events surrounding Joseph Massino's arrest on January 9, 2003, came from interviews of Massino's wife and two daughters on May 23, 2004, for a story that ran in *New York Newsday*, as well as from interviews with FBI Special Agents Jeffrey Sallet and Kimberly McCaffrey and McCaffrey's testimony during Massino's trial in 2004. Information about Massino's prior problems with law enforcement came from his 1982 and 1985 federal indictments and court records of those cases. Details of the news conference announcing Massino's arrest were provided by newspaper articles and press releases from the Brooklyn U.S. Attorney's Office.

2. Amici The story of the development of the Mafia in New York is found in several books, notably *Luciano: The Man Who Modernized American Mafia* by Tony Sciacca, *Honor Thy Father* by Gay Talese, *The Valachi Papers* by Peter Maas, *The Five Families* by Selwyn Rabb, *The Crime Confederation* by Ralph Salerno, *The Mob: 200 Years of Organized Crime in New York* by Virgil Peterson, and *American Mafia: A History of Its Rise to Power* by Thomas Repetto.

3. The Toughest Kid on the Block The background on the families of Joseph and Josephine Massino was derived from the May 23, 2004, interview with Josephine and from confidential sources. Details about Joseph Bonanno's development as a major Mafia boss are contained in his autobiography *Man of Honor,* cowritten with Sergio Lalli. Bonanno's son, Salvatore, also known as "Bill," gave his own perspective of his father's life in *Bound by Honor: A Mafioso's Life*. The kidnapping of Joseph Bonanno was described in his autobiography and in contemporary news accounts.

4. Maspeth Joe Salvatore Bonanno's meeting with Philip Rastelli and others the day President John F. Kennedy was assassinated is described in *Bound by Honor*. Rastelli's life as a career criminal is contained in the 1970 *Report of the New York State Joint Legislative Committee on Crime, Its Causes and Effect on Society* and in various newspaper articles. The Bonanno crime family wars was detailed in the *New York Times*. Duane Leisenheimer testified about his friendship and work with Joseph Massino during Massino's 2004 trial. Salvatore Vitale also testified at Massino's trial about his background in crime. Similar information about Vitale is contained in reports of his interviews with the FBI. Background on the federal investigation of the garment industry is contained in a series written by me for *Womens Wear Daily* in 1977. Joseph Bonanno's travels to Sicily were detailed in his autobiography.

5. A Piece of Work The murders of Vito Borelli and Joseph Pastore were described by Vitale in his interviews with the FBI and in documents filed in the case *U.S. v. Joseph Massino,* 02-cr-0307 (EDNY). Pastore's murder is also discussed in *U.S. v. Joseph Massino,* SS81-cr-803 (SDNY).

6. "I Don't Do Nothing" Testimony about the Hemingway truck hijacking is found in *U.S. v. Joseph Massino, and Ray*

Wean, 75-cr-471 (EDNY). Massino's testimony is also contained in the court file. Former FBI agent Patrick Colgan was interviewed about the Hemingway case.

7. Power Play The description of the scene outside Casa Bella Restaurant is contained in *Donnie Brasco: My Life Undercover in the Mafia* by Joseph Pistone and Richard Woodley. The Pistone-Woodley book is also the primary source for information about Pistone's infiltration of the Bonanno crime family. Details of Pistone's undercover work is also contained in the trial record of *U.S. v Napolitano et.al.*, 81-cr-803 (SDNY). Carmine Galante's rise to power in the 1970s was described in a 1977 article in the *New York Times*. Galante's assassination was described in various newspaper accounts. The Pistone-Woodley account also describes the effects of the Galante murder within the Bonanno crime family.

8. The Three Captains The Pistone-Woodley book describes the way Benjamin Ruggiero and Dominick Napolitano came to know and trust "Donnie Brasco." The plotting within the Bonanno crime family that led to the deaths of the three captains is described in a variety of sources. The Pistone-Woodley book gives some background on those murders but most of the details are derived from the trial record in *U.S. v. Massino*, 02-cr-0307 (EDNY) and the testimony of Frank Lino and Salvatore Vitale. FBI agent Vincent Savadel testified in *U.S. v. Napolitano*. FBI agent Charles Rooney was interviewed by me on a number of occasions. Donna Trinchera testified about the last time she saw her husband in the trial of *U.S. v. Massino*, 02-cr-0307 (EDNY).

9. The Inside Man The aftermath of the murder of the three captains is detailed in the Pistone-Woodley book and in Pistone's testimony in the trial of *U.S. v Napolitano*. Former FBI agent Patrick Colgan was interviewed a number of times by me.

10. Up on the Roof Testimony of Pistone in *U.S. v. Napolitano*. Salvatore Vitale interview with FBI. Testimony of former FBI agent Doug Fencl in *U.S. v Napolitano* and *U.S. v. Massino* (2004).

11. Do It to Me One More Time My interviews of former FBI agent Patrick Marshall. Trial record in *United States v Napolitano*. Testimony of Lino in *U.S. v Massino* (2004).

12. The Gathering Storm The genesis of the Pizza Connection investigation was described to me by Rooney. Vitale's comments about Massino's strange trips were made during interviews with the FBI. Additional information in the chapter was provided by Patrick Colgan, by trial records of *U.S. v. Napolitano* and *U.S. v. Massino* (1981), and by contemporary news accounts of the trials.

13. Murder on the Lam Massino's time on the lam was described by Duane Leisenheimer and Salvatore Vitale in their testimony in *U.S. v. Massino* (2003). The Charles Rooney interview provided details about the Pizza Connection investigation and indictments. Vitale was interviewed by the FBI about the Bonventre murder and he also testified about the events, as did James Tartaglione in *U.S. v. Massino* (2004).

14. Return Attorney Jon Pollak described his blindfolded trip to see a fugitive Massino in an interview with me. Details of Massino's arraignment came from the transcript in *U.S. v. Massino* (1981).

15. Horatio Alger of the Mafia Patrick Marshall described the service of the wiretap notification in an interview with me. Anthony Salerno's and Salvatore Avellino's comments on surveillance tapes are contained in transcripts from the Commission Trial of 1986. Details of the trial of Philip Rastelli, Joseph Massino, and others in the moving industry case were taken from contemporary news accounts in the

New York Times and in reported court decisions. Attorney Bruce Cutler provided me with details about Massino's 1987 trial with Vitale. Other information about that case is contained in the trial record of *U.S. v Massino* SSS81-cr-803 (SDNY) and in accounts published in the *New York Times*.

16. By the Numbers Charles Rooney provided details of his conversation with Louis Freeh, as well as his theory of the Sciasica murder, to me in an interview. FBI agents Jeffrey Sallet and Kimberly McCaffrey, as well as supervisory agent Jack Stubing, were interviewed by me. Former prosecutor James Walden is the source of information about the Baldassare Amato and Anthony Spero cases. Former Assistant U.S. Attorney Ruth Nordenbrook was interviewed by me. Details about the Barry Weinberg connection are contained in the testimony of McCaffrey in the trial of *U.S. v. Massino* (2004). Frank Coppa testified about his cooperation in the 2004 Massino trial.

17. Ghosts Details of Massino's arraignment are contained in an audio taped record made by the Brooklyn federal court.

18. All in the Family Josephine Massino and her two daughters, Joanne and Adeline, gave an interview to me on May 23, 2004. Additional information about them was provided by confidential sources. Information about Vitale's decision to become a cooperating witness is contained in the 2004 Massino trial record, in Vitale's interviews with the FBI, and in accounts published in *Newsday*. Tartaglione's decision to cooperate was something he discussed in his trial testimony. Nordenbrook also provided details about Tartaglione. Information about Tartaglione's taping is contained in the Massino trial record and government documents.

19. "Let's Bring In the Jury" Details of the various Bonanno-related indictments are found in news releases distributed by the Brooklyn U.S. Attorney's Office and in court documents. The jury selection process in Massino's 2004 trial was observed by me and was the subject of some press accounts. The legal wrangling over pretrial motions in the Massino case are detailed in court filings and motions papers.

20. "They Didn't Die of Old Age" Trial transcript filed in *U.S. v. Massino*, 02-cr-0307 (EDNY), author's notes.

21. "They Thought They Might Get Killed" Trial transcript filed in *U.S. v. Massino*, 02-cr-0307 (EDNY), author's notes.

22. "I Didn't Want to Do No More Time" Trial transcript filed in *U.S. v. Massino*, 02-cr-0307 (EDNY), author's notes.

23. "This Is for Life" Trial transcript filed in *U.S. v. Massino*, 02-cr-0307 (EDNY), author's notes.

24. "He Is a Rat" Trial transcript filed in *U.S. v. Massino*, 02-cr-0307 (EDNY), author's notes.

25. "I Had Killed for Him" Trial transcript filed in *U.S. v. Massino*, 02-cr-0307 (EDNY), author's notes.

26. "Not One We Won" Trial transcript filed in *U.S. v. Massino*, 02-cr-0307 (EDNY), author's notes.

27. Endgame Two confidential sources provided me with information about Joseph Massino's monumental decision to become a cooperating witness. Details of his cooperation are contained in court records filed in *U.S. v. Basciano* (EDNY) and court proceedings the day Massino pled guilty to the murder of Gerlando Sciascia on June 23, 2005.

Bibliography

Books

Alexander, Shana. *The Pizza Connection: Lawyers, Money, Drugs, Mafia*. New York: Weidenfeld & Nicolson, 1988.

Blum, Howard. *Gangland: How the FBI Broke the Mob*. New York: Simon & Schuster, 1993.

Bonanno, Bill. *Bound by Honor: A Mafioso's Story*. New York: St. Martin's Press, 1999.

Bonanno, Joseph, and Sergio Lalli. *A Man of Honor: The Autobiography of Joseph Bonanno*. New York: Simon and Schuster, 1983.

Capeci, Jerry. *The Complete Idiot's Guide to the Mafia* (2nd ed.) New York: Penguin, 2004.

Giovina, Andrea, and Gary Brozek. *Divorced from the Mob: My Journey from Organized Crime to Independent Woman*. New York: Carroll & Graf, 2004.

Jackson, Kenneth T. *The Encyclopedia of New York City*. New Haven, CT: Yale University Press, 1995.

Jacobs, James B., Christopher Panarella, and Jay Worthington. *Busting the Mob: United States v. Cosa Nostra*. New York: New York University Press, 1994.

Lewis, Norman. *The Honored Society: A Searching Look at the Mafia*. New York: Putnam, 1964.

Longrigg, Claire. *No Questions Asked: The Secret Life of Women in the Mob*. New York: Hyperion, 2004.

Maas, Peter. *The Valachi Papers*. New York: Putnam, 1968.

———. *Underboss: Sammy the Bull Gravano's Story of Life in the Mafia*. New York: HarperCollins, 1997.

O'Brien, Joseph F., and Andris Kurins. *Boss of Bosses: The Fall of the Godfather: The FBI and Paul Castellano*. New York: Simon & Schuster, 1991.

Peterson, Virgil. *The Mob: 200 Years of Organized Crime in New York*. Ottawa, IL: Green Hill, 1983.

Pistone, Joseph D. *The Way of the Wise Guy*. Philadelphia: Running Press, 2004.

———, and Richard Woodley. *Donnie Brasco: My Life Undercover in the Mafia*. New York: New American Library, 1987.

Rabb, Selwyn. *Five Families: The Rise, Decline, and Resurgence of America's Most Powerful Mafia Empires*. New York: Thomas Dunne, 2005.

Repetto, Thomas. *American Mafia: A History of Its Rise to Power*. New York: Henry Holt, 2004.

Saggio, Frankie, and Fred Rosen. *Born to the Mob*. New York: Thunder's Mouth Press, 2004.

Salerno, Ralph, and John S. Tompkins. *The Crime Confederation*. Garden City, NY.: Doubleday, 1969.

Sciacca, Tony. *Luciano: The Man Who Modernized the American Mafia*. New York: Pinnacle, 1975.

Servadio, Gaia. *Mafioso: A History of the Mafia from Its Origins to the Present*. New York: Dell, 1976.

Talese, Gay. *Honor Thy Father*. New York: Dell, 1981.

Teresa, Vincent, with Thomas C. Renner. *Vinnie Teresa's Mafia: A First Person Account of Life as a Hunted Informer*. Garden City, NY: Doubleday, 1975.

Volkman, Ernest. *Gangbusters: The Destruction of Amer-

ica's Last Great Mafia Dynasty. Winchester, MA: Faber and Faber, 1998.

Volz, Joseph, and Peter J. Bridge, eds. *The Mafia Talks*. Greenwich, CT: Fawcett, 1969.

Court Documents and Cases

People of the State of New York v. Philip Rastelli, 37 N.Y. 2d, 240 (1975).

U.S. v. Patrick DeFilippo, 03-cr-929, United States District Court for the Eastern District of New York.

U.S. v. Ronald Filocomo, 02-cr-0307, United States District Court for the Eastern District of New York.

U.S. v. Gennaro Langella and Carmine Persico, 804 F.2d 889 (1986).

U.S. v. Dominic Mariani, 851 F.2d 595 (1988).

U.S. v. Joseph Massino, 02-cr-0307, United States District Court for the Eastern District of New York.

U.S. v. Joseph Massino, SS81-cr-803, United States District Court for the Southern District of New York.

U.S. v. Joseph Massino and Salvatore Vitale, SSS81-cr-803, United States District Court for the Southern District of New York.

U.S. v. Joseph Massino and Ray Wean, 75-cr-471, United States District Court for the Eastern District of New York.

U.S. v. Philip Rastelli, et.al., 85-cr-354, United States District Court for the Eastern District of New York.

U.S. v. Philip Rastelli, et.al., 551 F.2d (1977).

U.S. v. Philip Rastelli, et.al., 870 F.2d 822 (1989).

U.S. v. Benjamin Ruggiero, et.al., 81-cr-803, United States District Court for the Southern District of New York.

U.S. v. Anthony Salerno, et.al., 85-cr-139, United States District Court for the Southern District of New York.

U.S. v. Anthony Salerno, et.al., 868 F.2d 524 (1989).

U.S. v. Anthony Spero, et.al., 331 F.3d 57 (2003).

U.S. v Anthony Urso, et.al., 03-cr-1382, United States District Court for the Eastern District of New York.

Government Publications

New York State Joint Legislative Committee on Crime, Its Causes, Control and Effect on Society. Report for 1970, September 1970.

Presidential Commission on Organized Crime. *Record of Hearings*, Vols. 1–7. Washington, DC: U.S. Government Printing Office, 1983–1985.

Newspapers Consulted

Daily News
Newsday (Long Island)
New York Newsday
New York Post
New York Times
Record (Hackensack, New Jersey)
Womens Wear Daily

Other Periodicals

Lombardi, John. "The Dumbest Don." *New York Magazine*, January 17, 2005.

Plate, Thomas, ed. *The Mafia at War*. NYM Corporation, 1972.

Web Sites

www.crimelibrary.com
www.fbi.gov
www.findagrave.com
www.ganglandnews.com

www.Lexis.com
www.Mafia-International.com
www.Nexis.com
www.usdoj.gov/usao/nye (U.S. Attorney's office, Eastern District of New York)

Acknowledgments

A book like this, covering decades of the history of the American Mafia in general and the Bonanno crime family in particular, is the result of a lot of research. Along the way, there were numerous people who helped with this work and I want to acknowledge them all at this time. Some were only able to assist me with the proviso that their identities be kept secret and confidential. They know who they are and they, too, have my thanks.

First, I would like to thank my editor at Kensington Publishing, Gary Goldstein. Usually, editors are the last to be thanked by authors. But Gary came to me out of the blue one day in late 2004 with the idea of a book about Joseph Massino. He had followed my *Newsday* coverage of the Massino trial that year and liked what he read. With his encouragement, I put together a proposal that he patiently shepherded through the editorial process until a deal was struck. For his continuous support and encouragement, I thank him.

Among those in law enforcement, I would like to thank several people in the Brooklyn U.S. Attorney's Office: prosecutors Greg Andres, Robert Henoch, Mitra Hormozi; press spokesman Robert Nardoza; and paralegal Samantha Ward.

At the New York Office of the FBI, invaluable assistance was given by Special Agents James Margolin and Kimberly McCaffrey. In Washington, Special Agent Jeffrey Sallet gave the same kind of help and guidance, as did Jack Stubing in White Plains, New York.

Several former FBI agents were also generous with their time, spending hours with me in interviews and conversations about an important and exciting time in law enforcement history. They are Patrick Colgan, Patrick Marshall, Steve Morrill, and Charles Rooney.

David Breitbart and Flora Edwards, two defense lawyers who represented Joseph Massino and who I got to know during his 2004 trial, deserve special thanks for the patient help they gave me in understanding the dynamics of the case from their perspective.

A number of other private attorneys who I came to know over my years of work as a journalist covering organized crime and legal affairs were treasure troves of information. Some of them had served as prosecutors and had firsthand knowledge of the events portrayed in this book. Others had (and still do) worked as defense attorneys and were involved in some of the criminal cases that served as the spine for the story of Joseph Massino and his life. This group of lawyers includes Frank Bari, Bruce Cutler, James DiPietro, Ronald Fischetti, Steven K. Frankel, Barry Levin, Jon Pollok, Murray Richman, Ephraim Savitt, Gerald Shargel, James Walden, and Joel Winograd. Special mention goes to Ruth Nordenbrook, a former member of the Brooklyn U.S. Attorney's Office, who was instrumental in bringing some of the early cases to my attention that proved to be a vital part of this story and was very generous with her time.

Private investigator and security expert Eugene Sampieri, an old friend who was one of the first in his profession to realize the usefulness of computerization, gave helpful advice and historical perspective.

As is often the case in Mafia stories, the reporting of

other writers, and newspaper and magazine journalists was relied on and I would like to mention those whose work proved helpful. They are Justo Bautista, Bill Bonanno, Pete Bowles, Jimmy Breslin, Leonard Buder, Jerry Capeci, Kati Cornell, Robert Greene, Charles Grutzner, Glenn Fowler, Stephen Fox, William Glaberson, Zach Haberman, David Hafetz, Adrian Humphreys (Canada), Tom Hays, Lee Lamothe (Canada), Arnold H. Lubasch, John Marzulli, Allan May, Alexandra Mosca, Gene Mustain, Tom Perrotta, Nicholas Pileggi, Joseph Pistone, Selwyn Raab, Will Rashbaum, Thomas C. Renner, Ralph Salerno, Tony Sciacca, Max H. Seigel, Greg Smith, Gay Talese, Michael Weissenstein, and Richard Woodley.

Books about crime figures are often mainly distilled from police and law enforcement sources. But in reporting the story of Joseph Massino, through his 2004 trial and beyond, I had the unique opportunity of receiving the courtesy and consideration of his immediate family. Massino's wife, Josephine, gave me an exclusive interview at the start of her husband's trial that was published in *Newsday* and was trusting enough, despite what she was going through, to talk with me throughout that proceeding. Her daughters Adeline and Joanne also participated in the interview with their mother and talked to me as trial events warranted. They showed a tremendous amount of class and civility through a very difficult time. They may not like everything that is contained in this story but I hope they find my account of Joseph Massino's life to be fair and accurate.

I made one accommodation to the Massino women in my dealings with them. Joanne and Adeline asked that neither their married names nor the names of their children be used as a way of protecting the youngsters' privacy. That seemed reasonable. The children had been shielded from public pressure and as of this writing really do not know the full details of what happened to their grandfather and what he did with his life. At some point, the Massino grandchildren will learn about what happened and make up their own minds about him. I hope this book helps them in some way to understand.

I also want to thank my colleagues at *Newsday* for giving me the freedom and time to pursue this book. Special thanks to my editor John Mancini, managing editor Mary Ann Skinner, associate managing editor Les Payne, photo editors Chris Hatch and Jeff Schamberry, city editor Diane Davis, and assistant city editor Melanie Lefkowitz. My colleague and friend, columnist Jimmy Breslin, gave me a lot of encouragement as well.

Susan, and our dog, Ollie, had to put up with my moods and inattention as I worked the many months on the writing and research. They get special thanks for keeping the faith and offering encouragement every step of the way.

Finally, I want to thank my agent, Jill Marsal at the Sandra Dijkstra Literary Agency, contracts expert Elisabeth James, and subrights manager Taryn Fagerness for carefully guiding me through the process of getting this book published.